ALSO BY THERESA RIZZO

Just Destiny
He Belongs to Me

Just BEGINNING

A PREQUEL TO JUST DESTINY

THERESA RIZZO

Published by Theresa Rizzo
www.theresarizzo.com

Print ISBN 978-0-9890450-4-9
eBook ISBN 978-0-9890450-5-6

Cover design by Kim Killion, Killion Group
Cover photo by
Trevor Allen, Trevor Allen Photography
Book design by Donna Cook

Printed in the United States of America

For my old pen pal, Bob Dircks, Sr.,
the first person to delight in my writing,
and the first to suggest I had a real gift
as a storyteller to share with the world.

A million thanks for years of encouragement.
Rest in peace,
Mr. Dircks.

Acknowledgments

My sincerest thanks go to the many people who helped with this book. To Dr. Paul Rizzo, for letting me harass him endlessly with medical and Grosse Pointe questions. To JE DeSequera for advice on motorcycles. To Anasheh Satoorian, Patricia Clark-Martin, Joan Reiber, Amy Krueger Malow, Kristen Strauss, Allison Brooks, and Laura Rizzo for brainstorming help.

To writing pals, Kaki Warner and Kimberly Savage, fabulous cover designer, Kim Killion, and editor extraordinaire, Kerri-Leigh Grady. To Donna Cook, my wonderful formatter, who makes my print copy look great. To the very talented photographer, Trevor Allen, who shot the lovely cover photo. To Mandi and Mark Fanning for sharing their beautiful wedding rings with me.

To Wendy Gerome and her terrific 7th graders at Grosse Pointe Academy, for their stellar research work, confirming that it takes a LOT of force to do more than crack a cell phone screen.

To my invaluable beta readers, Jessica Peters and Jillian Cullinane—you guys keep me honest and help make each book exponentially stronger. To my brilliant webmaster, business manager, and my husband, John, for years of encouragement and help.

Chapter 1

Two-thirty in the morning, Jenny Campbell stared at the brightly lit, quiet ER entrance. Slipping by the guard during the chaos of last night's emergency had been easy; tonight would be trickier.

Maybe... She went to the hospital's side door and tugged. Nope. Not just stuck, the heavy steel door firmly resisted her attempts to open it. *Not getting in that way.* She'd have to take her chances going through the ER. As Jenny eased through the dark night toward the sliding doors, she studied the waiting room occupants.

A pregnant lady sat in a wheelchair at the admissions desk. Her eyebrows banded tightly together as she massaged her beach ball stomach in a circular motion. The clerk assisting her alternately poked at the computer screen with a silver wand and glanced at the closed doorway a nurse had disappeared through as if worried the expectant mother would throw herself on the floor, spread her legs wide, and demand he deliver her baby.

Ignoring the half dozen sleepy people waiting for treatment, the security guard puffed out his chest as he hitched his pants under his protruding stomach and flirted with the blushing night secretary.

A young man carrying an overnight case and a bright, fluffy duck brushed past Jenny through the sliding doors. *Yes.* Jenny dashed behind and followed him to the admissions desk, hoping it would look like they were together. When the guard dismissed them with a cursory glance, Jenny broke away from the husband and headed for the stairway, like a nervous mouse seeking the safety of her tunnel.

She eased the door closed and had almost reached the bend in the stairs, when the door creaked open behind her. Fighting the urge to either freeze or bolt up the remaining steps, Jenny lightened her tread and continued climbing. It could be night personnel using the stairs to get some exercise.

"Miss, can I help you?" The guard called out.

She considered pretending she hadn't heard him, but his voice echoed loudly in the empty stairwell. Jenny stopped and curved her lips into a friendly smile, before turning to face him. "No thanks. I'm fine."

Below her, he took a step toward the bottom stair and cocked his head. "Visiting hours are over."

"I had to work late tonight and couldn't visit my son earlier. The nurse said I could come by when I got off." The lie rolled off Jenny's tongue as she pasted a worried expression on her face. "That's okay, isn't it?"

He propped a foot on the first step and pursed his lips. "Son? You hardly look old enough to have a kid."

"Trust me." She forced a chuckle. "I feel old enough."

"I'll have to call up to get permission. Got to follow protocol."

Of course you do. For an instant, Jenny calculated her chances of sprinting up the stairs to lose the overweight guard. The hospital had dozens of rooms, closets, and alcoves where she could hide. But she eased to the other foot, deciding to play it cool.

"Sure, no problem." Jenny retraced her steps and breezed past him.

Standing next to the guard at the front desk, she projected a look of bored indifference while observing the other occupants to see if they noticed her detention. What would he do when he discovered her lie?

When nobody seemed interested in her predicament, she focused her attention on the telephone, willing the nurse to allow her up to see Michael.

"Helen? This is Bob Cullen in security. You got a patient..." He looked expectantly at her.

"Michael Campbell."

"Michael Campbell. His mom's down here wantin' to come up. Said someone told her she could visit when she got off work." With one beefy hand planted on his hip, his dark, large eyes watched her. He hung up the phone with a loud click and faced her. "Go on up."

Smiling to cover her relief, Jenny thanked the guard. She returned to the stairwell and slowly climbed the steps, praying the night nurse had never met her mother.

Jenny snuck onto the darkened floor and hurried down the carpeted hall to room 496. Guided by the muted light from the slightly open bathroom door, she crossed to the window side of the bed, away from the I.V. pole and the quietly whooshing suction machine.

Her gaze swept the sleeping boy—from the crown of his honey blonde head down the length of him—noting the tube protruding from one nostril, the long I.V. tubing taped to his arm, and the fresh fiberglass cast encircling his left wrist. She brushed damp bangs from his forehead. Her caress traveled down his good arm, past the white gauze and tape holding the I.V. needle in place on his uninjured hand.

Michael's dark brown eyes, heavy from pain medication, blinked at her. The corners of his mouth lifted in a slight smile as he took her hand and his eyelids fluttered shut. With a contented sigh, Michael drifted back to sleep. Jenny hooked an ankle around the chair leg and dragged it near so she could perch on the edge without relinquishing her hold.

The night nurse whisked into the room, making no more noise than the gentle rustling of leaves on a windy night. A tentative smile hovered on Jenny's lips, as she tried to look friendly and harmless while preparing to beg she be allowed to stay. To her relief, the nurse said nothing, seeming to barely register her presence. But she knew those sharp, dark eyes that surveyed the occupants and machines in one sweeping glance had noticed her.

With an economy of motions, the nurse replaced the depleted I.V. bag and noted the level of stomach fluids intermittently plopping into the plastic collection jar, before running a light hand around Michael's face, checking for fever as a mother would—a competent specter tending her patient without disturbing his peace.

The nurse nodded toward the door and drew Jenny into the hall. She crossed her arms over her animal print scrub top and under generous breasts, then shook her dark head. "Mother, huh?" She cocked her head. "And I'm Aretha Franklin."

"Sister, actually." Jenny shrugged. "I didn't think the guard would let me up if I wasn't a parent."

"He does have eyes, you know."

"He didn't know how old Michael was. Besides, I couldn't take the chance he'd turn me away."

"And sneakin' in here every night isn't taking chances?"

Jenny shrugged but relaxed, as it seemed the nurse wouldn't kick her out. "I promised."

Black brows arched over the nurse's wide eyes, as if preparing to lecture her. Jenny glanced at her index finger, expecting it to wag in her face any minute for emphasis. "Only reason I'm lettin' you stay is 'cause you don't cause any trouble and he sleeps a whole lot better with you here."

Jenny looked through the door, checking on Michael. "He worries about me."

"Whatever." The nurse waved a dismissing hand. "He's a sweet kid. Don't have a mouth on him like most his age."

"Don't let him fool you. He can be a pain." Jenny smiled, removing the sting from the insult. "Do you know what time his doctor will be in this morning?"

"Dr. Harrison?"

Jenny nodded. That was the name stitched in navy on the lab coat of the doctor she'd run into—literally—yesterday morning.

Jenny's stomach quivered at the memory of his strong, warm hands on her arms as he'd steadied her after the collision. He had kind, pewter gray eyes that crinkled at the edges when he smiled and a deep rich voice capable of soothing a Tasmanian devil.

"He usually makes rounds about seven." The nurse looked at her out of the corner of her eye with sudden interest, as if sizing her up. "Why? You need to talk to him?"

Seven? She might still be here then. Jenny shook her head. "Nothing important."

The bleeping phone at the nurses' station called the woman back to work. Grateful for the distraction, Jenny quietly reentered the room. Michael shifted in his sleep and frowned. She pulled the chair close to the bed and gently smoothed the hair away from his forehead until his expression relaxed.

As a baby, Michael had been remarkably touch-sensitive. He'd loved to be cuddled, have his back patted or rubbed, his head scratched... But lately, she didn't dare show him much affection—especially in front of his friends. Not cool now that he was in middle school. However, when he was sick Michael still enjoyed a back rub.

Jenny rested her chin on her folded arms and willed him to get well.

∾ ∾ ∾

Gabe Harrison felt every one of the twenty-four hours he'd been awake. A short two-hour nap didn't cut it anymore. He pressed his fingers over stinging eyes and then finished typing in the post-op orders. His long night on call had ended with an emergency appendectomy. He'd catch up on sleep today, but before heading home he needed to check on a patient's latest lab results.

Michael Campbell worried him. Two days ago he'd removed the boy's ruptured spleen. Healthy before his accident, the twelve-year-old should have bounced back faster, yet his hemoglobin remained low and he just didn't look right.

Gabe yawned, scraped a hand over bristly cheeks, and scrolled through Michael's latest blood work. Not bad, but not good. He glanced at the wall clock. Six. He'd examine the incision and see if Michael was better. His partner would check the boy during morning rounds, but Gabe would sleep better having checked on Michael himself.

Might as well. Gabe had no plans today other than picking up his laundry from the cleaners on the way to Wednesday afternoon tennis. He pushed the tablet back in the charging rack and blew out a deep breath before heaving to his feet and crossing the hall to room 496. He paused in the open doorway.

A young woman slept half-sitting in a chair, half-draped across the bed next to Michael. Her slim hand held the boy's, as she pillowed her head in the crook of her folded arms. Beautiful brown hair the color of a rich, warm dark ale cascaded down her back to a shapely buttocks, perched on one bent leg.

Wonder if her hair's as silky and heavy as it looks. Probably smells great too. All fresh and sexy. Gabe jammed his hands in his lab coat pocket. She'd pulled it back in a ponytail yesterday morning, but he was pretty sure she was the same woman who ran into him.

Gabe cocked his head and frowned. *How can she sleep that way? That can't be comfortable.* This must be the mystery lady claiming to be Michael's mother, and he knew for a fact she was not. Mary Campbell was a slight woman with short auburn hair, probably in her late forties, early fifties. Careful not to wake them, Gabe stepped closer, moving to the foot of Michael's bed.

The pair shared a similarity in their delicate features and heart-shaped faces, but whereas Michael's came from youth, the woman's came from femininity. Disregarding hair colors, he detected a strong likeness. She was too old to be his sister and Mary Campbell looked too young to have a daughter this age. An aunt? Why visit in the middle of the night?

The pair looked so innocent and defenseless in sleep, Gabe had the strange urge to fold both of them in his arms and hold on tight.

The scene reminded him of the many nights he'd come home from a late night call and wandered in to check on his children. Standing by their beds watching them sleep had reassured him. Now he came home to an empty house.

Examine the patient, Harrison. Gabe cleared his throat then slapped his feet down loudly as he approached the bed.

The young woman's eyes popped open, revealing pale irises ringed in deep blue.

What stunning eyes.

They stared at each other several long seconds before she eased away from the boy and pushed mussed hair away from her face. Tugging her sweater down in the back where it rode up, she continued to watch him through wide eyes, as if trying to gauge his mood.

Gabe flashed her a brief smile, then turned to Michael, who rubbed his face. "Hey buddy, how're you feeling?"

The door pushed wide open, circulating fresh air into the stuffy room. Michael's sleepy gaze settled beyond Gabe to where Mary Campbell breezed into the room. Guilt flashed across the boy's face but was instantly replaced by wide-eyed anxiety as he looked at the young woman at his side. He clutched her hand in a white-knuckled grasp.

His mother came to an abrupt halt. Her soft welcoming smile evaporated the second she spotted the young woman. Stiffening, she scowled at Michael's visitor.

"What're you doing here, Jenny?"

Chapter 2

Jenny. His mystery lady had a name. Michael's mother knew who she was and apparently didn't like her much.

Jenny's cheeks flushed, and she glanced at him out of the corner of her eye before turning in her seat to face Michael's mother.

Michael winced as he struggled to sit up. "Don't be mad."

"What're you doing here?" she asked in a quiet deliberate tone. Mary Campbell sat on the bed, smoothly inserting her body between the pair. She patted Michael's leg as if reassuring him, yet Gabe noted the possessive display.

Jenny slid her hand out of Michael's grasp and backed away from the bed. "Giving you a break. You've been here all day. I thought if Michael had good nights you'd rest better."

"Mom, it's okay. I asked her to come." He turned toward Gabe, pleading. "Dr. Harrison, tell her it's okay."

Tell her it's okay? The room hummed with heightened emotions and nonverbal aggression. Maternal anger pummeled his tired brain. The last thing he wanted to do was to try to untangle the nuances of battling female minds and sensibilities.

Ignoring the mother's simmering anger, Jenny smiled fondly at Michael. "It's okay. Don't worry, kiddo." She faced Mary Campbell. "I just sat with him."

"Haven't you done enough?" Lips drawn tight, Mary Campbell's laser-sharp blue eyes threatened to disintegrate the girl on the spot. The angry flush blotching her face effectively hid her abundant freckles.

"Mom." Michael fought back tears with quick sobs that bordered on hyperventilating.

Jenny scowled. "I didn't hurt—"

"Can I talk to you both outside?" The last thing the boy needed was these women battling over him. Gabe ushered the ladies into the hall and firmly closed the door behind them.

"Ladies, you're going to have to work this out somewhere else." He turned to Michael's mom, holding her gaze. "Michael feels like shit, and this arguing isn't helping. His blood work isn't as good as it should be, and if things don't improve soon, he'll need a blood transfusion. I don't know what your problem with this young lady is, and frankly I don't care, but if Michael wants her here, I recommend you let her stay."

Jenny's eyes widened in concern. "Transfusion? Do you have his type? I can give blood if—"

"*If* Michael needs blood, his father or I will donate it." Mary scowled at the younger woman. "We're A-positive, too."

Gabe held up a pacifying hand. "You can all donate blood. We're always appreciative of any donation."

Jenny folded her arms and glanced sideways at the older woman. "I just wanted to help."

Mary turned toward Gabe. "Michael needs his rest. She shouldn't be here."

"Is that what Michael wants?" Gabe asked.

Mary Campbell drew herself up to her full five foot three inches and pinned him with a steady gaze. "Doctor Harrison, if you can't keep her from disturbing my son, I'll find another doctor who can." She whirled and stalked into Michael's room, shutting the door firmly behind her.

Gabe dropped his head to his chest in defeat. *That went well.* No wonder he made it a policy to avoid patient's family disputes. It was much easier letting the nurses handle it.

Jenny sighed and stared at the golden wood grain of the closed door. "I'm sorry you got dragged into this."

He held out his hand. "Gabe Harrison, Michael's surgeon."

"Jenny Campbell." She shook his hand with a firm grip, then quickly released it. "Michael's sister."

Sister. Mary Campbell must be older than she looked. She was tough enough to have lived three lifetimes.

"General or orthopedic?"

"General. I took out your brother's spleen."

Jenny pulled her brown hair to the side, so it wrapped around her neck and trailed over one shoulder. She crammed her hands deep into her jean pockets until they stretched tight across trim hips, while small white teeth momentarily trapped her bottom lip. "Will he really need a transfusion?"

Gabe tried to concentrate on her question instead of staring at the way her hair cascaded past her breast in a silky, sable waterfall, but lack of sleep made him slow. He gave himself a mental shake and concentrated on her concern, her brother.

"Maybe. But it's really no big deal."

Smooth, Harrison. He'd meant to be reassuring and confident, but he'd sounded uncaring. He frowned, wondering how to recover.

She silently nodded, seemingly equally at a loss to know what to say next. "Well... Okay then."

"Um... The Pancake House is just down the street. You wouldn't want to get some breakfast, would you?"

Anyone willing to sneak into the hospital in the middle of the night and brave Mary Campbell's considerable fury to comfort her brother piqued Gabe's interest. The fact that she was gorgeous was a secondary benefit.

"I'd like to, but I don't have time. I was just going to grab a quick cup of coffee from the machine before trekking to the back forty."

"Back forty?" Gabe raised an eyebrow.

"I parked way in the back next to the employee parking lot."

"Why don't you wait here while I take a quick look at Michael, and then I'll walk you out?"

"I don't want to put you out. Don't doctors have a separate parking lot?"

"I could use the exercise."

"Yeah," she eyed his chest and flat stomach. "You really look out of shape."

He grinned and resisted the urge to puff out his chest. "It feels good to stretch my muscles after hours in surgery."

"Okay. Stretch away."

"Be right back."

Jenny stood to the side of the nurses' station, trying not to feel conspicuous. Dr. Harrison's invitation to breakfast had caught her off guard. She wanted to go with him, but really couldn't afford the time away from work.

She should be mortified he'd witnessed that humiliating scene with her mother; it'd hardly been one of Mom's finest moments. She couldn't imagine why he'd asked her out instead of running in the opposite direction, but she was glad he had.

Five minutes later, Gabe caught up with her. With a warm hand at her back, he turned her toward the elevator. Several nurses cast admiring glances at the doctor walking by her side. Smiling broadly, they all greeted him with a friendly "good morning," to which he responded with a nod and brief "morning" as they passed.

They probably wonder what he's doing with me.

Gabe stood a good six inches taller than her, closing in on six feet—big enough to make her aware of him, but not enough to feel dwarfed. She liked the way his light brown hair laid close-cropped to his head in tidy layers. Though not pretty-boy handsome, he had that slightly rugged, everyday gorgeous look.

As they waited at the elevator, Jenny glanced at Gabe, then looked away. She gathered her hair to one side of her neck and smoothed it down. "Sorry about my mom. She's rather overprotective."

The elevator chimed. Gabe stepped to the side to allow the people from the elevator to pass, then reached for the padded door to hold it open for her. Leaning close so the other occupants wouldn't hear, he lowered his voice. "You're her daughter."

"Michael's her late-in-life baby." She shrugged. "She has a hard time letting go."

"She overreacted," Gabe said.

"A little." To an outsider Mom's reaction probably seemed harsh. He didn't know Jenny deserved it.

His steady, earnest gaze made her want to squirm. She didn't want his pity. She couldn't exactly name what she wanted from him right then, but it definitely wasn't pity. Looking away, she hurried through the open door and waited while he helped an elderly volunteer wrestle a library cart onto the elevator.

Jenny paused at the droning vending machine and Gabe reached into his pocket for change. Coins clinked and jingled down the slot.

"What's your pleasure?" Gabe asked.

"Coffee with cream, please."

Gabe handed her the cup. "Careful. It's hot."

"Aren't you having any?" Jenny blew on her drink and took a tentative swallow.

"Not if I want to sleep."

She focused on sipping her beverage as they walked through the ER waiting room. The last thing she needed was to spill hot coffee on herself. She searched for a neutral topic. "You seemed pretty comfortable with Michael. Do you have kids?"

"Two. A boy and girl."

"Dr. Harrison?" The emergency room nurse hurried over.

Gabe slowed and turned toward the approaching nurse, saying to Jenny, "I'll only be a minute."

Jenny tuned out their medical conversation. He had kids. Her heart dropped. Was he married? She glanced at his bare left hand. Divorced? Widowed? Maybe he just didn't wear a ring. Maybe she'd misread the signals and he wasn't attracted to her at all.

When he finished talking to the nurse, they walked out of the hospital in silence. She peeked at him, wondering what he was thinking. Finally, she couldn't take it anymore. "So, you have kids..."

His gray eyes twinkled. "And an ex-wife." His amusement melted away. "I'm divorced."

Divorced. Her heart lightened and she bit her lip to keep from smiling. Jenny'd made her share of mistakes—more than her share, actually—but dating married men wasn't one of them. She'd never been that dumb.

Long divorced or rebound divorced? She peeked at Gabe as they left the hospital and walked into the brisk morning air. Kids? Huh. She liked kids. "How old are your children?"

He put a hand to her back and urged her out of the way of a large blue Navigator cruising for a parking spot. "Alex is sixteen, and Ted's eighteen."

Jenny sipped her coffee to hide her surprise and buy a little time. Sixteen and eighteen? They weren't kids. She'd been expecting six and eight or eight and ten. Sixteen and eighteen were teenagers.

She made a face at Gabe. "Teenagers. Not the most pleasant years I hear." Hers had been a nightmare.

"Not bad. They're good kids."

She smiled up at him with a knowing glint in her eye. "And living with their mother most of the time."

He chuckled and inclined his head in concession.

They walked through the huge asphalt parking lot, with her taking occasional sips of coffee and him slowing to her pace. Jenny thought about the earlier confrontation with her mother and his reaction.

When they reached her old maroon Jeep, she faced him. "Dr. Harrison—"

"Gabe."

"Okay, Gabe." She paused. "I think we gave you the wrong impression back there." She looked back toward the hospital. "My mom's really not..." She sighed. "Mom was right to be pissed at me."

"What? You beat your brother up?"

Jenny smiled, appreciating his attempt to lighten her mood. "I bought him the skateboard. Mom forbade him to get it, but I thought it'd be fine as long as he had a helmet and pads."

"What'd he run into?"

"A parked car." She stared at the distant maple trees lining the parking lot chain link fence. "I was experimenting with a new camera. Michael was showing off when he went flying into a parked car."

Gabe winced. "He's not the first kid to get hurt on a skateboard. He's probably learned his lesson."

"I learned mine." She'd never forget the terror of seeing Michael lying in the street, broken.

"It was an accident."

"It's my fault he got hurt. If I hadn't given him the skateboard— then had him posing for pictures—"

"She should love you regardless."

"She does." Jenny frowned, not wanting him to think her mother didn't love her. "It's just that when you screw up repeatedly, you have to earn love back."

"I disagree." He pressed his lips together and shook his head. "There's nothing my kids could do that would make me stop loving them." He inclined his head in an acknowledging nod. "Sure, they could disappoint me or damage my trust. But not my love."

"That's not how it works in our family." Jenny crossed her arms, careful not to spill the remains of her coffee.

Had she ever been loved that way, unconditionally? If she had, her memories were overshadowed by rough teenage years. Her adolescence had tried her parents' patience and love, but to be fair, they'd gone above and beyond supporting her—until now. This had been Mom's last straw.

Gabe rested his hip on the side of her car and then watched her with a curious expression. Jenny eased back, a bit unnerved at their closeness. He might not dwarf her as some men did, but he had a powerful presence that made her a little uneasy.

"So what do you do when you're not corrupting your little brother?"

She breathed a sigh of relief, grateful for the change in topic. "I'm a journalist. I freelance."

"Interesting. Would I recognize anything you've done?"

"Last month I did a piece on Joe Scarfili's work in laparoscopic surgery. Do you know him?"

"Sure. He's talented."

"So I learned. That piece spawned a four part series on the inner city clinic he and his wife Gianna run." Jenny checked her watch. "That reminds me, I've got to call her to set up tomorrow's tour."

"Where's the clinic?"

"Detroit. On Connor off of Mack. Not the best side of town. It's an interesting story, actually." She smiled as she warmed to her topic. Jenny loved her job investigating other people's lives, work, and interests, then sharing their stories with her readers. Through her interviews, Jenny had a unique opportunity to briefly enter another person's world and understand what made them tick and what was important to them. It fascinated her, and she never tired of sharing her work.

"Gianna's mother died from multiple sclerosis. Her death affected the entire family. Gianna went to nursing school because of it and her father became a champion of the disabled and underprivileged. He started this clinic as a memorial to his wife, and Gianna kept it going after her father passed on."

"Do they only do immunizations and peds, or can they handle trauma?"

"I'm not exactly sure. If you're really interested, you could come to the clinic with me tomorrow and find out. I'm sure Gianna would love to meet you." Gianna was always looking for volunteers—especially doctors.

"What time?"

"Late afternoon. I can let you know after I confirm."

He pulled his phone from his pocket, poked and swiped it a few times before looking up. "I'm swamped the next couple of days. How about joining me for dinner Saturday? You can tell me about it then."

"Dinner?" As in a date or an easy way to get more info about the clinic without having to worry about being pressured into volunteering?

"Dinner. The main meal eaten in early evening."

Jenny hitched her purse higher onto her shoulder. No, it felt like a date. With her brother's doctor. That probably would *not* help her situation with her mom... Then again Mom didn't have to know. It was one evening, and it might not go anywhere. She peeked at the sexy guy in scrubs leaning against her car. They might realize they have nothing in common. But she'd sure like to find out.

She frowned as if mentally checking her calendar, though she knew very well her weekend was wide open. "What time?"

"I've got surgery, and I think I'm on call—I need to double check with my partner. Can I call you?"

"Sure." She fished a pen from her purse, turned her empty coffee cup sideways, and wrote her phone number on the outside with clear, precise strokes, then ripped a chunk out of the Styrofoam cup and handed it to him. She snatched her hand back to wipe a lingering brown coffee drip off the piece before offering it to him again.

Gabe took the bit of plastic, lightly brushing his finger by hers, and dropped it in his breast pocket. He pushed off the car, leaving her just enough room to move by him. "Great. I'll get back to you tonight."

Jenny retrieved her chunk of keys from her purse. "Well... Thanks for the coffee."

"You're welcome."

She unlocked her car door and opened it, conscious that he stood watching her. "Can I give you a ride to your car?"

"No thanks. I'll walk."

"Okay. Well...bye."

"Good bye, Jenny."

She got in the car, twisted the key in the ignition, and rolled down the window. "Have a good nap."

He nodded and tapped the top of the car twice, as if giving her the all-clear signal.

Jenny drove off, watching Gabe grow smaller and smaller in her rear view mirror. Good thing the parking lot wasn't crowded; it would have been embarrassing to run into a parked car while he was watching.

On the drive home, she didn't even try to curb her silly grin. He'd called her Jenny. She'd never thought of her name as anything special. Plain Jenny. Jenny Wren. But Gabe's deep timber made her name sound like a sensual promise.

She shivered and clutched the steering wheel. She'd met a great guy. He was confident, caring, and sexy as all get out.

And she'd get to see him again Saturday.

Chapter 3

Six forty-five Saturday night, Gabe pulled up outside Jenny's apartment, an old beige brick bungalow that had been converted into two apartments. He blew out a deep breath, wiped sweaty palms on his Dockers, and climbed out of the car.

"What're you doing here, Harrison?" he muttered. Slamming the door closed, Gabe looked at the house and drummed his fingers on the car roof. It'd been years since he'd had a real date, and Jenny was no Judith he could talk shop with. In fact, work and the kids were all that'd kept him and his ex-wife together. With Jenny, Gabe had neither.

"Come on, man, it hasn't been that long; how different could it be?" He crammed a restless hand in his pant pocket, rounded the car and walked up the steps. Maybe he should've called his son to subtly solicit a few pointers. He laughed at the absurdity.

For cripes sake, Harrison. Get a grip. He reached out to ring the doorbell. What could Ted teach him he didn't already know?

Whether you'll need a condom tonight or not.

"Shit." His hand abruptly fell away as the door whipped open.

Bright-eyed and grinning broadly, Jenny pushed the screen door open and looked past him. "Hi. Who're you talking to?"

His tension drained away at the sight of her. Jenny was dressed in a gauzy top and flowery skirt that fell to just above her ankles, revealing shiny blue toenails and sandals. She'd twisted the sides of her hair into some complicated braid, then left the rest free. Damp ends of her hair curled slightly below her breasts, releasing a fresh lemon aroma that made him want to pull her close, close his eyes, and fill his lungs with the summery, sunshine scent of her.

"I... Nobody. Just reviewing a few things I forgot to do before I left the hospital," he improvised. "You look great."

A gentle smile brightened her face. "Thanks. Do you need to call somebody to give them instructions?"

Would that he could. "Naw, it's fine. Ready?"

"Yup." She lowered the dark sunglasses perched on the crown of her head, pulled the door closed behind her, and started down the walkway.

Gabe trailed behind, watching her swaying skirt for a moment before tearing his glance away and swallowing hard. *Oh, Harrison, are you in trouble.*

He helped her into the car, then rushed around and got in. As he pulled away from the curb, he saw Jenny looking around the interior of the car. He made a quick inspection—nope, no forgotten lab specimen jars sat in the cup holder to gross her out, and he'd thrown out all the clutter before leaving home.

Jenny picked up his travel mug and studied the picture of him, Alex, and Ted taken outside the Hogwarts School gate. "You took the kids to the Wizarding World of Harry Potter? Oh my God. How was it?"

"Impressive. We had a great time. You're a Harry Potter fan?"

"Who isn't?" She put the mug back.

He felt her gaze on him, but when he looked at her, she immediately found the dashboard fascinating. He made a left at the light, and out of the corner of his eye watched her checking out his car again.

A slight frown wrinkled her brow—not in disgust but... What was she thinking? Was she having second thoughts? Was he overdressed in khakis and navy suit coat? He'd forgone the tie, but... He made a mental note to ditch the jacket as soon as possible.

He turned down Lakeshore Drive and headed north. Jenny casually—too casually—glanced over her shoulder into the old Volvo's backseat. What was she looking at?

"What?" he finally asked.

"What, what?" she feigned ignorance.

He studied her for several long seconds before returning his attention to the light evening traffic. "What's the matter?"

Her mouth opened and then closed as if trying to frame her comment tactfully. "You drive a station wagon."

"What's wrong with a station wagon?"

"Nothing. I just expected..."

So that was it. His station wagon didn't mesh with his doctor image. Relief flooded him and he suppressed a grin. "A BMW? Audi? Mercedes?"

"Well... Yeah." She squirmed in her seat, clearly uncomfortably. "I'm not a snob—really I'm not. It's just that I'd never have guessed a station wagon."

"Maybe I can't afford a better car?"

"Does that mean I'm paying for dinner?"

He laughed. "Of course not." He glanced at her and raised an eyebrow. "Maybe I'm not a very good doctor?"

"And you admit this to your patient's sister?"

"Gonna sue me?"

"Only if you screw up."

"Fair enough." He shrugged. "I don't need to impress anybody. The wagon suits me fine."

She bit her lip, hesitating before pressing to the heart of her discomfort. "It's black."

"What?"

"The car. It's black."

"I like black."

"No offense, but It looks like a hearse."

He scowled and reared his head back in surprise. "A what?"

She sniffed the air, as if searching for the noxious scent of formaldehyde or the sweet cloying odor of ripe flowers. "A hearse. You know, those black funeral cars that carry dead people around."

"I *know* what a hearse is." Silence filled the car a good five seconds before Gabe could think of a reply. "It does not."

Eyebrows raised, she tilted her head and winced in apology. "Yeah, it does. I'm sorry, but it reminds me of a hearse. All it needs is the little funeral flag."

"Very funny."

"Well, it does." A cute blush tinted her earnest face.

"At least you're honest," he chuckled. "Morbid, but honest."

What an interesting perspective on life, amusing and spontaneous. Refreshing.

They turned into the Hunt Club and drove down the long asphalt driveway under interlacing maple trees. Four green, freshly resurfaced outdoor tennis courts stood to the left of the entrance, and on the far side of them, farthest from the musty hay and horse smells, sat the club's pristine pool and red brick clubhouse.

From the big red and white barn straight ahead, a large brown horse with a jagged white mark bisecting his nose bobbed his head over his stall door. He nickered loudly to a fat gray pony standing in the shade, flicking his tail and chewing lazily as a groom sluiced water over his broad back.

Gabe exited the car to the rhythmic *clip clop* of a horse's hooves tapping the asphalt as a young girl urged her horse into a quick walk across the drive to the dirt corral. Alex had loved taking riding lessons here; she still enjoyed walking through the barns, petting a horse here and there and sneaking the gray fat pony carrots purloined from dinner.

The indoor tennis courts and riding rink were housed in the brown brick building next to the u-shaped stables. Colorful impatiens and daylilies circled the buildings. Altogether, the pastoral environment, secretly nestled in the heavily populated residential area, had a soothing effect on him. This was the kind of feeling he'd always wanted to come home to, but what was the point of creating this haven only for himself?

Standing beside the open car door, Jenny's wide eyes took it all in. "Wow. This is great. So peaceful."

Gabe smiled and stood a little taller. Shrugging out of his suit coat, he tossed it in the backseat. He took her elbow and moved her away from the car so he could lock it.

Walking toward the clubhouse, Jenny suddenly grabbed his hand and pulled him to a stop. She arched a brow. "Wait. You drive a station wagon, but have a membership to The Hunt Club?"

He relinquished her hand to pull open the dark wooden door. With a firm nudge at her back, he urged her through the entrance. "I play a lot of tennis."

"A *private club?*"

"The food's terrific."

Jenny laughed, a light airy sound that brushed away his defensiveness. "I'm sure it is."

At his request, the hostess seated them on the enclosed patio overlooking the swimming pool and outdoor tennis courts. She took their drink order and left them looking over the menu.

Jenny closed the menu and put it aside. "So when can Michael come home?"

"Tomorrow. He's done great since the transfusion." The waiter interrupted him to take their order. When he left, Gabe settled the cloth napkin across his lap. "So, how was your week? Did you get your article done?"

"Part one. I sent it in yesterday." He listened with interest as she detailed the kind of medical assistance the clinic offered and what the directors hoped to achieve, with special emphasis on how it was largely run by volunteer medical professionals.

She told him about the heartbreaking poverty she'd witnessed and the air of hopelessness permeating the neighborhood. "Hopefully, my article will spur some positive interest in the clinic."

Her impassioned talk reminded him of similar speeches he'd heard when his parents had solicited donations for their latest cause. "It's a large project."

"They want to make a difference."

"Don't we all?" He sipped his red wine and then reached for a hard roll. With quick mechanical thrusts, he slapped whipped butter on the bread.

Resting her elbows on the table, Jenny laced fingers around wine glass and tilted her head to the side. "What're you thinking?"

His attention snapped back to her. "Nothing really. I just hope they haven't taken on more than they can handle."

"Seemed pretty realistic to me."

"I've had a little experience with hospital politics. This clinic is a more complex issue than you've been led to believe. I don't think they can do it relying that heavily on volunteers. They need an enormous amount of capital, state or federally funded. Private sector donations aren't going to cut it."

"You seem to know a lot about it. Why don't you help?"

"I could," he allowed, reluctant yet intrigued. His practice kept him so busy that it'd been ages since he'd volunteered for anything. "My parents were in the Peace Corps," he said.

"And..."

"They died in a poor little village in Columbia."

"I'm sorry. What happened?"

"They caught amoebic dysentery. I was only twelve when they died. Before that, I'd traveled with them around the world wherever they were sent. It was a great adventure for a little boy—and a sad education. The people were so poor." In his mind's eye, he could still clearly picture the flimsy tin lean-tos. "The lucky ones had stick huts with tin roofs, and the wealthy ones had sandals. After my folks died, I went to live with my aunt and uncle."

Sympathy softened her expression. "I'm sorry. That must have been tough."

"Could have been worse. Aunt Adele and Uncle George were great. They were never able to have kids of their own, so it seemed like we were meant to be together."

"What an eventful childhood." She put her wine glass down. "Did you ever want to follow in your parents' footsteps, or did you resent their life?"

"I never resented what happened. Uncle George was angry enough for all of us. He was close to my mom and blamed my father and the Peace Corps for her death. But my parents loved helping others. They'd needed to try and make a difference—it's who they were. They often gave up their own quinine tablets so that the less hardy locals wouldn't get sick."

"What about you?" she asked softly.

"I always had quinine."

The conversation had turned uncomfortably personal and serious for a first date. Gabe hadn't thought about his parents and his unusual childhood in years. He had a lot of happy memories—his parents had been loving and generous, but their early deaths left a scar. Being orphaned was tough—even when raised by family.

The waiter delivered their dinner, and they ate in comfortable silence.

"After college, I considered joining the Corps," Gabe admitted.

"And?"

"Uncle George had a fit. He was hurt and betrayed. He even threatened to disinherit me." Gabe chuckled, a dry mirthless sound. "I wanted to join the Peace Corps—like I cared about money."

"What'd you do?"

"I stayed. He took me in and raised me." He shrugged. "I couldn't hurt him like that."

"What about your aunt?"

"Aunt Adele died of a stroke when I was fifteen."

Jenny blew out a dramatic breath. "Mother died, aunt died, wife divorced. Women don't last long around you do they, Harrison?"

He chuckled. "Guess not." The he held her gaze. "It'd take a special woman to stay with me."

The waiter interrupted to clear their plates. Declining dessert and coffee, they paid the bill and left the club.

Gabe groaned and patted his flat stomach. "I could use some exercise. Want to walk along the lake?"

"Sure."

They parked at the bottom of Woodland Shores Drive and crossed Lakeshore. The breeze lofted strands of Jenny's long hair before settling dark tendrils across his navy jacket arm, clinging like a sticky web. He jammed his hands deep in his pockets to keep from reaching out, gathering the escaped locks, and rubbing them to see if they were as soft as he imagined them to be.

Instead, Gabe scanned the glossy water dotted with hopeful sailboats and sighed. "It's beautiful here."

Beautiful woman. Beautiful sunset. Beautiful night. If he put his arm around Jenny, would she lean into him and rest her head on his shoulder while soaking in the serenity of the lake or was it too soon?

She stood with her arms crossed under her breasts, looking out across the water.

"Cold?" he asked.

"It's a little chilly."

He shrugged out of his jacket and draped it over her shoulders. She reached behind her to free her hair, but then the jacket began sliding off. Gabe brushed her hands aside. "I got it."

While she held onto the lapels, he gathered the hair at the nape of her neck and pulled the long strands free of his jacket, reluctantly releasing them to tumble down her back. Softer than he'd imagined, with the light airy scent of springtime.

"Thanks." Jenny shot him a quick, bright smile as they began walking. "I'd love to have a house on the water. Can you imagine how amazing it'd be to come home to this every day? It'd be the perfect place to write—so beautiful and quiet. How could you not be creative, surrounded by all that?" She paused. "We lived in San Diego for a while. I couldn't wait to get back to Michigan."

"Missed the humidity and bugs, did you?" He took her hand and pulled her away from a swarm of gnats, then didn't let go. Her small hand disappeared beneath his big paw, and he loved how it automatically curled into his. There was something intimate yet comforting about walking hand-in-hand. He'd missed this connection.

"Hardly," she said dryly. "I missed the huge green trees, the space, and seasons. I love the colors and smells in the fall, the biting winter, ice storms and all. And the spring—I can't imagine a more beautiful place in the spring with all the trees flowering. The summer may be a little hot, but if I could live by the lake, it'd be worth it."

"I agree. A lot of people aren't as blessed."

"Yeah, but we all have something to be thankful for."

"Tell that to the poor folks living in roach-infested dumps, struggling to eke out a living, trying to feed and clothe their kids while protecting them from gangs. I bet they have a little trouble finding blessings to count."

Jenny's sideways, cautious look told him he'd been a little too emphatic.

"Sorry. Guess I feel a little guilty. We've had a great meal and are enjoying this beautiful lake, while those poor people at that clinic have next to nothing. Comparatively."

"So why don't you help? Give them some time at the clinic? They're always looking for doctors to volunteer. One afternoon a week would be a huge help."

He pursed his lips in consideration. He could. "Maybe I will. It'd be good to feel useful again."

The pager on his hip sounded. *No. Not now. Damn it.*

Gabe released her hand to check the number. His shoulders drooped. "ICU I'm sorry; I've got to answer this."

"It's okay." She smiled. "I don't mind."

His hand went to his belt and the empty phone case, and then he patted his pockets.

"It's in your car. Charging."

"Right." *Damn.* "I hate to cut our walk short, but—"

"You have to answer the page." Jenny took his arm and turned them around. "If you weren't having a good time you could've taken me straight home. No need to have your buddy page you with a fake emergency."

"Wha—?" He frowned and his pace slowed before halting completely as he got it. "Hey, no. This is for real. I—"

Her lips spread in a wide grin. "I'm teasing you." His pager sounded again. Jenny tugged on his arm. "Come on. Let's go. You need to save a life."

She'd been kidding? "Have you done that often?"

"Tease?"

"Have a friend text you to get you out of an awful date?"

She gave him an impish look. "Maybe a time or two. You haven't?"

"Nope. No need." He lightly squeezed her hand. "I'm an excellent judge of character."

"And. It never occurred to you."

He grinned. No way he was going to admit that. They hurried back to the car, where Gabe could answer the page in relative privacy.

Tuning out his conversation, Jenny settled back in the cloth seat and blew out a contented sigh. Nice dinner followed by a pleasant walk by the lake and not much first date awkwardness. Gabe was intelligent, interesting, and caring. So where was his fatal flaw?

She peeked at Gabe out of the corner of her eye, admiring his handsome face, kind eyes, and the soothing timbre of his voice. He was polished, she'd give him that, and when he smiled he was irresistible. His smile literally made her heart flutter. This guy had definite potential. She pulled his jacket tighter around her. But his car definitely was weird. It really did remind her of a hearse—she hadn't been teasing him about that.

Gabe held out his phone to her. "Say hello to Betty."

"Wha—?" Jenny automatically took the phone. Then she glimpsed the sparkle in his eyes.

He nodded at the phone. "Go on."

She brought the phone to her ear. "Hello?"

"Hi, Jenny. My name is Betty and I'm a nurse in the ICU"

Jenny's eyes grew wide as she stared at Gabe, who watched her intently.

Are you kidding me right now?

"Dr. Harrison wanted me to assure you that he's having a marvelous time on his date, and he's heartbroken that he has to cut your evening short, but he *really* does need to go to work and this *really* is an emergency."

Seriously? She looked at Gabe's amused expression, knowing he could easily hear every word. *Touché, Doctor.*

"And how much is Dr. Harrison paying you to say that?"

Betty laughed. "Nothing. We love Dr. Harrison. He's a real sweetie."

"Say goodbye," Gabe ordered as he held out his hand. Was that a blush darkening his cheeks?

"He doesn't date nearly enough," Betty said.

"Is that so?" Jenny gave him a sly look, and leaned away as he tried to snatch his phone.

"Which was why I was so sorry to have to bother him tonight, but—"

Jenny grinned at Gabe's scowl and took pity on him. "Goodbye, Betty. It was nice chatting with you." She handed Gabe his cell.

Gabe mumbled a goodbye, turned on the car, and drove away from the peaceful lake. "You seem to have trust issues. I thought you might need proof that I wasn't ditching you."

"Thanks," she said dryly. "Now she's gonna think I'm some clingy, insecure woman."

"Hardly. She's going to think I'm pitiful and inept since I needed her to vouch for me. But if Betty met you..." He gave her a warm, admiring look that curled her toes. "She'd know I'm a very lucky guy."

Well, heck. It's hard to tease someone when he's so darn sweet. Tonight had been great; Jenny didn't want it to end so soon. "I'm surprised you *didn't* bring me in and make Betty tell me to my face."

"I don't dare," he muttered.

"What?"

"I thought of it, but I wasn't sure how long I'd be and I'd hate to keep you waiting."

"And considerate, too." Jenny smiled. "Somebody raised you right, Harrison."

"Why, thank you, ma'am."

At her apartment, Gabe walked Jenny to the door. She faced him and smiled. "Thanks for dinner. I had a great time."

"Me, too. Sorry we had to cut our walk short."

"Me, too." She looked down, feeling stupid at having mimicked his words. She was a journalist for pity's sake; she ought to be able to come up with her own words.

He glanced back at his car. "I'd better get going."

Ordinarily she would have invited him in, but a patient was waiting for him. Should she kiss him? A quick glance up the street showed that her neighbors had retired for the night.

Gabe lifted her chin and brushed a light kiss across her lips, a little more than a taste really, then turned and walked away.

Jenny opened her eyes and frowned at the empty space in front of her, then found his retreating back. *That's it? That's all she got?* Gabe was nearly at his car when she called out, "Gabe, wait."

He stopped and turned around.

"You forgot something."

Gabe retraced his steps, and she met him halfway. Jenny's gaze locked onto his gray eyes, willing him to kiss her again. Hands pressed against his warm chest, she held on tight. His head lowered and his eyelids drifted shut in a lazy, sensual promise. She rose up on tiptoe and leaned into him. She longed to snuggle into his neck where the faint, yet heady, scent of cologne and male tantalized her.

Her breath quickened with the effort to keep her hands from exploring the hard muscles beneath her damp palms. In all honesty, she'd been curious about this since she'd first awakened in Michael's room and seen him watching them sleep.

Lips glided over hers; their warm breath mingled. She wound her arms around his collar so that her fingertips trailed on a seductive quest through crisp, short hair at the nape of his neck. His hands dropped to her waist, and he pulled her firmly against him in a hold so intimate that Jenny had to quell the instinct to press her hips against his.

His heart pounded against her breast, an ardent, undeniable appeal. His breath came in short bursts, between deepening, wet kisses she relished. Groaning, Gabe's fingers dug into her waist as he pushed her away, putting a good half of a foot between their heated bodies. He rested his forehead against hers, while drawing in several deep breaths. "I should go."

Gabe didn't lift his head or remove his hands from her waist, and Jenny's hands remained locked around his neck.

"I have to go."

Mind numb, Jenny's consciousness lagged several seconds behind. She released him, and trailed hands down his chest. "Okay."

"Geeze. We're standing in your front yard making out like teenagers when I should be taking care of poor Mr. Rogers." He shook his head, bemused. "You're a bad influence, Jenny Campbell."

No kidding. Wasn't the first time she'd heard that, but this time she didn't mind in the least.

"Yeah, but you like me anyway." She flashed him a sassy smile. "'Night." Pulling out of his arms, she scooted into the house before she gave into the temptation to invite him in and the hell with Mr. Rogers.

Now *that* was a proper kiss. Jenny shut the door, closed her eyes, and leaned against the hard wood, staying that way until she heard his car pull away. Great kisser. Great guy.

Taking a deep breath, she pushed away from the door, kicked off her shoes, and tossed her keys and purse onto the table. Jenny poured herself a Sprite Zero and sat at her desk. She jotted down a quick note to call her editor at ten-thirty Monday morning then scrolled through the messages on her phone. Nothing from Starbucks.

What ever happened to common courtesy? She'd interviewed with them more than a week ago; they couldn't even take the time to drop her a note letting her know she'd been passed over? Or were they still interviewing candidates? Maybe she needed to do an article on the demise of polite social behavior. *Yeah, that'll get you a job.*

Jenny opened her Gmail. Eureka! An email from Nordstrom's. Working retail again wasn't her first choice, but it wouldn't be the worst thing either. Jenny opened the email, then drooped into her seat. *Dear Jenny, I appreciate you coming out and interviewing, but the position has been filled. We will keep you in mind...* Yada yada yada.

"Don't bother," she muttered and tossed the phone onto the desk. She needed the extra money now. She *had* to start whittling away at that balance on her credit cards.

Jenny'd indulged herself a little too much lately, buying her MacBook Air, Cannon DSLR, computer backpack, several new outfits, and a few other costly accessories she needed for work.

After all, if she expected people to take her seriously, if she wanted her editor to trust her with the choice assignments, she needed to look like a professional. But when the bill came in, she'd been shocked at the price of chic professionalism.

Not to mention that darn hundred and twenty-five-dollar Zorlac. Considering all Michael's medical bills, that had to be the most expensive skateboard on the face of the earth.

To be fair, the Jeep repair was not her fault; the transmission died on her. Unfortunately, resuscitating the Jeep added another three thousand dollars to her already stressed VISA and MasterCard—she'd had to split the payment between them.

Jenny scowled and pursed her lips. She needed to make money, and fast. Even taking in a roommate hadn't helped as much as she'd hoped. She fingered a sheet of paper with her roommate's suggestion. Cindy paid for extra goodies and vacations being a part-time nanny. Sittercity.com, eh?

Jenny hadn't babysat anyone other than Michael, and that'd been a long time ago. But there was a lot of flexibility in nannying. And it paid well. She wrinkled her nose at the thought of changing dirty, smelly diapers and being slobbered on. She glanced at the email reminding her that Citibank had her statement ready. Sighing, she opened her computer and typed in the website.

"Of course. Another log-in and stupid password to remember."

Jenny sat back in her chair and crossed her arms over her stomach. Then again, if she couldn't get a job working retail—something she had experience in—what made her think anybody would trust her with their kids? There had to be another way to make money... Selling body parts? Did she really need that spare kidney?

If she didn't find something soon, she'd have to ask Dad for a loan, but that was absolutely her last resort. Mom couldn't find out that she'd gotten herself in a financial bind. Jenny'd never live that down.

Chapter 4

Jenny spent most of the next week at her computer. She visited Michael shortly after he got home from the hospital but didn't stay long. Her mother hovered around them, finding any excuse to stay by Michael's side, continually reminding Jenny not to tire him.

Jenny found conversations with her brother were far easier conducted over the telephone—especially when timed during Mom's favorite evening TV programs *The Voice, CSI, Downton Abby,* or *Modern Family* re-runs.

Stretching her arms over her head, then across her body in a firm hug to relieve her bunched shoulder muscles, Jenny pushed away from her computer. She looked at her watch. Nearly dinnertime; Mom would be busy preparing supper. Jenny picked up the phone and dialed. Slouching in her chair, she propped one foot on the desk.

"Hi, Mom. How's it going?"

"Not bad. Michael had a good day. He's a little tired from our walk to the mailbox, but he's getting stronger. I'm glad you called." Mom lowered her voice. "Michael said you went out to dinner with his doctor the other night." She paused. "You weren't actually on a date, were you?"

"How—?" It'd been a great first date, but nothing Mom needed to worry about. Gabe had kids and she had bills and a career to establish. Despite that completely unprofessional, toe-curling kiss in her front yard, she had her priorities straight. "It was business, Mom. He wanted some information about an article I did."

"Oh, good. Did you have a good time?"

"Yes, Mom. He's very nice." Nice guy, nice sense of humor, and a *very* nice body that tempted her to forget his teenagers, her responsibilities, and her mother, she really didn't want to disappoint again. Jenny cleared her throat. "Is Michael around?"

"Sure, I'll get him."

"Hey, Jen. When're you comin' over?" Michael asked.

"Not sure. Why, what'd ya need?" Jenny pulled her hair back and over one shoulder.

"Food. Mom won't give me anything good—only healthy stuff to build up my blood," he said, raising his voice, mimicking their mother, then sighed dramatically. "I'd kill for a burger and a bag of Doritos."

"Good to see you're recovering your appetite. Eat the veggies Mom gives you and I'll smuggle you in some Burger King tomorrow." She divided her hair into three hanks, untangling and smoothing each section.

"Cool. Hey, Jen?" His voice lowered. "I didn't mean to get you in trouble."

"What trouble?"

"You know. The skateboard. You and Dr. Harrison. I thought she knew."

"Don't worry about it." Jenny expertly flipped one section of hair over and the other under.

"But you and Mom—"

"Are fine. It has nothing to do with you."

"Is she mad you're dating Dr. Harrison?"

Jenny raised her eyebrows. Her hands stilled. "What makes you think I'm dating Dr. Harrison?"

"He was asking a bunch of questions about you. And none of the other kids' doctors visited them that much, so I figured either he had a crush on you or I was dying."

She smiled at his logic and continued weaving her hair. "He doesn't have a crush on me. He took me to dinner once—to talk about the Donnatelli clinic."

"Whatever. *Is* Mom mad you're dating him?"

"Why would she be?" She twisted a hair tie at the bottom of her braid.

"He's old."

Jenny could imagine that, 'well, duhhh' look Michael gave her whenever he thought she was being dense. "He's *not* old."

"A lot older than you."

She knew he'd rolled his eyes at her. "Not much."

"Wa-a-y."

"Besides, age doesn't matter so much the older you get." Especially when he had a great body and a sexy smile.

"Well, I like him."

"Me too." The doorbell rang. "Gotta go, Kiddo. Someone's at the door. Be good."

Jenny clicked off the phone and looked through the peek hole to see Gabe's distorted face. It'd been a week and a half since she'd last seen him, although he had called several times. They'd mostly spent the week playing phone tag.

She took in her bare feet, jeans, and Mickey Mouse T-shirt. With her hair pulled back and braided, Jenny knew she looked young and unsophisticated—not exactly the image she wanted to project around her older guy friend. She toyed with the idea of pretending she wasn't home, but his handsome face on the other side of the door pulled at her. She'd missed him.

Jenny's dilemma ended as she looked beyond Gabe to her approaching roommate. She bolted to the kitchen, yanked the dishwasher door open, turned the water on, and began scrubbing dishes.

"Jen, you home?" Cindy called out.

"In here."

Cindy appeared in the kitchen doorway, with Gabe looking over her shoulder. She jerked a thumb toward him. "Look who I found outside. He says he's a friend of yours."

Casually dressed in jeans, a white polo shirt, and sneakers, Gabe flashed a tentative smile. "Hi."

Smiling, Jenny turned the water off, then wiped her hands on a nearby dishtowel. "Yeah, I know him."

"Well..." Cindy backed down the hallway. "I'll catch up with you guys later."

Suddenly alone, Jenny tugged at her worn T-shirt and propped one bare foot on top of the other as if hiding the fact that she was barefoot. Jenny suddenly wished she were one of those girls that put on makeup as soon as they rolled out of bed.

Gabe stood in her tiny kitchen, shifting his weight from one foot to the other, watching her reaction as if unsure of his welcome. "I was on my way back from a Tiger's game, and... kind of ended up here. Want to get a Dairy Queen?"

Had he taken his kids or a date to the ballgame? Don't be silly; he wasn't the kind of guy to go from one woman to the next. Was he? "Did they win?"

"No. It was pretty boring, but Uncle George had free tickets."

His uncle, she cheered. "Free's hard to pass up. Where's your uncle?"

"I ditched him. I'll buy you a cone—or a blizzard, or you might want a sundae... whatever you want." His voice trailed off.

Jenny inwardly smiled. He was nervous—how cute. She raised her eyebrows. "Large, chocolate-dipped?"

"Sure."

Jenny passed him. "Let me get my shoes and a sweater."

After she was suitably attired, Gabe pulled the apartment door closed behind them and followed her into the front yard. Although spring was here and they had the rains to prove it, the late afternoons held a definite chill.

Jenny drew in a deep breath of crisp, pure air and looked around, loving the way the new green leaves were beginning to unfold on the huge trees. The pale lime shoots contrasted against the dark brown branches, looking like delicate lacy veils covering the huge trees. Beautiful.

She hesitated as they approached the hearse. "Let's walk. I could use the exercise."

"How far is it?"

"Not more than a mile or two."

"One way?" He stood on the sidewalk with keys in hand, looking at her in surprise. "You hate my car that much?"

"I don't hate it." She glanced away, rueful. "Exactly."

Laughing, he pocketed his keys and took her hand. "I love your honesty. Lead the way."

Jenny loved the way his larger hand dwarfed hers in a light, possessive hold. They walked down the block, with Jenny returning neighbors' greetings.

"I started work at the clinic. I'll be there every Tuesday," Gabe announced.

"You did? That's great." He'd actually taken her suggestion to volunteer. She was flattered—and nervous. What if it didn't work out? What if his car got broken into or his partners got mad at the loss of income, or if one of the indigent patients sued him? Would he blame her? "How was it?"

"Interesting. I treated a pregnant fifteen-year-old who didn't tell anyone she was pregnant until she was eight months along, and there were the usual U.R.I.s—upper respiratory infections—and allergies, common this time of year. But then there was a guy who got beat up with a tire iron and a carpenter who shot himself in the thigh with a nail gun."

"Yow." She winced. "Sounds like they kept you busy."

"For sure."

"What do your partners think?"

"They're not crazy about it. But they were mollified by a cut in my salary."

She slowed and turned to him. "Oh, no. *I'm sorry.* I never thought—"

He squeezed and tugged her hand. "Don't worry."

"But your partners—"

"Are fine."

She should have kept her big mouth shut. Now because of her Gabe was making less money. She peeked at him. With his loose stroll and relaxed expression, he didn't seem concerned. Maybe he could afford it. "But you're happy with your decision?"

"You know... I am," he said, sounding like this was the first he'd recognized it. "I went into medicine, for the usual reasons—"

"Money?" She couldn't resist ribbing him.

Gabe nodded, smiling. "Right, money. Anyhow, work had become so routine, I hadn't realized how bored I was until you and the clinic came along."

Her heart swelled with pride that he was crediting her with being a positive influence in his life. That was a first. But doubt crept back. "Don't go thanking me yet. See how you like it a year from now."

"Yeah, but I have a good feeling about it, like I do about you." He smiled warmly and squeezed her hand. "My instincts about these things are never wrong."

She hoped not 'cause she really liked him too.

As they approached the red and white hut, Gabe perused the ice cream selections. "What do you want?"

To continue that conversation about the good feelings you have for me, she thought. "Small vanilla cone, dipped please."

"Small? What happened to large?"

She grinned and shrugged. "Just wanted to see if you were a big spender."

They sat at a picnic bench licking their cones. "So if your instincts are never wrong, what happened with your first marriage?"

"We married and had kids too young." He tossed the end of his orange sugar cone in the aluminum garbage can, wiped his face, and threw the paper napkin away. "She fell in love with another guy. We divorced. They had two more kids and have been happily married for the past ten years."

"No waaay." She couldn't imagine any woman turning down Gabe for another guy. She'd had him; they had two kids together. She must have cared for him. How could she have broken his heart? "What about you?"

"The divorce was hard." He nodded and pursed his lips. "But I adjusted. We all did."

She stared at him, the ice cream in her hands forgotten. His dispassionate tone shocked her. His life had fallen apart, yet he recited it like recounting his morning dressing ritual. He'd lost not just a wife, but his whole family.

"You let them go, just like that? What about your kids?"

Gabe's face darkened. "That's how it works. And Dave's a good man. What was I supposed to do, make her miserable staying with me? I loved Judith, but I wasn't *in love* with her—not the way Dave loves her." He paused letting his words sink in. "She deserved to be happy. So I let her go."

Wow. His selfless logic blew her away. His wife fell in love with another man and he'd put her happiness above his own. Jenny looked at him, curious. "What about the kids?"

"What about them? They've got two dads. Dave's a great father. He's never tried to usurp my position with Ted and Alex, and he fills in for me whenever I have to work. I have joint custody. Now that they're older and can drive, I never know when they'll drop in on me."

"Amazing." Eyes locked on Gabe, she ignored the chilly ice cream dripping down her hand. She'd never been more attracted to a man. "You're a very special guy, Doctor Harrison."

Gabe brought her sticky hand to his mouth. With quick little strokes that faintly tickled, he licked the ice cream trailing down her fingers. At her quick intake of breath, he tilted his head so that his darkened gaze met hers. "You're pretty special yourself, Ms. Campbell."

"Gabe?" An older man on a mountain bike pulled up next to them. A Wayne State sweatshirt stretched tightly across his protruding belly. He swiped at the sweat running in rivulets down the sides of his flushed face to his jowls as he caught his breath. "I thought that was you. How're you doing?"

Gabe released her hand, turned and nodded. "Fine, Ken. You?"

Jenny took the opportunity to throw out the rest of her cone and wipe her hand.

"Great, just out for a ride, trying to work off those old love handles. Taking my kids up north next weekend. My son thinks he's gonna leave his old Pop in the dust." He glanced at Jenny, nodding. "This must be your daughter. She's beautiful—takes after her mother, eh?"

Daughter? She and Alex looked nothing alike. Jenny glanced at Gabe out of the corner of her eye to gauge his reaction.

"This is my friend, Jenny." Unperturbed, Gabe turned to her. "Jenny, Ken. Ken's Chief of Neurology at St. Francis. Been riding long, Ken?"

He paused briefly, as if considering Gabe's question, before giving himself a mental shake. With one last curious look at Jenny, he patted his gut. "Try to do ten miles three times a week. Great exercise. You should try it."

"I don't have love handles."

"Not yet, but you're getting up there. It pays to keep in shape."

"Thanks, I'll remember that. You'd better get going before it gets dark."

"Right." Ken's cheerful facade wilted. With a muffled groan, he pushed away from the curb. "See ya around."

Jenny moved close to Gabe, giggling. "Daughter?"

He stared at her, assessing. "You could be. With your hair like that and no makeup, you could pass for a teenager."

"Yeah," she drawled. "If you'd been a really precocious boy."

"We have similar coloring."

"And that's about it." She wrapped an arm around his trim waist and leaned into him. "We could really give them something to talk about," she whispered, pulling his head down. "But, of course, it might ruin your reputation to be caught necking with your daughter."

Tongue poking his cheek, he looked over her head, pretending to consider it, before turning sparkling eyes to her. "I'm willing to risk it."

∾ ∾ ∾

"Gabe? I'm starvin'. Ready to go?" George Turner called as he let himself into Gabe's little house and wandered into the kitchen.

"Just out of the shower," Gabe yelled from down the hall. "Help yourself to a beer."

George snagged a Molson's from the fridge, pawed through several cupboards before he found the Lays potato chips his nephew always kept in the house. After twisting off the cap and tossing it onto the counter, he grabbed a handful of chips and pulled out a stool.

Squeak, screech, whizz.

"What the hell?" George scowled at Gabe's phone as it made a racket again. *What the hell is wrong with the thing?*

He picked it up and saw Alex's pretty face. He poked the text message and smiled at a picture of Alex and her best friend, Jamie. At sixteen, his great niece was turning into a pretty young lady. She'd grown into her gangly pubescent limbs. The persistent freckles across the bridge of her pert nose and her mischievous grin gave her away. She would look younger than her years for quite a while still, despite her curves and makeup.

He took a long pull on his beer, closed the text, and poked Gabe's photo icon. What other pictures did Gabe have of the kids? There were the three of them at Ted's graduation. Then a few shots of Gabe and Ted washing Ted's new car, a '90 Ford Mustang convertible. Ted's pride and joy.

Although divorced, Judith and Gabe had done a good job with those kids. They raised them right. He hadn't seen his great niece and nephew in a while. Maybe he should take them out to dinner to catch up.

He swiped through some group pictures of people on a sailboat, pausing on a shot of Gabe and some girl. The wind ruffled Gabe's hair as he grinned carefree into the lens. One arm draped casually around the girl, who held a handful of long, brown hair away from her face while she posed for the camera. The next picture caught the girl perched at the bow, looking wistfully out over the water. Then a close-up of the same picture. What a looker. Who was she?

George gazed out the window, trying to remember if he'd ever met her. His glance lit on a red car parked in Gabe's driveway. Frowning, he took a gulp of his beer, then called out, "Hey, there's a fire-engine parked in your drive."

Gabe rounded the corner, finger brushing his damp hair. Ducking, he looked out the window. "The car? It's mine."

"You got a new car? What's wrong with the old one?"

Gabe got himself a beer. "Nothing. I repainted it. Got tired of the black."

He put the phone down. "Your phone was squeaking and squawkin'."

"That's my text alert. Recognize it?"

"Should I?"

"You know it." Gabe picked it up, poked the phone a couple of times, and set it off.

George cocked his head. It was kind of familiar...

"R2-D2. *Star Wars.*"

Of course. "Oh, yeah." He and Gabe had a tradition of seeing each movie the day it came out. "I'm not supposed to know the girl, too, am I?"

"Who? Alex's friend?"

"Naw, I know Jamie." George took Gabe's phone and flipped through to the picture of the brunette with the long hair. He angled the phone toward Gabe. "This one."

Leaning close, Gabe craned his head sideways to get a better look. He'd taken the picture of Jenny out on the sailboat on the fourth of July. Her long silky hair blew free in the wind as she hugged her slender, shapely legs tight against her chest. He loved the sexy, carefree smile she'd given him. A smile full of promise. Just for him. God, she made him feel like a king. He'd have to print that one.

"Jenny. We went out with friends on the Fourth." He popped a chip in his mouth.

"You're *dating* her?" George riffled back to the shot of the two of them, she looked older there, maybe early twenties, but in the one on the bow with her hair blowing in the breeze, she could've been Alex's age.

Gabe nodded and swallowed. No denying Jenny looked young for her age, but she acted a lot older. An old soul. Yes, he was dating her and loving it. Before Jenny, he'd been idling along, especially since his buddy had gotten married and moved to New York six months ago.

He'd turned to his children to fill his free time, but his kids were mostly grown and didn't need him. In fact, he got the feeling they allowed him to hang out with them and their friends out of pity. They felt sorry for him because he was alone. Which he wasn't— really. He had Uncle George to play golf with, a thriving practice, and Wednesday night tennis league.

It wasn't as if he'd never dated—not seriously, until Jenny. He'd never taken the time to get serious. After the divorce, he and Judith devoted a lot of time ensuring that the children were okay with their new lives, and his life had gradually slipped into a routine existence.

Even his work became habitual. Gallbladders, bowel resections, mastectomies, hernias, and so on. His life had turned gray, but since being with Jenny, he was seeing bright colors. Brilliant hues he'd never noticed before. No matter what they did, whether it was a simple walk down the street, a concert under the stars, or grocery shopping, with Jenny he noticed the beauty in life.

She reminded him of the good and the bad that he used to see before he'd gotten bogged down in routine. Now he took the time to rediscover life outside his family and hospital. Took time to rediscover himself. He redirected his energies to caring outside him, and it felt good. Hell, it felt great.

"Since when're you into cradle robbing?" Eyes narrowing, Uncle George stared at Jenny's picture. "I swear I've seen her before."

"Probably in the paper. A couple of weeks ago her story about teenage runaways was the cover story for the magazine insert in the *Free Press*. She's really good."

Uncle George's lips tightened in anger. Face contorting in disgust, he tossed the phone onto the mail like it oozed toxic waste. "You're dating a reporter? A child reporter at that?"

"Journalist."

"Are you nuts, man?"

"She freelances, Uncle George. Human interest stories."

"Snoop stories that tell things better left untold. They justify them as 'human interest,' when they print some trash about you."

Gabe's face remained impassive. He was *not* going to argue about this. Uncle George couldn't be swayed by logical arguments when it came to reporters.

"After what they did to Adele, how could you date anybody in the press?"

Gabe drained his beer and placed the bottle in the recycle bin. "Let's go."

Uncle George swiveled on his stool, stubbornly refused to budge. "I'm *not* ready to go."

Gabe gave him a patient look. "Look, Jenny's a great lady. I'm not going to justify her career choice to you. She's not a threat to you, or anybody. She helps people, and I admire her for that."

And I'm not about to let you scare her away.

He'd purposely kept Uncle George away from Jenny these past few months, knowing that not many women appreciated his uncle's bluntness. Uncle George was a little rough around the edges—not exactly a people person.

Usually, Gabe didn't care much if Uncle George upset his dates—he was a good test—but Jenny was special. He didn't want Uncle George scaring her off. He sighed. Now that Uncle George knew about her, their meeting was inevitable. Maybe he'd like her. He could behave himself when he liked someone. He could be charming when he wanted to be. What wasn't there to like about Jenny?

She was beautiful, spunky, and quick-witted. Much like his mother, Uncle George's little sister. She was also a great cook, like Aunt Adele. And compassionate and seemingly very tolerant, like both Mom and Aunt Adele. He looked at Uncle George's suspicious expression, and his heart fell. Yup. He was going to test Jenny's compassion. No doubt about it.

George's eyes narrowed in comprehension. He pointed an accusing finger at Gabe. "She's the one that got you goin' on that clinic in the ghetto."

"She didn't 'get me going' on anything."

"She did. She wrote those articles about that clinic you're wasting your time on. How long till you're done impressing her, son?"

Gabe frowned. "I'm not working there to impress her. I enjoy it."

"My ass. Just like you didn't break your arm on the trampoline showing off for little Julie Rider in sixth grade."

Because at forty, I still have the social skills of a twelve-year-old. Gabe knew better than to feed into his uncle's taunting.

"Do you enjoy not getting paid, too?"

Gabe raised his eyebrows, nodding. "As a matter of a fact, I do."

He snorted. "I thought I taught you better. What about your responsibility to your partners?" Then his expression lightened in comprehension. "It's a tax write-off, right? You keep track of the money you could be charging for working at the clinic and they give you a slip for the IRS, like donating old clothes to AM Vets, right?"

What? Gabe tilted his head sideways and squinted as he tried to follow the man's skewed logic. "No, I can't write it off on my taxes. Look, I know you mean well, but drop it."

"Drop it?" he echoed. "What? Do you enjoy keeping me up nights worryin' about you? That place is dangerous. Nothing but gangbangers and junkies. I sent you to med school to keep you out of neighborhoods like that."

"And I'm grateful, but even poor people need medical treatment. Most of the patients at the clinic are good honest folks trying to make a living. Instead of griping about them you should be trying to help them, the way you helped me."

From Uncle George's narrowed, thoughtful expression Gabe knew that he suspected he was being placated with flattery and reasoning. But it was working.

Gabe pressed his advantage. "You took me in when you didn't have to. You took care of me. Taught me right from wrong, and told me I had to get an education. If it hadn't been for you, I might have ended up in some foster family or out on the street. I'm just giving back a little, Uncle George. I'm doing the responsible thing—and you know it."

Uncle George hated admitting when Gabe was right. He hefted himself off the stool, tossed his bottle in the trash, and headed for the door, mumbling, "Couldn't you just write them a check?"

Gabe laughed and slapped him on the back. "You write the check."

George grunted. He wasn't going to win this one. Once Gabe made up his mind, he rarely changed it. His mother had been stubborn like that. The obsession to help the downtrodden must have been passed along in the genes, 'cause Lord knew he tried hard enough to teach Gabe that he needn't put himself on the line to help people.

He'd guilted him out of that stupid Peace Corp tour. It already took his sister; George wasn't going to give it another life in Gabe, so he'd talked him out of signing up—without a twinge of guilt. But apparently he hadn't extinguished the compulsion altogether.

It hadn't even been that hard to get Gabe to forget the Peace Corp. Gabe felt indebted to him—not that he'd ever done anything to make him feel this way, but he hadn't discouraged the thinking either.

Honorable to a fault, Gabe always did the right thing; it was only that sometimes being honorable led to heartbreak. Like when Gabe married Judith 'cause she'd gotten pregnant, then the shmuck simply stepped aside and let that Dave character steal his wife and family.

Too nice for his own good, Gabe still needed watching after. It was a job George'd grown used to doing. They walked out the door, and he paused while Gabe locked it. "So tell me about this girl."

"What about her?"

"Are you sleeping with her?"

"No comment."

He hadn't really thought Gabe would tell him, but you never know. "You're using protection, right?"

Gabe scowled over the car roof at him. "No. Comment."

"How long you been dating her?"

"A few months."

"Months?" George leaned his forearm against the windshield. Hmm. Months was more than a few dates in. Sounded like a relationship. Although an infatuation could go on for months. Didn't have to be serious. Cocking his head he squinted at Gabe. "She know you have kids?"

"Yup."

"Why wasn't she at Ted's graduation?"

Gabe slid in the car and popped the lock. "Out of town."

"What kind of woman doesn't make your kid's graduation?" George pulled the car door open and got in.

"The kind who honors a previous commitment. She was a bridesmaid in a friend's wedding in Kentucky."

"What do the kids think of her?"

"They like her."

"They're not bothered by your cradle-robbing?"

"Nope."

"Aw, come on."

"Sorry. They like her just fine."

Gabe didn't sound the least bit apologetic. "They have any idea you're serious about her?"

"Don't know. Don't care. Look," Gabe turned on the car and faced him. "Stop looking for trouble. I'm sorry about what happened with Aunt Adele. I agree that if it wasn't for that stupid article, she'd probably still be alive today. But Jenny's not like that, and she's not responsible for Aunt Adele's death, so don't take it out on her." Gabe gave him a stern look. "Jenny's special. She means a lot to me, so when you meet her, *be nice.*"

Gabe's serious expression and lecture made George nervous. This wench had really got under his skin. But how far? "You're not going to marry her, are you? I mean you're not *that* serious, right?"

"Let's eat." Gabe pulled out of the driveway and headed toward The Hill.

Chapter 5

Jenny sat at her Mac editing her piece on a program that helped homebound elderly people. One last pass, and she could send it in. She smiled at the champagne-colored sweetheart roses standing in her grandmother's crystal vase on the corner of her desk. Still fresh after a week.

Taking one perfect, newly opened bud, she brought it to her lips, marveling at its cool silkiness. Jenny closed her eyes and inhaled the light, slightly citrusy scent that would forever remind her of that awesome weekend.

After a wonderful day out on his boat, she and Gabe had run to Kroger and Nino Salvaggio's and strolled the food aisles selecting fresh veggies to grill along with their steaks. Lays potato chips, double chocolate ice cream, fresh raspberries and blueberries to accompany their bagels and cream cheese breakfast also found the way into their cart. Jenny threw in a bag of plums, grapes, a Sanders bittersweet chocolate topping for the ice cream, double chocolate milk, and shaving cream.

ດບ ດບ ດບ

They returned to Gabe's place and unpacked the groceries. Romantic candlelight softly lit the tiny kitchen and mellow show tunes soothed them as they ate the delicious dinner. Jenny, hands buried deep in warm, sudsy water washed a spatula, when a stinging snap bit her butt.

"Youch!" she jumped and spun around. "What the—?"

Gabe stood near the table giving the platter he was drying undue attention. He looked up and frowned. "You okay?"

She scowled at his innocent expression. "Cute, Harrison."

Jenny turned back to the dishes. In the window reflection, she caught sight of Gabe winding his towel seconds before a crack sounded and her other buttock smarted.

"Ow!" She whirled around. "Knock it off." She rubbed her stinging butt. "That hurts."

Gabe widened his eyes and raised his eyebrows. "Did a bee sting you?"

"I'll show you bee sting," she muttered, glaring.

"Me?" He managed to keep a straight face, but his eyes were smiling—the brat. Jenny had never mastered the wrist-flick necessary to whip a towel, but she'd get even.

Head down, she diligently scrubbed a pot while watching his reflection in the window. He wound the towel once, twice, three times. As he pulled back, she spun around and turned freezing cold water on her tormenter.

"Wha—?" Gabe held his hands up to block the spray. "Are you crazy?"

His blue dress shirt turned navy as water bounced off the saturated shirt. He backed away, then dodged right, then left. Jenny relentlessly kept the spray trained on him, refusing to show any mercy. Gabe charged her, trying to wrestle the hose from her grasp.

"I." She twisted in his arms and held the nozzle as far away from him as she could. "Warned. You," Jenny huffed.

Instead of going for the hose, Gabe attacked her ribs, tickling.

Squirming, Jenny dropped the nozzle and slid out of his hold.

Gabe grabbed the hose, tossed it in the sink, and slapped the water off.

"Not fair," she wheezed.

"You call this fair?" He gestured to the water dripping off the cabinets, streaking the stainless steel refrigerator, puddling on the stove. He shook his head, like a shaggy dog, sending water spraying everywhere.

Oh my God. Jenny grimaced at the dripping kitchen and water pooling all over his hardwood floors. What'd gotten into her? Gaze never leaving Gabe's face, Jenny tried to gauge how angry he was as she backed away. What kind of retaliation would he exact? Her mouth gapped open and closed. "I'm... I'm... I'm so sor—"

Gabe lunged forward, grabbed her wrist, and yanked her forward, plastering her against his cold, soaked body.

"I'm sorry. I'm sorry. I—" She twisted and squirmed, but his grip didn't loosen a bit. Pursing her lips, she reared back to break his hold, then froze when she saw the humor in his eyes. He wasn't angry; he was amused—and aroused. Now still, Jenny felt his erection throb against her belly. Like a light switch flicked, her shortness of breath and adrenaline rush took on an entirely different feeling. *That* type of retribution she was willing to take.

Jenny relaxed into his embrace and pulled Gabe's head down for a long, deep kiss. Through wet, clinging clothes, the heat of his body and pound of his heart called to her. She fumbled with his buttons, impatient to peel the shirt from his body. Gabe brushed her hands aside, ripped the remaining buttons, and yanked his shirt free from the waistband.

"Think you can distract me with a few pretty kisses?" he growled.

Jenny shivered as his warm breath tickled her ear. She ran her hand over his goose bumpy chest to his puckered nipples. Leaning forward, she licked one nub. Cold and rough. Hmm. She took it in her mouth and suckled, then a little harder as she felt the rumbling of Gabe's groan against her lips. He liked it. She released his nipple with a kiss.

"Is it working?"

Gabe groaned again and burrowed into her neck. "Maybe."

Good to know. Jenny tugged on his belt and unbuttoned his jeans. He stood still, allowing her to divest him of the soggy clothes.

"In that case," she purred and pressed close, pushing his bare back against the refrigerator. Ignoring his quick hiss, she rose up on tiptoes, slipped her arms around his neck. "I intend to distract you a whole lot more."

Gabe picked her up and carried her down the hall into the bathroom.

Reaching around her, he twisted the shower, set her on the counter, then quickly stripped. Jenny followed his every move with hungry eyes, enjoying his striptease. Naked, Gabe braced hands on either side of her hips and kissed her again. Only lips touching skin-to-skin, Jenny grabbed his shoulders, dug in her nails to bring Gabe closer to give her better access to damp body.

So much bare skin to explore, Jenny wasn't sure where she wanted to start. When Gabe held her waist and lifted her, Jenny's legs instinctively circled him as she pulled closer and feathered kisses along his jaw.

Gabe carried her into the shower, and Jenny hid her face against his neck as the hot, steamy water sluiced over her head, arm, and soaked half her body. Beneath the hot, steamy water, Gabe returned the favor of stripping Jenny, paying special attention to the long forgotten stings on her bottom, which had started the whole war.

Who said fighting and making up wasn't fun?

Jenny woke alone in Gabe's bed and watched dust motes dance in soft morning light. A note lay on his pillow next to a perfect, pale rose bud, telling her he'd been called away to the hospital.

Wandering into his kitchen, Jenny found three more roses, wrapped in cellophane, sitting in a drinking glass on the kitchen table next to a mushy Hallmark card. What a sweetie; Gabe had remembered their four-month anniversary.

The bleeping of her telephone interrupted her musings. Startled, Jenny dropped her rose and sifted through the papers, looking for her phone. There it was, under the mail.

"Hello?"

"Hi, Jen. What are you doing?" Gabe asked.

"Working. What about you? I thought you were operating all day?"

"My last case got cancelled. I'm meeting a realtor to look at a house. Want to come?"

She did. She hadn't seen Gabe in a couple of days and she missed him. It didn't really matter what they did—being with him made her happy. But on deadline, she needed to finish her article before she went for a job interview at La Trattoria at four. She needed that waitress job to pay off the balance on her VISA. Rent was due soon, and she still owed her dad from last month.

"Tempting, but I have to work."

"You're not working now."

She dropped the rose, feeling guilty. "I was before you called."

"Don't lie."

"I'm not lying," she claimed in an indignant voice.

"You're sitting there, probably with one bare foot propped up on your desk, daydreaming. About me, I hope."

Jenny froze. "How—?"

"I'm glad you like the roses, Jen, but come out with me."

Jenny bolted out of her chair. She looked at the closed apartment door, then the kitchen and the hallway. He must be here, somehow watching her. "Where are you?"

A shadow outside the window caught her attention. He was on the deck. Gabe held up his cell phone and waved.

"Rat," she chuckled.

"Please? It'll only take an hour and a half, max, then I'll bring you right back to work."

Please. She sighed. She'd always been a sucker for a man with manners. Jenny hung up the phone, slipped into her shoes, grabbed her purse, and walked to the door. Tossing her long hair over one shoulder, she arched a brow. "An hour and a half? I'm going to hold you to that, Harrison."

He smiled and closed the door behind her. "Hello to you, too."

໑ ໑ ໑

They headed north on Lake Shore Drive. The drive along the water relaxed Jenny as usual. She loved watching the twinkling green water with gliding sailboats, racing speedboats, and profusion of fat Canadian geese waddling along the shoreline or the elegant swan pair that had taken up residence around the Crescent Club.

They passed Saint Paul's Church, the Farms Pier, then the Yacht Club to Grosse Pointe Shores. Gabe turned down a narrow gravel drive and parked in front of a medium-size brick house.

She perked up and looked around with interest. "It's on the water?"

"It's smaller than I'd wanted, but the realtor thought there'd be room to add on." He switched off the ignition. "That must be her."

The house sat dwarfed by a huge oak tree, looking somewhat sad and neglected amongst weed-filled dried-out grass, overgrown yews, and dogwoods. Jenny lifted her hair off her sticky neck and stepped into the shade. Even in this humidity, the lawn needed watering. She glanced at the water beyond the driveway. Wonder if they were allowed to use the lake to water their yards. Probably not.

Gabe took her hand, and they walked up the cracked cement sidewalk to where wooden barrels of wilting impatiens flanked the porch in an obvious attempt to infuse the house with some cheerful color. The owners didn't have much of a green thumb.

A smiling blonde stood in the doorway of the house, framed by peeling white-painted brick and covered by a slanted red tile roof. Her high heels showed off shapely calves, and her welcoming smile was much, much wider than the brief skirt that *almost* covered her butt.

Jenny frowned and cocked her head to the side. How the heck did she manage to sit in that thing without giving all nearby males a cheap thrill? As Barbie realtor batted her big doe eyes at Gabe, Jenny's imaginary hackles rose.

With one delicate claw on his arm, Barbie tried to draw Gabe into the house.

Gabe disentangled himself from the woman's grasp, pulled the door wide, and with a warm caressing hand at her back, urged Jenny forward. She inwardly smiled in feminine satisfaction as she brushed past the other woman.

The realtor chatted brightly while giving them the tour, handed Gabe information, and then left them alone in the house while she went to her car to make some phone calls. Jenny stood in the family room before the wall of glass admiring the lake.

"Not much of a backyard with that slope," Gabe observed. "Must be a pain to cut the grass."

Jenny looked at the dried out straw masquerading as a lawn. "It's not *that* steep. Healthy green grass would look lovely. I bet a good landscaper could come up with a fabulous design. Maybe something terraced...besides, you'd have a whole lake for your back yard. It even has a boat dock."

"What do you think of the house though? It needs work. Plumbing and electricity need updating. Undoubtedly a new roof." He frowned and glanced at the kitchen. "Kitchen needs to be completely redone and opened up, bathrooms gutted..."

"And the yard needs reworking and it's just crying for an enclosed porch off the dining room." She bit her thumbnail, thinking about how her parents' home flooded periodically and how much work it was to clean up the basement. "The foundation looked solid—no cracks or sign of flooding or water damage, but you'd have to have it inspected."

"Lot of work. And I'd want it done right away—enclosed before the winter."

"It's vacant, so you wouldn't have to wait for the owners to move out, but getting a builder and permits immediately would be challenging. Winter seems ambitious."

"Not if you know the right people and are willing to pay. Still, it's a lot of work."

"Yeah. But look at that view." Jenny sighed and pivoted toward the lake. "And it's close enough to the hospital and your office. I like it."

Gabe wrapped his arms around Jenny, back to chest, and rested his chin on her head. "You do?"

She tilted back until she leaned flush against him. "Yup."

"Enough to help me remodel it?"

"Sure." It'd be a fun project.

Lulled into a lazy, satisfied complacency, she stared at the lake. The calm water gently lapped at the concrete retaining wall. Miles away, a huge gray freighter, flying a flag Jenny couldn't quite make out, lumbered by, not even coming close to obscuring their view of Canada.

It must be wonderful to watch the sunrise each morning from here.

"Enough to share it with me?"

Jenny turned to the side, craning in his arms to look at his face. "You want to live together?"

Gabe's hands slid down her arms and turned her to face him. Taking her hands in his, he threaded his fingers through hers. "I want to marry you."

"Marry?" As in, get married? As in wedding? As in husband and wife, marry?

He nodded. "We're good together—great together. And you make me happy. You're so..." He frowned, struggling to find the right words, "passionate and sincere." Pausing, his eyes locked onto hers. "I love you, Jenny. Will you marry me?"

Jenny's heart lifted, and her breathing slowed. He loved her. The thought both thrilled and humbled her. Wow. Gabe wanted to marry her. "But we've only been together four months."

"I knew after four days—after our first date. This just feels right. We're right. I know you feel it too."

She nodded. She did feel it. She felt good, strong, and complete when she was with Gabe. Jenny enjoyed every moment they spent together, but she'd never really thought about marriage.

Jenny Harrison? It sounded good. It sounded great. As Jenny Harrison, she could forget her screwed-up past and begin anew. As Gabe's wife, and Alex and Ted's stepmother, she could wipe the slate clean. Marriage to this wonderful, sexy man would allow her to put those haunting mistakes to rest and become reborn, a completely new and better person. She could do it. She could.

Tell him. Tell him now, an inner voice urged. *He wants to marry you—he has a right to know. It'll be okay; he loves you. He believes in unconditional love*, the voice reminded.

Jenny's hands suddenly felt cold in his larger, warmer ones. Her gaze dropped to scrutinize his shirt button, peeking out from beneath the protection of his skewed silk tie. Unconditional love—for his children.

She bit her lip, knowing that the love from a parent to a child was far different than this. Gabe had loved his children for eighteen years. They were a part of him—flesh of his flesh. Would he be so forgiving with a love he'd only had for mere months? She wanted to believe so.

Besides, he respected and loved her honesty. How could she tell him she lived a lie? She couldn't. She couldn't bear to see regret and disillusionment cloud his eyes. He may still love her, but she couldn't take that risk.

She'd always had to earn love, and she was willing to work for Gabe's. But if he knew about her past, she'd never have a chance. She'd lose his respect for sure, and she couldn't live with that loss—another loss.

"Jenny?" he prompted. "Don't fall all over yourself accepting. I'm not sure my ego could take it."

Conscience prodding her, Jenny pulled out of his embrace. She couldn't believe she was going to blow this, but she had to be fair—for his sake. Avoiding his earnest gaze, she looked down and wrapped taut arms over her nervous stomach.

"Umm... I... I haven't made very good decisions in the past." She frowned and looked away.

"I've made a few bad calls, too. Who hasn't?"

"I don't trust my instincts anymore."

"Then trust mine." Gabe moved closer until she could feel the heat from his body and smell his sexy cologne. He hooked a gentle finger beneath Jenny's chin, lifting it until she met his warm gaze. "My instincts say you should marry me and we'll be crazy happy together."

Jenny closed her eyes and pulled away. "But what if we're not? What if I screw it up?" That was what she did. Jenny was a master at getting herself in trouble, and after all Gabe had been through, she couldn't stand the thought of disappointing him. "I don't want to hurt you."

"You won't. You couldn't."

Jenny's eyes popped open, and she cocked her head. *Oh, don't challenge me that way. If only you knew.*

But it wasn't a challenge. His unwavering stare spoke of confidence and sincerity. He had that much faith. He believed in her, in them. This wasn't some spontaneous suggestion blurted out; Gabe seriously wanted to spend the rest of his life with her. Her stomach quivered in excitement that he loved her that much.

"Trust me." He took her cold hands and warmed them between his. "Do I make you happy?"

"Yes."

He paused, searching her face. "Do you love me?"

She swallowed hard. *With all my heart.* "Yes."

His face lightened, but still he didn't smile. He squeezed her hands. "Then marry me."

Could it really be that simple? *He makes me happy. I love him. He loves me.* Of course he made her happy, happier than she'd ever been. And she loved him more than anything. He believed in her. He completed her in a way no other could. In such a short time, he'd become so very important to her that she couldn't imagine life without him. But could it really be that simple?

Frightened to say the words aloud as if she'd jinx them if she did, Jenny looked at him and nodded.

"Yes?" Widening eyes matched his emerging smile.

She nodded again, grinning.

"You're sure? You're not just marrying me for this fancy house on the lake and my car?"

Her credit card balance and rent money problem flashed to mind, but Jenny promptly pushed those worries away. She'd get that waitress job and wouldn't spend a cent until she'd paid off all her debts. She loved this man, and she was going to marry him.

Jenny shook her head and threw her arms around his neck. "Your body. I'm marrying you for your sexy body."

∽ ∽ ∽

Mary Campbell stood in their family room. With her arms tightly wound around her stomach, she leveled a flat stare at Jenny. "Are you pregnant?"

"Mary," her father put a warning hand on her shoulder.

"What?" Surely Jenny hadn't heard right. "*No*, I'm not pregnant." Bewilderment turned to anger, and Jenny came off the couch to face her mother. "Why? You think the only way I could get a man like Gabe is by trapping him?"

"You've only known each other a few weeks, and he *is* quite a bit older than you," her mother said.

"Surprise, Mom." Jenny glared through narrow, hurt-filled eyes. "He loves me."

They'd been together more than a *few weeks*—long enough to know this wasn't puppy love. She and Gabe were old enough to know their minds. Jenny didn't understand her mom's reaction. Gabe was a good, honest man, not like her immature first love, Danny Sullivan. Most mothers would be thrilled their daughter was marrying a doctor. Why couldn't she be happy for them?

"How well does he know you, Jennifer?" her mother asked with a pointed look.

Gabe stood and put a reassuring arm around Jenny's shoulder. "Mrs. Campbell, I know this seems a bit sudden, but we've been dating for months, and I love your daughter very much. I'm fourteen years older than Jenny, but that's not an issue for either of us. I'm sorry if you have a problem with it."

"Fourteen years is a long time, Dr. Harrison—almost middle-aged."

"Forty is hardly middle-aged, Mom," Jenny protested. "Not anymore."

"Please, call me Gabe. Jenny and I love each other, and we're getting married. We're not asking permission, we're inviting you to share our happiness." He paused, "Naturally, we'd like your blessing."

"Yesss," Michael hissed from the doorway. Mom's instant glare wiped the smile from his face. He settled into a recliner and pulled out his iPod, pretending to play a game.

Her mother returned her attention to them. "This is so sudden. What's the hurry?"

"No hurry. There's just no reason to wait." Gabe slipped a hand under Jenny's hair to massage her tense neck muscles.

The warm, intimate look he gave Jenny both curled her toes and lifted her heart. This was right. The most right thing she'd ever done. Jenny looked at her parents and raised an impish eyebrow. "Would you rather we moved in together and lived in sin?"

"Maybe."

"Really?" Jenny searched her mom's face trying to discern if she was serious or just testing her. Why in the world would her conservative, Catholic mom prefer that they live together without being married? She was condoning premarital sex? That went against everything her mom believed in.

"If that's what it takes. You've always been impulsive, and it usually gets you into trouble." She faced Jenny. "Have you *really* thought everything through? Marriage is a huge commitment."

Her father thrust his hands deep in his pockets and raised a dark eyebrow at Gabe. "What about children? You'd be in your sixties when your children graduate college."

"We're not going to have any," Jenny blurted out.

Gabe stiffened at her side.

They'd never talked about children, but Jenny didn't want to admit they'd overlooked this important issue, confirming Mom's belief that they were rushing things. Besides marriage, step parenting and jump-starting her career would fill her life; Jenny couldn't imagine children on top of that.

"I have a daughter and son from my first marriage," Gabe admitted. "If Jenny doesn't want children, that's fine with me. Even if we change our minds, we'll figure it out; just like you did when Michael came along. Mr. Campbell, I love your daughter and will do my best to make her happy."

Jenny took Gabe's arm and snuggled close, needing his warmth and strength against her father's concern and her mother's doubts.

Dad stared at them ten long seconds before smiling broadly. "It seems the feeling's reciprocated." Her father held out his hand. "But I'd have a hard time with 'Dad', call me Mike. Welcome to the family."

Her mother's lips tightened to a thin line as she stared hard at her husband, sending him a silent, disapproving message.

"Let it go, Mary." He smiled at Jenny. "Look how happy she is."

Mom stared at them one long, considering minute. Concern flickered across her face. "It's just so sudden. I'm worried you haven't had enough time to really get to know each other. Marriage is *hard* and you have to have a solid foundation to weather the challenges all married couples face—the irritating habits, career stress, disagreements over raising children." She glanced at Michael.

"Unplanned pregnancies, money problems... Speaking of money, does Gabe know about your debt, Jennifer?"

With a sinking stomach, Jenny couldn't prevent a peek at her father. How'd she find out? Dad promised not to tell Mom about the loan. Jenny couldn't bear disappointing her mother again, but when Dad offered the short-term loan, she hadn't been able to turn it down either. Attempting to salvage Jenny's pride, Dad suggested they keep it between the two of them.

Her father frowned at her mother. "What're you talking about, Mary?"

"I'm talking about your *little loan* and how Jenny can't pay her bills." She frowned, hurt and betrayal stamped all over her stubborn Irish face.

Damn. Jenny shook her head. This was exactly what she hadn't wanted. She should have told Mom about the loan. Now not only was Mom disappointed that Jenny'd failed again, but she felt excluded and hurt, thinking they were hiding things from her— which they were.

"So Jenny had a little cash flow problem this month. It's no big deal."

"And the month before that, and the four months before that?" Her mother raised her eyebrows.

It'd been a long time since Jenny'd been at the center of a parental argument, and the guilt and the sick feeling in her stomach didn't feel any better now than it had then. Worse, Gabe and Michael were witnessing it, and she didn't know how to stop it.

Jenny bent her head, unable to look at Gabe. She wished for a magic mirror to step into another world—any other world would make more sense than this and be far less embarrassing. She was afraid to even think of what Gabe was making of all this.

"I know about Jenny's financial situation, and we'll be taking care of it right away," Gabe said. "So there's no problem."

Jenny turned astonished eyes to Gabe, who squeezed her shoulder a little harder than reassurance warranted. When she began to protest, the pressure on her shoulder increased until she closed her lips.

"See, Mary." Her father beamed. "Everything's taken care of."

Indecision replaced the hurt in her mother's eyes. Jenny silently prayed Mom would take the opportunity to let the past rest, but her optimism died when her mother turned steady eyes to her. Her freckles stood out in her pale face with the weight of her decision. "I hope you'll be very happy together."

Jenny deflated; not exactly the endorsement she'd been hoping for, but she'd take it.

Her father put an encouraging arm around her. "I've got a bottle of Moet & Chandon chilling for a special occasion, and I think this definitely qualifies."

Jenny summoned a smile and returned her father's hug.

Dad poured champagne for the adults and ginger ale for Michael. He proposed a simple, eloquent toast and they clicked glasses, yet her mother didn't smile once. She brought the crystal flute to her lips but barely sipped the sparkling wine.

Turning to her fiancé, Jenny smiled and finished her champagne in two quick swallows. "Thanks for the champagne, but we've really gotta run. Gabe's got to get back to the hospital, and I've got to work."

Jenny and Gabe left her parents' house and drove down the street. Making a left, Gabe pulled the car over as soon as they were out of sight of the house. Throwing the gear into park, he faced her. "When were you going to tell me?"

Chapter 6

Jenny didn't even pretend to misunderstand. Gabe had a right to be angry. She watched a man on a tractor whirl around a front yard while another gardener pulled weed from the lush flowerbeds. "I wasn't."

"What do you mean, you *weren't?*" he nearly shouted. "Did you think I wouldn't notice when you got kicked out of your apartment? Or was your dad going to subsidize you forever?"

"No." She gave him a sharp look. "I was going to get—" She slapped a hand to her mouth, then groaned. "I was going to get a second job, but now I've missed the interview. Crap."

"Well, *excuse* me, for proposing."

"You knew I didn't have much time," she grumbled.

His mouth dropped open. "It was *your* idea to run over and tell your folks."

"Well, you got me all excited about a new house and new life. There was so much to think about, to plan."

"I would've waited if I'd known how it would turn out." He slammed the gear into drive and hit the accelerator with enough force to press her into the upholstery, yet not hard enough to burn rubber.

Jenny gripped her seat, afraid to look at him; she'd never seen Gabe angry before. They flew under an arguably red light, missing the turn to her street.

"Where're we going?" She peeked at him, discouraged by his frown and clenched jaw.

"My place."

"What for?"

"To get my checkbook. Then we're going to your bank, so you can make a deposit. Tomorrow you can cut your father a check and pay him back, so we can start free and clear."

Tears flooded her eyes. After that nasty little surprise, Gabe was going to pay her debt and forget about it. "No, we're not."

"Yes. We are."

She could imagine what Mom would have to say about *that*. "I can't take your money."

"Yes, you can."

"I *won't* take your money." Jenny took a tissue from her purse and dabbed at her eyes. "Besides... I owe, a bit more than that. Don't worry," she hurried to reassure. "I'm going to get a job waitressing and pay it all off before we're married."

"Pay all *what* off?" His foot eased off the accelerator.

"We're going to start our new life free and clear. A clean slate."

"Jenny?" The quiet, biting word came out as a warning.

She shifted in her seat. "I've run up a little bit of a balance on my credit cards, too, but—"

"How much?" The car slowed beneath the posted forty-five mile an hour speed limit, forcing traffic to pull out around them to pass. The drivers cast them curious looks.

She struggled not to wince—or lie. "Which card?"

Gabe swerved to the side of the road. The car behind them laid on the horn, long and loud. He shoved the gear into park, punched on the hazard warning lights, and turned toward her. "How many credit cards do you have?"

"Including Target, Macy's, and Nordstrom's? Or just, VISA and MasterCard?"

Gabe cursed under his breath.

"Look, it's okay. I'm going to take care of it."

"How much do you owe on your credit cards, Jenny?"

"You're not listening. I'm going to get a job waitressing—"

"*How* much?"

"I'll even take in another roommate to speed it up if I need to. Please don't worry about this. We're *not* getting married until I'm debt-free."

"I don't want to wait years."

"Funny." She frowned at him. "It's not *that* much."

Gabe glowered at the street before turning back to her. "Look, I respect that you want to deal with this yourself, but there's no need. Let me help."

"I don't want your money. I love you, but this is something I need to do." She smiled. "You won't have to wait years. I promise."

"It's only money."

"To you. To me it's respect."

Gabe opened his mouth to protest, but Jenny rubbed a comforting hand up and down his arm. "Thank you for understanding."

He turned off the hazards and put the car into gear. "I don't like it."

"That's okay." *You don't have to like it. As long as you respect me and allow me to pay my own debt.*

Gabe checked the traffic in his mirrors, then made a U-turn and headed back to her townhouse.

Jenny blew out a satisfied breath. They'd had their first fight, and it'd been okay. Gabe still loved her. She smiled to herself. Everything was going to work out.

❧ ❧ ❧

Thump. Thump. Thump, thump, thump. Errrr—aaaaa—ck. The nail gun rapid-fired to the accompaniment of a screeching saw. *Boom.* Jenny winced and ducked as a stack of planks dropped directly above her head. *Time to go.*

Jenny grabbed her coffee mug, gathered up her laptop and wedding bible, and moved out to the flagstaff patio. She cranked open the hunter green umbrella and settled down at the old iron and glass patio set that'd come with the house. Looking out over the lazily rippling lake, Jenny sipped her coffee and appreciated the cool morning breeze, knowing it wouldn't last. In a few hours the oppressive summer heat and humidity would drive her into air conditioning. But for now, she'd enjoy working outside.

Jenny rolled spongy orange earplugs, wedged them in her ears, and lifted the lid on her laptop. They'd had a seven-thirty meeting at the new house with the landscaper to finalize the yard work to start next week. After that, she'd have no safe haven on site to work.

With machinery digging in the yard throwing dirt everywhere and carpenters and drywallers dusting up the house, Jenny'd have no clean, relatively quiet space to work, but as long as they kept making progress at this rate, she didn't mind.

Things were coming along nicely. In a couple of weeks, they'd added a third garage, her study over it, and a glass-enclosed porch off the dining room. The electrician would complete rewiring this week, and the plumber should finish up next week. The kitchen and bathrooms would be attacked next, ripping out all the outdated appliances, cupboards, and cabinets, replacing them with designer cherry cabinets and pink-flecked, black granite surfaces.

All the bathrooms would have new flooring, wood cabinets, and lovely designer touches like vessel and copper sinks, bronze faucets, and a steam shower for Gabe to help him relax after a rough day on his feet.

After the birch hardwood floors were sanded and refinished, the whole house would be treated to a fresh coat of paint. Then they'd be done, hopefully by Christmas. Then they'd be comfortably settled for their February wedding.

Jenny opened the guest list spreadsheet. They'd whittled it down to a hundred fifty people, but something still nagged at her. Chin propped on her folded hands, she stared harder at the list. Jenny'd always dreamt about a small, intimate wedding, fifty people max. Nothing elaborate, just elegant. A hundred fifty wasn't exactly small, but Gabe requested so little, she couldn't complain when his list included forty colleagues.

She opened her wedding bible. The summer she'd been thirteen, Jenny and her best friend, Jackie, had driven her mom crazy. Too young to get real jobs and too old for camps, the girls had been bored out of their minds. To keep the boy-crazed girls out of trouble, Mom took them to Jo-Ann's craft store and bought them each scrapbooks, the beginning of her wedding bible.

Through the years, Jenny'd cut out pictures and added to it. Then along came Pinterest with millions more ideas, and the bible had been relegated to her closet, but she still referred to it for an idea or two.

Jenny frowned at the colorful wedding collage. Maybe it was the orchids. She liked the way they looked, but they were kind of stinky. Perhaps... She flipped to the flower pages. Maybe something like tulips would be more suitable? Then again, tulips might not be available in February. Shoot.

Her mother was supposed to be here, giving her opinion. Planning Jenny's wedding was supposed to be their girl bonding time. Never in a million years had Jenny ever imagined her mother wouldn't be excited and involved in her wedding, but she wouldn't force it on her.

Mom's enthusiasm for the wedding hadn't grown any—not even when Gabe insisted on splitting the cost to compensate for his extra guests and Jenny'd mostly repaid her loan.

Following a strict regimen, Jenny succeeded in paying down the bulk of her debt.

Savings from adding the second roommate, plus the additional income waitressing weekends provided, and she was on track to be completely debt-free very soon.

Though her free time, social life, and sleep had been severely compromised, Jenny didn't mind 'cause she'd remained disciplined. She'd done it. All by herself. As soon as her paycheck cleared, she'd pay off Mom and Dad, and then she'd have a small balance on her

VISA for a few more weeks before she'd experience the sweet relief and pride of fiscal freedom.

All she had to do was dredge up the energy to continuing waitressing until Thanksgiving, and then she'd have enough money saved for Christmas presents and a tidy little bonus to pay for extra wedding goodies.

Jenny smiled. Life was good. Close to debt-free and closing in on her favorite season. She loved the fall with all its autumn earth colors and coziness. Life seemed to slow a little in Michigan: the kids were back in school, summer vacations were over, and people worked in their yards raking leaves, winterizing their houses, putting snow tires on their cars... Families drew inward concentrating on hunkering down for the winter and preparing for the holidays.

She looked forward to spending lots of quality time hibernating with her love in their new home, but first, their perfect wedding. Jenny took a fortifying sip of coffee and opened the Google doc spreadsheet. Today she needed to analyze the three photographers' bids and pick one, proof the invitations, then at three she had an appointment with French's Flowers in Livonia to finalize the bouquets, boutonnieres, and centerpieces.

The florist was a long-time friend of her mom's. Ordinarily they didn't work in Grosse Pointe, but Judie made an exception for Jenny, and Jenny hoped giving her mom's friend the business and added exposure would please her.

Jenny looked out over the water. With or without Mom's help, she'd have an amazing wedding that would force her mother to see Jenny as a capable, grown woman.

It's okay, Mom, I don't need your help. I can do this.

Jenny slouched in her chair. Though it'd be a lot more fun with Mom. She wanted her mom to be happy for her, to share in this special time. That's the way it was supposed to be. She pushed out a deep sigh.

Suddenly, a big hand stroked her head. Gabe brushed her hair aside and gently pulled a plug from her ear. "Hey, Baby. What's wrong?"

Plucking the other earplug out, Jenny forced a smile and cheerful tone to her voice. "Hey. What're you doing here? Aren't you supposed to be in surgery?"

"Forgot my phone." Gabe reached across the table and pocketed his Galaxy. He took a step back and looked at her. "What's the matter?"

The temptation to let it all spill out and have a good cry in his arms swamped her, but Jenny refused to burden Gabe with her silly family problems. With the clinic and having to rearrange his schedule to accommodate these frequent builder meetings, and his own wedding to-do list, Gabe had enough stress.

She smiled broadly. "Nothing. I'm fine."

"Damn it Jenny, you're exhausted. Why won't you let me help?"

"I'm fine."

"At least let me finish paying off your credit card. You've made your point: you're an independent woman. I respect that, but I also respect someone who knows her limits and asks for help when she needs it."

"And I will if I need it. But I don't. I'm fine, and you've got to get to work."

"Let me hire a wedding planner for you."

"I don't want a wedding planner." She smiled at Gabe. "I've been planning this day since I was a little girl."

"I don't want you stressing over this. You're spread too thin."

Jenny raised an eyebrow. "Have you always been this bossy?"

"Have you always been this stubborn?

She nodded. "Pretty much." Jenny wondered if he bossed Judith around like this, somehow she doubted it. His ex-wife was pretty strong-willed. Ex-wife. Hmm. "Hey, Gabe? What was your first wedding like?"

"Doesn't matter. This is your wedding."

Because naturally, Jenny was destined to crash and burn and would go running to her parents to pick up the pieces. Jenny raised her chin. "I wouldn't ask you to."

She didn't even mind burning that bridge. A divorce would be painful, but unlike before, she could deal with that on her own. And seriously—she and Gabe were meant to be. There would be no divorce.

"Dealing with an ex can be difficult and being a stepmom...even harder. You've never had to be the bad guy or take responsibility for a child before. It's tougher than you'd think."

"Not a problem." Jenny sat back against the couch, tucked one bent leg beneath her and fully faced her mom. "Judith's this big-shot heart surgeon, and she and her second husband have two kids of their own, so she's too busy to bother with us.

"And Gabe's kids are great—we get along fine. Besides, they're nearly raised. Ted left for school in Ann Arbor a few weeks ago, and Alex just got her driver's license and Judith bought her a car, so I won't even have to drive her around." She shrugged. "Easy peasy.

"Besides, Gabe, Judith, and Dave have been juggling the parenting stuff for years. They've got it down. There's nothing for me to do but stay out of their way and do my own thing with Gabe. It's perfect."

"Famous last words," Mom muttered.

"Don't worry. I know what I'm doing." Jenny pursed her lip and cocked her head, trying to read her mom. "Sooo you're okay with our marrying?"

"No." She shook her head. "I still think you're making a mistake. But there's no way I'm going to let a man come between us. You're my baby girl, and I love you."

Not the full endorsement she'd hoped for, but it was something. Time and Gabe would eventually allay her fears. "He's a good man, Mom."

"I never doubted that."

Right. She never doubted Gabe, just me.

"However." Mom took a deep breath. "I was hoping that maybe you'd consider extending your engagement and get married in the summer instead of February."

Do what? Jenny's eyes grew wide and her jaw dropped. "Why would we do that?"

"Six more months would give us opportunity to get to know your future husband and his children. It'd give you and Gabe more time to get to know each other better and be certain that you *really* want to spend the rest of your lives together.

"You could move in together and have a trial run to make sure you're compatible and give you confidence in your decision, which I think is critical when children are involved." She looked Jenny in the eye. "Just consider it?"

That's not going to happen.

Jenny got a heavy feeling in the pit of her stomach as Mom laid out her plan. She'd clearly thought things through, and it was logical, but it wasn't going to happen, and she wouldn't understand. Mom was going to see this as another example of her being "impulsive." Jenny was going to disappoint her mother again, and she hated it.

"I…I'd like to give you that peace of mind, but we can't. That's the other reason I'm here today. We've had a change of plans."

Mom's eyes narrowed, and she grew still.

"Instead of getting married at The Academy, having the reception at the Country Club in February with a hundred and fifty of our closest friends and family…we're getting married on a beach in Maui, next month, with the family, Cindy, and her boyfriend, Dillon."

"Next month." Mom raised her eyebrows and stared hard. "You're moving the wedding up."

Jenny put a hand on her arm. "Don't freak out. And, no, I'm still not pregnant. We'll totally reimburse you for any deposits we lose, and Gabe wants to pay for everybody's trip. It's our gift to the family."

"Your gift or his? Because last time I checked, you didn't have that kind of money."

Jenny rolled her eyes. *Fine.* "His."

"Why *in the world* would you move it *up?*"

"It's just that all the wedding plans were stressing me out, and I hated that everything I'd planned was a repeat of Gabe's first wedding."

"What do *his* parents think of this?"

"They're dead. It's—"

"Which we *would have known*, if you weren't in such a rush to—"

"They died when Gabe was twelve. His uncle George raised him."

"So you're canceling *everything* you've dreamed of for the past decade, for him?"

Seeing the color flush her mother's cheeks and the glint of battle lighting her eyes, Jenny hurried on, but not before noting the irony of Mom's protective reaction. Her mother didn't approve of her marrying Gabe, but if they were going to do it, apparently she wanted it to be everything Jenny'd dreamed of.

"Not only for Gabe, for both of us. I was getting stressed out by all the millions of little details—"

"If it's *that* stressful, you're obviously not—"

"That's only part of it." She broke in, not wanting to hear more of her mom's negativity. "I need this day to mean as much to Gabe as it does to me. I don't want a redo of his first wedding. It *has* to be perfect for both of us."

"But you've planned this day since you were a little girl."

"I know, but my tastes have changed. We found this amazing all-inclusive five-star resort in Maui that's perfect. We met with their wedding planner and got it all worked out. I've got my soul mate, my dream dress, the perfect bouquet, a wonderful meal, and dancing—we can even have the butterfly release.

"The only really disappointing thing is that the wedding cake comes with that nasty fondant icing—there are no other options. But I can live with that as long as the family's all there.

"It's October eighteenth—during Ted's fall break. We got permission from Judith to take the kids, and I know you'll have to take Michael out of school, and I know it's short notice. And I know it's a long way to go, but please, say you'll come."

Please, please, please. They have to come. Jenny wasn't even sure she could get married without her parents and Michael.

"Where do I even begin?" her mother muttered. "One month is not a lot of notice, and did you even think to consult anybody before finalizing a date? No. You expect everybody to drop everything and fly to Maui because you two want us to?

"Jennifer, weddings aren't all about you two—that's romantic marketing nonsense. Weddings are an art in negotiation, compromising what the bride and groom, and both families want. The way you start your marriage sets a tone for your future relationships and interactions with both sets of in-laws, and his kids. I'm sure you didn't think of that."

Jenny wanted to shrink under her critical stare. "Not exactly like that."

"I'll have to talk to Michael's teachers and try to get his school assignments, and I have no idea if your father has a business trip scheduled then, but it's likely he does, so you're asking him to rearrange his work schedule.

"And you're mighty cavalier about losing thousands of dollars in deposit money. I'd hoped when you showed up with that check, it meant you'd learned some fiscal responsibility, but obviously I was wrong." She sighed. "We'll do our best to make it to your wedding. However, we will pay our own way. We do *not* want to start out our relationship with your husband paying for us—he can't buy his way into this family or our good graces."

What? Jenny scowled at the unfair accusation. Gabe was a sweet, generous man. Buying his way into the family was the last thing he'd think of. "He *wasn't* trying to. Why do you have to make it sound so dirty? We realize what an inconvenience it would be, and he wanted to make up for that by doing something nice."

Mom opened her eyes wide and tilted her head. "Did it ever occur to you that maybe we *wanted* to be more included in our only daughter's wedding? More included than writing a check—oh, right, now you've taken that away for us, so we don't even have the opportunity to give our only daughter a beautiful wedding."

Are you kidding me right now? This is so unfair. Never in a million years did Jenny expect this reaction.

"It's as if you decided that by paying for everything yourself, you'd be able to have everything your way, and we could either fall in with your plans or not. Is that the type of relationship we can count on in the future? You two make all the decisions, and we can choose to participate or not? I have to say, I'm really hurt. I thought we raised you to be more considerate and family-oriented than that."

Jenny sat quiet for a minute, letting her mom's painful words sink in.

"I don't even know what to say. Apparently I can't do anything right." Tears glistened in Jenny's eyes, and disappointment roughened her voice. She was so tired of fighting—and losing. She sighed. "There's no grand plot here, Mom. We aren't trying to exclude you and Dad in any decisions. Your reaction to our engagement made it crystal clear that you weren't enthusiastic about our wedding, so *why* would I think you'd want to be involved?

"I'm *sorry* we didn't consult you about the date. It never occurred to us that it might be inopportune for Dad—we were trying to minimize the time out of school for Ted, since it's hard to make up college classes. And you can pay for whatever you want. I'm not trying to deprive you of anything. The resort we picked is really nice and rather pricey, so Gabe didn't want you stressing out about the cost, since we *did* pick it without consulting anybody.

"And true, nobody's had a chance to meet and get to know each other, which is exactly why we thought a week's vacation in Maui with the family would be so great."

"So we're all going on your honeymoon with you?"

"No, we're staying two weeks." Jenny sighed. "I'm sorry for this mess. Gabe and I are spontaneous. We didn't think it'd be this big of deal for everyone. We thought it'd be fun. But we're totally willing to change the date to one that's more convenient for you guys if it's a problem."

"Haven't you put down a deposit?"

"Yes, but it shouldn't be a problem to change the date. It's not exactly Maui's high season. Besides. You're my family, and you have to be there. Please say you'll come."

"I'll talk to your dad, check with Michael's teachers, and see what we can work out." "Thank you." Jenny looked at Mom. "If you have time, I'd love to get your opinion of the stuff we chose. There are a couple of things I'm waffling about. It's all online."

"Sure." Mom sighed, and worry replaced the tightness in her features. "But I still have one big problem. I have no idea what the mother of the bride is supposed to wear to a beach wedding."

The tightness in her stomach unwound, and Jenny offered her mom a smile of relief. "I can help you with that."

∾ ∾ ∾

George moved around the wooden sawhorses and stack of drywall to the backyard where one of the workmen had told him he could find Jenny. Stepping over a pile of debris, he frowned at the ripped-apart house. No way was this worth all the money Gabe was plowing into it.

So it was on the lake? He could get the same house for half the price if he just walked across the street and up the hill a block. He shook his head; this lavish renovation wasn't like Gabe. He'd never cared about comfort things or money. It must be her.

George rounded the corner and found Jenny hunched over her computer. Her fingers flew like pistons, punching the keys, undoubtedly crafting more lies. He tripped over the uneven flagstone and cursed. He looked up to apologize for swearing, but Jenny was apparently deep in concentration. He moved closer and tapped her shoulder.

She jumped, and then smiled. Putting a hand to her ears, she pulled out orange striped cones. "George. Hi." She held them up. "Ear plugs, so I can work."

He smiled and nodded. Without waiting for an invitation, he took the chair next to hers and fiddled with the envelope in hand. "I was on my way to the driving range and thought I'd stop by for a visit."

She watched him, a tad wary. "Gabe's not here."

"That's okay. I wanted to speak to you."

She stood. "Can I get you something to drink? A pop or something?"

"Coke would be fine." He followed her onto the new glass enclosed porch. The gas fireplace and the windows still had stickers on them, but the tile floor and drywall looked finished. A small refrigerator with plastic cups, cookies, and a fruit bowl atop it was tucked into a corner.

"The house is coming along."

"It's a mess right now, but it'll be great when we're done." She raised her voice to be heard over the pounding, and grabbed a Ziploc bag of cookies. "Let's go outside and talk. It's a little quieter—at least while the landscapers are at lunch."

He followed her back to the patio, and she pushed her computer aside. "I was just getting a little work done." She opened the bag and held it out to him. "Cookie?"

"Thanks. What're you working on?" he asked, trying to sound interested to put her at ease. He bit into the cookie, savoring the rich chocolate filling his mouth. Chocolate chip, his favorite. Was that pecans, too? He loved nuts. "This is great. You make them?"

She nodded. "I was finishing an article covering the Literacy Run next month." She paused, watched him polish off the cookie, and then put her drink down. "But you didn't stop by to ask me about work. What can I do for you?"

He eyed the bag of cookies. "May I?"

She tilted the open bag toward him, and then sat back, waiting.

He took a big bite of cookie and chewed it slowly. "Mmmm, you're a great cook. My wife was a great cook," he mused. "Gabe's a lucky man."

She didn't answer, just sat patiently watching him, making him feel like a blabbering old fool. "Anyhow, I wanted to talk with you about your marriage." He looked sideways at her. "You know why athletes and actors have agents?"

"To guide their careers."

"Right." He smiled. "And to take care of the money stuff. The talent like to concentrate on the job at hand and not be distracted by finances."

Jenny sat silent, waiting. Her expression, polite.

"Well, Gabe needs an agent. He's so busy with you and the house, and that new clinic job, he doesn't have time to look out for the little stuff."

She raised an eyebrow.

"So I'm doing it for him."

"Doing what for him?"

"Talking with you about a prenuptial agreement." He raised a hand. "Now don't panic, just hear me out. A prenup is practically standard these days. With the divorce rate still at fifty percent, it's only smart to play it safe. I mean, nobody gets married thinkin' they'll get divorced, right?"

Her blank look gave nothing away. She wasn't nodding in agreement, and she hadn't told him to go to hell—yet, so he pressed on.

"Grosse Pointe's a small community. And...well, to be honest, people are talking about you and Gabe. Family, friends, colleagues—

everybody. And frankly, honey," he paused, tilting his head, trying to look honest and sympathetic, "what they're saying isn't kind. Because of the age difference." He gave her a pained look. "They're saying you're marrying him for his money." He paused for dramatic effect, feeling elated when her eyes widened in surprise. This might be easier than he'd thought.

"A prenuptial agreement would protect both of you. It makes sure that whatever you have before you marry, remains yours. It proves you're not marrying Gabe for his money and shuts up those gossips." George pushed a copy toward her. "Here. Take a look. This is only a sample, but I have a friend who could draw one up for you, if you want."

She studied him with those spooky pale eyes, then reached out and took the documents. She held them, not looking at them, staring at him.

"What do you think, George?" she asked, sounding more curious than baiting. "Am I marrying Gabe for his money?"

"Me? To be honest," he widened his eyes and leaned close, trying to look sincere. "I don't know you well enough to make that call. But I didn't raise a fool. My boy thinks the world of you and you make him happy, so I'm willing to give you the benefit of the doubt."

Seemingly satisfied with his answer, Jenny withdrew the fat document from the envelope. She leafed through the three pages.

Good girl. Keep reading. Maybe she was as innocent as Gabe thought, or maybe she was so blind in love she'd be willing to sign a prenup to shut up his fictitious gossips who considered her a gold digger. Either way he didn't give a damn, as long as she signed one.

She read on, skimming through the stipulations. George leaned forward, reading with her. She paused, frowning, at the Presentation of Assets and Liabilities.

"Gabe's father came from money," he explained. "I don't know if he told you, but he inherited quite a bit—not that that should matter," George amended. "But it's common knowledge among our family and friends."

Jenny flipped back, skimmed through the rest before laying it down, her expression unreadable.

What was she thinking? Would she buy it? He studied her carefully. "You can have your own attorney draw one up, but my friend would do it for free—as a courtesy to me."

"Why didn't Gabe come to me himself with this?"

"Probably didn't think of it. He's been so busy with the house, and Teddy goin' off to school, then there's that clinic you got him involved with—probably slipped his mind." George shook his head. "After Judith, he should've. A smart man would have. Or could be he hasn't heard the rumors, or if he did, didn't care."

He shook his head and patted her hand, sympathetic like. "He's a guy." He made a disparaging face. "We're really not all that sensitive. He probably thinks that just 'cause gossip doesn't bother him, it won't bother you either."

Just agree to the damn thing.

"But he's not the one people are whisperin' ugly things about." Taking a third cookie, he munched appreciatively, pausing to let that sink in. "Well? Shall I tell my friend you're interested?"

"I'll think about it."

His heart pounded, almost there. Now came the tricky part.

"Sure. Think about it," he nodded agreeably. "But I wouldn't take too long. People are talking. If you do go ahead, it would probably be best for you to have your side all drawn up, so Gabe can see you're serious about it. He may be a bit testy at first," he warned. "But once Gabe sees how much this means to you, I'm sure he'll sign it, and then you can thumb your nose at all those jerks sayin' you married Gabe for his money." He cracked a warm, friendly smile, as if triumphant on her behalf.

Jenny didn't look relieved or thrilled at his solution, merely contemplative.

"I know you'll do the right thing." Beaming, he stood and pulled her into his arms. "You're no gold digger. One look at that face, and I could tell you really loved my boy. Welcome to the family, honey."

Of course you're not, just 'cause you got Gabe to buy you that whopping diamond ring and foot the bill for a Hawaiian wedding for ten at that fancy five–star resort. Naw, you're no gold digger. He resisted the urge to snort his derision.

Gabe wouldn't be rushing around marrying her in secret if he wasn't ashamed of being led around by his dick and being taken for a fool. *Good God, I hope she's not pregnant.* His gaze dropped to her trim waist. Naw, Gabe wouldn't make the same mistake twice. Besides, he would've told him.

Gabe might be annoyed at this little intervention, but he'd get over it. Later, when she divorced poor Gabe, he'd be glad good old Uncle George had watched out for him. Again. Too bad he hadn't thought of this for Gabe's first marriage.

He should have thought of it then, but Judith never would have gone for it—she was too savvy. She'd been impossible to manipulate. Oh well, live and learn. Gabe would thank him for this one day.

He handed Jenny his friend's business card. "Call Stan and tell him we talked. He'll take good care of you." George looked at his watch, then glanced at the bag of cookies. Damn they were good. Patting his belly, he turned away.

"Good cookies. Well, I've got to get going."

She walked him around the workmen's trucks to his silver Saab.

George opened the car door. "Jenny."

She turned back, eyebrows raised.

"I can see how much you love my boy. I'm sure you'll do the right thing."

Jenny nodded, looking distracted. He'd seen her surprise and hurt when he'd told her people were gossiping about her. She cared what people thought. Where Gabe was concerned, she wore her heart on her sleeve; she wouldn't want people thinking badly of Gabe for marrying her. A bleeding heart like her would get the prenup for Gabe; she'd want to protect him more than prove herself.

"Okay." George climbed into the car and backed out of the drive.

That had gone fairly well. The girl might pull this off for him. She seemed open to the idea, and Gabe was so besotted he'd give the little chit whatever she wanted. And lord, she could cook too. He wished he'd brought a few of those cookies home for dessert. Adele would have loved that recipe. She loved her chocolate. She surely had.

Jenny watched George back out of the drive. All during the conversation, she'd studied him carefully, searching for some indication that he knew about her past financial troubles. She'd always distrusted pretty-boy handsome men, assuming they were adept liars, but George had the kind of craggy face that might more easily betray his true feelings.

Rather heavy-set with slight jowls and a thick nose, he wheezed with each sentence. His large head was mostly bald, except for the sparse salt and pepper hair above his ears and ringing the back of his head. A single tall hair protruded from a bushy black eyebrow, like a wiry antenna. He'd seemed sincere enough, but she still didn't trust or like him. He might have known about her debt; she couldn't tell.

Gabe wouldn't have told anyone about her financial mess, would he? She'd paid off the last of the VISA, and lately she'd been diligent about only using cash and detailing all her expenditures. No, he wouldn't have told George.

Jenny turned and walked up the drive. How rich was Gabe? From the sound of it, everyone else knew. Were the Harrisons old money? She didn't need that complication. Maybe she should do some digging. She couldn't stand it if Gabe thought she'd married him for money. Surely Mom didn't think that, did she?

Jenny'd made some mistakes in the past, but they'd been foolish, honest mistakes, and she'd done her best to make up for them. She'd never be so cold and calculating as to marry for money. If Gabe even hinted that he thought a prenup was a good idea, she'd go along with it. She tossed the business card on top of the sample prenup. But she'd get her own lawyer.

Jenny wished she could discuss this prenup stuff with her parents, but she needed to take care of this alone. She sighed and blew out a deep sigh. Just when she was getting a handle on her finances, this expense had to come along. Legal fees would likely cost her another month or two—if she was lucky—of waitressing, but it was unavoidable; she wasn't stupid enough to trust George's crony.

Chapter 8

The burger sizzled loudly as George tossed it onto the grill and took a long pull of his beer. Productive week, he mused as he moved into the kitchen and cut the ends off the ear of corn and popped it in the microwave. "Hmm, was that six or ten minutes?" He shrugged and set the timer for six minutes.

Not only had he trimmed his golf score by ten strokes, he'd convinced Jenny to get a prenup—at least he assumed she was goin' through with it since she hadn't heard otherwise in the past few days. He held out the half-drunk bottle and studied the label. *Not a bad week's work. Not bad at all.*

George nudged the mail across the table, away from his dinner plate and set the table. He pulled the *Newsweek* back to scan the cover.

The front door opened. "Uncle George?"

Speak of the devil.

"Kitchen." George went to the fridge and pulled out another beer. As Gabe stalked into the kitchen with Jenny trailing behind, George's smile faded and his arm dropped.

"What the hell is this?" Gabe asked in a low, menacing voice. The thick sheaf of papers Gabe threw down fanned out across the counter, burying the *Newsweek* George had been reading.

"Just let me turn my burger, and I'll take a look." George held out the beer. "Drink?"

"No," Gabe said. Jenny shook her head.

George set the beer on the counter and hurried outside to buy himself some time. Gabe was mad, and it didn't take a genius to guess why. The only question was how he should play it. He flipped the burger and turned off the grill. No use in ruining a perfectly good hamburger. He'd have to wing it.

George went back inside and picked up the papers. Unfolding his reading glasses, he put them on, turned the document right side up, and scanned it, though he could guess its contents.

Gabe, glaring, hovered over him, while Jenny waited at his side. Anchoring her long hair behind one ear, she shifted her weight from foot to foot and watched with an open expression on her face. Not smug and triumphant, nor angry, just...uncomfortable. Gabe made her come, and she clearly would've loved to have been anywhere but here.

He looked at Gabe over his reading glasses. "What's the problem, Gabe?"

"I want an explanation."

He didn't even consider playing dumb—it would only further anger Gabe. In this instance his nephew was very like him, they had absolutely no patience for fools. "Why're you upset? Jenny thought the prenup was a great idea."

"You lied to her," Gabe snapped. The muscles in his jaw worked a steady, angry beat.

George raised his eyebrows. "How so? You *are* wealthy, you *did* inherit a substantial amount of money, and people *are* talkin' about you both."

"But I'm *not* afraid to talk to Jenny about *anything*. We have complete transparency in our relationship. However, m*y finances*. Are *none* of your business," he exclaimed in clipped sentences. "If I'd wanted a prenup, I would've had one drawn up myself."

George shrugged and spread his arms wide. "I was just trying to help."

Gabe snorted and planted a hand on his hip.

"Okay, look." He stood and faced them. "People were talking about what a gold digger Jenny was, and before the rumors got back to you, or her, I wanted to squash them. By having a prenup, she's in the clear. Quit being selfish and think of her."

"I don't give a damn what people say."

He gave Jenny his best compassionate look. "Maybe Jenny does."

"She doesn't. Mind your own business." Gabe glared at him. "You owe her an apology."

An apology? Gabe wanted him to apologize to that gold-digging twit? He wanted him to apologize for looking out for his nephew's best interest as he'd done for the past thirty years? "It's for your own good—both of you. And besides, if her feelings are true, you'll never need it."

"It's distrustful, and I won't have it. Apologize."

Jenny put a calming hand on his arm. "Gabe."

Gabe's furious glare sharpened, as if his nephew was trying to incinerate him with his focused stare. *Quite effective.* George fought the urge to squirm.

"He had no right," Gabe said.

"It's not worth ruining a relationship over," she said softly.

He wanted to concur with Jenny but knew any comment might prod his nephew to violence. He'd sit back and let the girl do his peacemaking for him.

Gabe's angry stare never left his, like a pit bull with his jaw locked. "Stay away from us. You can tear up that plane ticket and vacation package we gave you; after all, I wouldn't want someone who's using me for my money at my wedding." Gabe turned, grabbed Jenny's wrist, and pulled her toward the door.

"Aw, now, you don't mean that."

Gabe continued his march through the house as if he hadn't even spoken. Wow, he was steamed. He'd never seen Gabe so angry. George hurried after them.

"Wait, come back. I'm sorry. Look, maybe I took things too far. I really just wanted to help." He clasped his hands together and looked at Jenny. "Jenny. I'm sorry."

Jenny tugged Gabe's arm, stopping him at the front door. Her arms at his waist, she turned Gabe around to face him. "Apology accepted."

Beaming in relief, he turned to Gabe. "Gabe? Forgive me?"

Gabe's set jaw eased slightly, but the hardness didn't leave his eyes. "If you *ever* do anything like this again—"

"Never."

"If you interfere again, or hurt Jenny, it's over. Understand, Uncle George?" Dark gray eyes bore into him. "I mean it."

"Okay." He nodded. *I understand she's got you happily wrapped around her little pinky, and is alienating you from your loved ones.* He tried to look contrite.

Well and truly, pussy whipped.

ᴔ ᴔ ᴔ

With a hand on her shoulder, Gabe led Jenny to the car, opened the door, and tucked her inside. She settled into the seat and put her seatbelt on, thinking she should've been thrilled her fiancé stood up for her instead of being consumed by this uneasiness.

Gabe was vehemently opposed to a prenup. Jenny would've signed one, and she wouldn't have been insulted or hurt. It made sense that if a marriage didn't work out that what each person brought into the marriage left with them. What was *earned* while they were married should be joint property, but before that...that was each person's. A prenup wasn't a barrier to trust and a good, solid marriage. But to Gabe it was.

The pride in his voice rang loud and pure when he claimed they had complete transparency between them. Jenny'd had to stifle the impulse to wince and mentally whispered, *almost*, as she reassured herself that nothing in her past affected her and Gabe's future.

Gabe stood outside the driver's side talking on the phone a minute before getting into the car. He tossed his phone onto the console between them. "Pizza okay with you?"

"Sure."

Actually, how well could one *really* know another person? After all, they'd both been around several decades; that was a lot of living and experiences to cover. It's *impossible* to know *everything* about another person. And wasn't that part of the fun in a relationship? Finding out new things about your person? Growing together? It kept things fresh. Well, that and sex. She smiled.

"What're you smiling about?" Gabe asked as they drove home.

"Nothing. Just happy."

"That was fun for you?"

Jenny cast him a sideways glance. "Hardly. I'm pleased you guys worked it out." She ran a hand along his well-muscled arm. From biceps over forearm, she enjoyed the definition and strength beneath her fingertips. "I'm glad the man I'm marrying has a forgiving heart. *That* makes me happy. I've chosen well."

"Oh yeah?"

"Absolutely."

"Well...when we get home..." Gabe slid his hand beneath her hair to massage her neck a minute before, running his hand over the crown of her head, past her sensitive ear and shoulder, slowly grazing her breast with his knuckles, to tug on the end. "I'll show you exactly how well you've chosen."

"Is that so?" Jenny reached over the space between their seats, and rested her hand on the top of his thigh. With slow, deliberate movements, she traced the crease from his hip to groin. On the second pass, she let her hand linger teasingly over his swelling erection.

"That, sounds like a promise," she said in a low, sultry voice, "I'm going to have to collect on next week."

"Next week?" Gabe raised an eyebrow and gave her a cocky look as he turned down Mt. Vernon. "I can do better than that."

"Don't think so." Jenny nodded to the car in Gabe's driveway. "Alex is with you until then."

His brashness vaporized into disappointment. "Well, shit."

"Poor baby." Jenny chuckled. "Only two more weeks of setting a good example and then we'll be free to frolic all we want behind closed doors."

"I *knew* we should have sent that kid to boarding school."

What, no protest? She'd thought for sure Gabe would take exception to her word choice, claiming that he'd never "frolicked" in his life. Poor guy must be really annoyed to pass that up. "Don't take your frustration out on your poor daughter."

He pulled in the drive and turned off the car. "You're enjoying this."

Jenny tried to keep a straight face, then gave in to a slow grin of feminine satisfaction. What woman didn't enjoy evidence that she had the power to get her guy all hot and bothered? "A little."

"A lot," Gabe groused as he got out of the car.

"Whatever." She linked an arm through his, lowered her voice, and growled, "Now feed me, man. I'm starving."

"So demanding. So this is what life with you's going to be like?"

Jenny turned and stood on the porch step above him so they were eye-to-eye. God, he had beautiful, intelligent pewter eyes. And she loved it when they were focused completely on her. Gorgeous man.

Resting her hands on Gabe's shoulders, Jenny pulled him close for an open-mouth kiss full of promise. Her hand cupped his stubble-roughened cheek as she leaned into him, tasting and teasing until their hearts raced and she couldn't tell his hot breath from hers.

With a growl deep in his throat, Gabe's arms tightened until her body was plastered against every millimeter of his strong torso, leaving no room for even air between them. The heat of his body warred with the pounding of his heart against her breast in a distinctive, primal calling that had Jenny's eyes drifting shut and her breath coming in short bursts.

Gabe's arms trembled slightly as he easily lifted Jenny off the stoop, and slowly slid her down his body to the tip of his erection. The friction pebbling her nipples and electrifying every nerve ending made Jenny want to fling her legs around Gabe's hips, bringing her closer to the fulfillment she craved.

A car in desperate need of a new muffler loudly rumbled by. Jenny's eyes popped open, and she frowned, stifling her own rumble of frustration.

Dirty Pool, Harrison; teasing me like that when we're on the front porch and your daughter's on the other side of that glass front door.

Jenny broke contact with his lips to bury her face in his neck and inhale his sexy cologne. With a quick nip to his neck, she squirmed against his erection and wiggled out of his arms. Oh, yes, this teasing followed by combustible chemistry was *exactly* what she intended their life to be like. She pulled out of his arms, pleased to note his unfocused gaze and the perspiration-beaded forehead.

"Yup. Get used to it." With a little extra sway in her hips, Jenny slipped through the front door.

"Well." Gabe raised his eyebrows and slowly nodded. "Okay, then."

He moved to the side of the porch near a huge overgrown bush to adjust the bulge in his pants. Jenny smiled. *Serves him right, the tease.* He collected the mail and riffled through it before pulling his phone from his pocket. "I'm just going to check my messages."

"Uh huh." And give himself time to cool down before greeting his observant teenage daughter. *Good idea, honey.*

Alex slouched in a chair with her bent knees propped on the coffee table. She rolled her head sideways. "Took you long enough. How's Uncle George?"

"Fine. What're you watching?" Jenny put her purse down and sat on the couch. A pregnant girl who must have been about ready to deliver sat, arguing with her mom and sister, next to a partially assembled crib.

With the phone to his ear, Gabe's expression darkened as he strolled into the living room.

Uh oh. What now?

"Sixteen and Pregnant."

Sliding his phone into his pocket, Gabe glanced at the TV and tossed the mail onto the coffee table. "Turn that crap off."

"It's not crap," Alex said. "It shows what it's like to be a pregnant teenager and the sucky choices they have to make."

"It glamorizes teen pregnancy."

"It does not," Alex shot back. "Right, Jenny?"

"I've never seen it." Jenny cocked her head at Gabe. "You have?" Gabe watched MTV?

"I treat girls like that every week at the clinic." He nodded toward the TV, then said to Jenny, "Gianna told me about it."

"You've obviously never even watched an episode; it doesn't glamorize anything." Alex reached for the controls and turned the TV off. "It shows how pregnant girls have to give up their youth and high school fun to make adult decisions—or live with the guilt of an abortion."

"And some of those girls got pregnant on purpose just to be on the show and pull a paycheck. Stupid. Where the hell are their parents?"

"Gabe," Jenny chided. *What happened to my forgiving, sweet man?* "Working with those girls should've given you insight into their problems and extenuating circumstances."

"Maybe the same place as Julie's parents when she got pregnant." Alex sprang from the chair and stomped into the kitchen.

Gabe froze. Mouth open, he glanced at Jenny.

Jenny shook her head and shrugged. "Who?" she mouthed.

"Old neighbors," he whispered.

He stared at the doorway his daughter went through. "Julie Denton's pregnant?" He called out.

The pantry door creaked opened and then clicked shut.

"Not anymore," Alex said. "But don't spread it around, it's not common knowledge."

Gabe dropped onto the couch next to Jenny and blew out a deep breath. Jenny rubbed a comforting hand across his back as Alex foraged through the snack cupboard. Elbows on knees and chin resting on tented arms, Gabe frowned at the floor as if collecting himself. He raised his head, then called out tentatively, "Wanna talk about it?"

"Nope. Are we having dinner tonight?"

"Pizza's on the way."

The refrigerator door slammed shut and Alex poked her head around the doorway. "And before you go judging the Dentons, people in glass houses..." Alex trailed off as she disappeared back into the kitchen.

What did that mean?

Gabe stiffened. "Having a baby at twenty-three is *hardly* the same as sixteen."

"You both were still in school."

"Med school."

"Whatever. Irresponsible," Alex trilled. "Do you want a drink?"

"Beer, please." He turned to her. "Jen?"

She shook her head. "No, thanks."

Gabe heaved to his feet and headed for the kitchen. He took the beer Alex handed him, twisted the cap off, and pitched it in the trash. Crossing his arms, he leaned against the doorframe. "Heard from your brother lately?"

Jenny eased past him and took a seat at the kitchen table. What was Gabe up to? His tone was a little too casual to be making small talk.

Alex glanced at her father out of the corner of her eye, before going back to pouring her soda. "We talked a few days ago."

"How's he doing?"

"Fine," Alex drew out.

The doorbell rang. Jenny got to her feet and waved Gabe away. "I'll get it."

Jenny paid for the pizza and brought it into the kitchen. Alex reached into the cabinets for plates, then spread forks and knives next to the pizza box.

"He's not having any trouble adjusting?" Gabe asked.

Alex hesitated, then threw the pizza lid open. "Not that I know of." She inhaled deeply and smiled. "This looks great. Mom and Dave hardly ever let us get pizza."

"You sure?" Gabe asked.

Alex drew out a slice and assiduously avoided looking at her father. "Why don't you ask him yourself?"

Gabe pushed off the door jam and moved over to the counter. "I have, but you'd know before I would if something's going on."

Judging by the tension in the room and Alex's body language, there was *definitely* something going on, but she wasn't about to rat her brother out, and it wasn't fair for Gabe to put her in that position. But this was between Gabe and his daughter. Jenny should stay out of it.

"If you want to know something, ask him yourself," Alex said.

"I have, but he claims everything's great," Gabe pressed.

Jenny ground her teeth together. *Stay out of it, Jenny. Not your business.*

Alex shrugged. "Then it must be."

"You guys know you can tell me anything, right?"

"I know."

Geeze, let her off the hook. It's the sibling code. She's not going to talk. Jenny picked up a plate. "One or two pieces?"

"Two. Thanks."

Jenny scooped up two slices of pizza and shoved them at Gabe. He took the plate and followed Alex to the table. "If either of you had a problem, I'd help."

Alex crammed more pizza in her mouth, as she raised her eyebrows. "Mmm huh."

Oh for God sake! Enough already. Jenny turned to Alex. "I'm going dress shopping with my mom tomorrow and then out to lunch. Want to come? She's all concerned about getting something that won't clash with your dress."

"Sure. Sounds fun."

"Great." Jenny and Alex chatted about wedding plans, never giving Gabe the opportunity to turn the conversation back around to Ted. After dinner, Alex excused herself to do homework while Jenny and Gabe cleaned up.

After he dried the pizza cutter and put it away, Jenny took Gabe's hand and led him out onto the back deck, the farthest she could get from Alex's bedroom. "*What's* going on?"

"What do you mean?"

"Why were you so mean to Alex? The show. Pumping her for information on Ted. That's not like you."

"I know." Gabe sighed. "I don't know. The thing with Uncle George, then I had a message from a friend who said he saw Ted in court today." He turned his head sideways to look at her. "Apparently he got written up for trying to buy booze from an undercover cop." He frowned. "Alex knew about Ted—I could see it in her eyes, but she *just* wouldn't admit it..."

"So you took it out on her? It's called loyalty, Gabe. She was protecting her brother. You should be proud."

"What about her loyalty to me?"

Jenny rolled her eyes at him and gave him a look that let him know how childish he'd sounded. "You're the parent. He's her brother. Siblings bond together. That's a good thing. It means you raised them right."

"I wasn't *that* mean." He scowled. "It just makes me so mad that my kids would lie to me. Am I that unapproachable?"

"You're a parent. Yes."

"It's not like I expect them not to screw up. They're kids. Was I shocked that Ted had a fake ID? No. I had one at his age. I did dumb things in college. I don't expect my kids to be perfect, but I *do* expect them not to lie to me."

"He didn't lie."

Gabe frowned at her. "By omission. We talk every week, and he said everything was fine. We talked about his classes, his roommates, the food—"

"And you *really* expected him to tell you about an alcohol ticket and court appearance?"

"Hoped."

"Why? He's protecting you. Apparently he manned up and dealt with it on his own. He didn't want you to be disappointed in him. I get it."

"It's dishonest. That's not how I raised my son."

"People have a right to their privacy—even your son. You don't need to know everything."

"Everything important, I do. And it's not a matter of privacy, it's a matter of honesty and trust. I want to be able to trust my kids, is that so bad?"

"No. No it's not." Jenny could sympathize, but with her recent growing pains with her own parents still fresh, she identified with Ted's decisions, too. "But you have to balance that with letting them make their own mistakes, deal with the consequences, and become their own person. You need to sit back and relax, and trust that you raised them right and that they'll come to you if they get in over their heads."

"They can do all that and still be honest with me. You've never had children so you don't understand the..." He frowned as he searched for the right word. "...incredible weight of responsibility for another person that comes as soon as that baby's born—even before. It's up to you to protect that child with your life and teach and guide him to be a loving, good person and productive member of society." He sighed. "No matter how old they get, that feeling doesn't seem to lessen."

"You don't have to be a parent to understand that."

"Yeah, you really do."

Jenny wasn't about to argue with him but thought back about the evening's conversations. "Can I ask you a question?"

"Anything."

"You didn't *choose* to have kids in med school. Ted was an accident, wasn't he?"

He shook his head. "We learned in med school that sperm and eggs are at optimal health around age twenty-five. After that, a man's sperm quality and the woman's eggs begin to degrade.

"Since we were in a financial position to hire a nanny, we decided to optimize our chances of having healthy, intelligent children." He pursed his lips. "Just so happens, Judith was twenty-five."

"So you *lied* to your children?"

Gabe frowned, and looked thoughtful. "I'm not sure it's ever come up, actually. But they're smart kids. I'm sure they've figured it out."

Jenny raised her eyebrows.

"Fine. Point taken. One could make an argument that we lied by omission." He put an arm around her waist. "Well, now that you've seen the good, the bad, and the ugly. Still want to marry me?"

"Aw don't be so hard on yourself. That wasn't your best effort earlier. We barely got started," she teased.

He frowned at her attempt at humor. "Interfering uncle and delinquent son. You're really willing to take us on?"

More than ever, now that she'd seen the man actually had a few flaws. Thank God. It'd be hard living with a saint—even a sexy one. So they disagreed on a few fundamental issues? She could respect his need for complete honesty, but he also had to respect loyalty. Hmm, if push came to shove she wondered which he'd put above the other. She'd choose loyalty.

"You've met my mother, yet you still proposed."

Gabe tipped his head and winced. "Still say I'm getting the better end of this deal."

Chapter 9

Two weeks flew by and before Jenny knew it, they were immersed in the wondrous magic of Maui. Upon arrival, they'd been welcomed with the traditional Hawaiian greeting of fragrant, colorful fresh flower leis, and from that minute on, their cares dissolved.

With Gabe and her whole family here, as well as her best friend Alex and Ted, Jenny had everything she needed to make her wedding perfect.

The clean ocean air, perfumed with hints of salt, sunshine, and sweet exotic flowers, enchanted Jenny. The gentle, warm sun and rhythmic breaking waves soothed her soul and swept her worries away. After only a few days, Jenny felt refreshed and ready for her new life. Even George couldn't spoil her good mood.

Jenny was relieved to note that Maui worked its magic on her mother, too—well Maui and the kids. Ted, Alex, and Michael never seemed far from Mom and Dad, whether at the pool, on the beach, shopping, or playing cards in the lobby. It was sweet to see how the generations enjoyed each other's company.

Days later, Jenny stood before the non-denominational officiant and her new husband feeling beautiful and chic in her strapless sweetheart gown. Beaded lace appliques covered the fitted bodice, then spread through a dropped waist in an ever-dispersing flow that gave way to the delicate tulle pleats beneath, reminding her of dozens of little mini waterfalls.

Between the puffy skirt that brushed against her legs with every move, the way her train ever so slightly tugged at her butt and hips with each step, and the feel of her gauzy veil flowing from the crown of her head around her shoulders, Jenny felt like a princess going to a ball.

She'd parted her hair slightly to the side and a light French braid framed her face. The rest cascaded down her back in long ringlets. Jenny had tried to coax Gabe into more comfortable island wedding attire, but he'd insisted upon wearing a suit.

Freshly shaved, slightly sunburned, with the wind rustling his hair, wearing a suit that emphasized his broad shoulders, Gabe made her heart swell with happiness. A slow smile of awe spread across his face, and he nodded in approval when their gazes met as Dad walked her down the aisle. Jenny's world was complete.

Then Jenny, Gabe, and the minister stood cocooned beneath a gauzy arch accented with white chiffon, pink roses, and hydrangea. A gentle late afternoon breeze skimmed her bare arms and shoulders in a cooling caress while the surf serenaded them, and the rest of the world dropped away until it was just Jenny and Gabe taking their vows and declaring their love. Rings exchanged and first kiss bestowed, they turned to the officiant.

"The butterfly symbolizes new beginnings, freedom, and happiness. In a few minutes, we're going to celebrate Jenny's and Gabe's love and new beginning with the release of these butterflies." He waved a hand at the white organza display that held a dozen sleepy Monarchs. Some of them clung to the side of the enclosure still while others slowly batted their wings as if fanning themselves.

"When Jenny was a little girl, she was enchanted with the American Indian legend that claimed that if one captured a butterfly, made a wish, and then freed it, in gratitude, the Great Spirit would always grant the wish. So in a minute I'm going to invite you to close your eyes and make a wish bestowing upon this couple our very best blessings to carry to God. But first, I'd like to read this poem Jenny and Gabe selected. *Learn to Fly* by Larry James."

Jenny faced Gabe and held his hands between hers, wishing she'd written the beautiful lines because it so spoke to her heart. When she looked into Gabe's dear face and saw his eyes glossy with unshed tears, she had to furiously blink back tears of her own. This poem was their truth and most fervent hope for their life together.

What happened before this day didn't matter. It was what they made of themselves and their marriage from this day forward that counted, how they learned to soar together.

Like a butterfly emerges
And unfolds its graceful wings,
A marriage grows and it develops
With the love each partner brings.

Your flight through life together
Is what you make it, so reach high
Spread your wings and learn to soar
As if with wings of a butterfly

Share together life's great adventure
Now the two of you are one
Shower your lover with butterfly kisses
Your infinite journey has just begun

Be a lover, friend, and playmate
Learn to listen, laugh, and cry
God has given you your wings,
But, you teach each other how to fly.

"Please close your eyes and make your wishes," the officiant instructed as he handed them the cage.

With unsteady hands, Jenny swiped a finger under each eye, hoping her mascara truly was waterproof. She blew out a deep breath and faced her new husband. Gabe held the box while Jenny reached for the lid.

Smiling, she looked up at Gabe. "One."

"Two," he said.

"Three," they chorused as Jenny pulled the top off, freeing the butterflies.

There was a round of applause as a half dozen Monarchs burst free in a graceful, elegant release. Jenny gently scooped her hand into the box to encourage the stragglers. One flew immediately to Gabe's boutonniere and settled there.

My favorite spot too, right over his heart.

ల ల ల

After an hour spent moving from one beautiful location to another to pose for photos, the group was led to a small, private room with a wall of windows overlooking the ocean. Doors swung open and the photographer rushed ahead of them to snap more photos.

Off to the side, one large, oval table was set with china and sparkling crystal. Different sized snow-white candles scattered throughout a wood bark vine strewn with leafy flowers in a variety of pinks and lavenders. Like a candle-lit walk through a forest. Perfect.

Jenny's gaze traveled the room from the table to the parquet dance floor, to—she froze and clutched Gabe's arm. Her eyes grew wide, and her mouth dropped open.

"Surprise!" An arm landed across her shoulder as a beaming Alex popped up between her and Gabe.

"Wha—?" Jenny slowly walked forward. *Oh my God.* But how?

She looked from Gabe to Alex to her parents and Michael. Cindy, her date, Dillon, and Ted stood grinning while George looked as puzzled as she felt.

George leaned toward Ted, muttering, "What's the big deal?"

"Are you kidding me right now?" Jenny looked at Gabe. "How?"

Gabe grinned and inclined his head toward her parents.

Picking up her poufy skirt, Jenny darted across the room and threw herself into her mom's arms whispering, "Thank you. Thank you. Thank you."

Mom squeezed back. "Someone who appreciates sweets as much as my girl deserves a delicious wedding cake."

"Oh, my God. It's not lemon with raspberry filling, too?"

"The top layer is. The other is chocolate with Bavarian cream, and then plain yellow for the bottom."

"But how? You didn't bring it all the way from home, did you? You couldn't—that's ridiculous." There was *no way* they could have transported that cake forty-three hundred miles on the plane, especially when there weren't any direct flights. And the caterer had been adamant about the desserts they would offer, and butter cream frosting had not been an option—no matter how sweetly Jenny'd requested it.

Mom smiled and stood a little taller. "Where there's a will..."

"It's right, isn't it? Just like in your book?" Alex asked.

Jenny nodded. It was more than right. It was perfect. An exact scaled-down replica of her wedding cake. The three-layer cake had a dozen silk butterflies winding and twisting up the side of the cake to a few small ones swirling around the feet of the bride and groom cake topper.

Wide-eyed, Jenny circled the cake. At the back, under a butterfly wing, she used her index finger to scoop up a healthy dollop of icing, half-afraid it was fondant masquerading as something tasty.

"That's it, right?" Gabe asked.

Jenny held her finger of icing up to him. "Buttercream?"

Gabe leaned forward and took the sweet into his mouth. Gaze locked on Jenny's face. His hot, wet tongue sucked the icing away, then swirled leisurely around her finger, the way he suckled and enjoyed tasting other parts of her.

Jenny held her breath, and her heart launched into triple time. She flipped her hair over one shoulder and tugged on her finger. Gabe grabbed her hand and held it steady.

"Gabe," she whispered and glanced at their audience. "Behave!"

With a last lick, Gabe released her, smiling. "Buttercream."

Flushed and hot, Jenny turned to the others. "Let's eat. I'm starving."

"Me too," Gabe murmured in her ear.

She pushed playfully at his chest.

Between sentimental champagne toasts, Jenny feasted on an amazing caprese salad while Gabe started with butternut squash soup, and they shared her pepper-crusted filet mignon and his butter poached Kona lobster, washing it down with a lovely mellow cabernet the wine steward recommended. Superb.

Cindy picked up a spoon and tapped it against her water glass and others—with the exception of George, who undoubtedly considered the custom silly—immediately chimed in in an insistent clinking until Gabe kissed Jenny.

Michael thought the tradition was great fun, thoroughly enjoying that they could make Gabe and Jenny stop whatever they were doing and kiss. He was often the instigator of many a kiss, until the zeal got the better of him, and Michael used his knife a little too hard and smashed his water glass.

Alex and Ted burst out laughing, enjoying Michael's red face and fluster as servers rushed forward to sop up his mess and replace his broken glass. Mom, on the other hand sent her wayward offspring a furious scowl. Jenny failed to hide her smile, unperturbed by one glass broken in a careless moment of enthusiasm. But Michael hung his head, sufficiently chastened.

Satiated by food and drink, Jenny and Gabe took to the dance floor for their first dance as husband and wife. They glided around the floor as Josh Groban sang "You Raise Me Up."

Snuggling close, Jenny looked up at Gabe, but his attention was focused across the room. This was their first dance; he should be paying attention to her. Jenny turned to see what Gabe was staring at. Beer in hand, Ted was talking to George.

Jenny leaned in, murmuring, "One beer at his father's wedding does not an alcoholic make."

"It's illegal."

"It's a special occasion."

"I thought the fine and alcohol class would've gotten through to him." Gabe scowled. "I talked to Ted on the plane. I thought we had an understanding."

"Well maybe you should've had that talk with George since he's the one who gave it to him. I'm sure Ted took it to save face."

"Great. Big help he is."

Jenny pushed on Gabe's shoulder, turning them so Gabe had his back to George and Ted. "Forget them and pay attention to me." She smiled. "I love this song but was surprised you even knew it. I wouldn't have taken you for a Josh Groban fan."

Gabe folded her hand in, tucking it close to his heart and lowered his head. "Truth? I barely knew his name before."

Jenny smiled and nodded. That's what she'd suspected.

"But when I heard the lyrics, I knew this was the one because meeting you and loving you have raised me up and made me want to be a better man, and I hope my love does the same for you."

Jenny scowled and sniffled, trying to hold back tears. She pinched his hand. "Stop saying such sweet things that make me cry." She rested her head on his chest. "I love you."

Gabe squeezed her tight and they danced until the end of the song, when he led her over to where Dad and Mom stood watching. Gabe gave her hand to Dad. "Thank you."

Her dad danced Jenny back to the center of the parquet floor to Rascal Flatt's "My Wish." Dad moved her around in the slow box step he'd taught her at her cousin's wedding when she'd been small enough to dance on the top of Dad's feet. "You look gorgeous today, Jenny."

"Thanks, Dad."

"At first I was concerned at your change in wedding plans, but this has worked out beautifully."

"Oh ye of little faith," Jenny teased. *Hope Mom thinks so, too.*

"I like Gabe and his kids. I'm enjoying getting to know them better. This vacation was a great idea."

Jenny searched out Gabe, who was sitting next to his uncle. He'd taken off his suit coat and rolled his sleeves. Jenny's gaze lingered on his muscular forearm, then Gabe winked at her. She drew back, a little surprised yet delighted, then rewarded him with a warm smile. "I'm pretty pleased with them myself."

"Though it might be nice if those kids had less luck at cards."

"Tired of losing to a couple of kids?" Playing Hearts, Euchre, and Spades was a favorite pastime Mom and Dad taught her and Michael at early ages. It actually started in elementary school. Dad had taught her cribbage to improve her addition skills. Ted and Alex delighted in embracing the Campbell tradition.

Her dad scowled at her. "Watch it, young lady."

"You'd better be nice to me, or I'll tell them to let you win."

"Don't you dare. I've been holding back since they're new to the game."

"Uh huh," Jenny said, her voice thick with doubt.

"To build their confidence. But they're getting a little cocky now. I think it's time to put them in their place."

Jenny chuckled. "Good luck with that."

Both Ted and Alex had strong card sense, and Dad notoriously had poor luck being dealt good cards. She'd put her money on the kids.

Dad looked at Mom, whose head was bent close to Alex's. "I especially appreciate you giving us older grandchildren so we missed the diaper changing phase."

Jenny chuckled. "Anything for you, Dad."

He twirled her around. "I'm not sure you've ever looked happier, little girl."

"Life is pretty good right now." Only one way it could be perfect. Jenny sought out Gabe where he sat talking to George. Okay, two maybe. George aside, one little conversation with Gabe would—

Don't be greedy. Be happy with what you have.

∾ ∾ ∾

Gabe took off his jacket, rolled up his sleeves, then settled in next to Uncle George to watch Jenny dance with her dad.

Damn, that woman's beautiful. And mine.

When Gabe caught his first glimpse of Jenny walking down the beach on her father's arm, all graceful and stunning in that beaded, gauzy dress, she'd taken his breath away. Literally; he forgot to breathe. But Lord help him, when she smiled for him—and it'd been *just* for him—she made his head spin faster than downing four straight shots of whiskey. He was the luckiest man in the world.

Jenny laughed at something her dad said then glanced at him. He winked. *I've got my eye on you, lady. Later you'll be laughing for me, and giggling, then moaning...*

Gabe shook his head to clear his brain. They had a ways to go tonight before he was free to see what it took to get Jenny out of that gown, and thinking that way would only lead to frustration.

He reached for his ice water and turned to his uncle. "Having a good time?"

"Dinner was pretty good." Uncle George frowned at him. "What's with her old man and that getup?" He nodded at Mike, dressed in a white embroidered Hawaiian dress shirt, khakis, and sandals.

"Jenny asked him to dress in traditional Hawaiian clothes, like the other guys." Ted, Michael, and Dillon were similarly dressed.

"That's fine for younger men, but he should know better. Looks ridiculous."

"He looks fine."

Uncle George raised an eyebrow. "You didn't."

"I'm the groom, not a guest."

He watched the way Jenny swayed to the music, her hair moving half a beat behind, brushing bare, silky skin, begging to be caressed.

Uncle George shook his head. "You gotta do something to keep a looker like that. Judith didn't look half that good, and, well, we both know how that turned out."

"Thanks, Uncle George."

"I'm just sayin' if you're gonna go to the trouble of marrying the girl, it's good to see you're trying to hang onto her. That ring. This wedding. You're certainly bringin' your A game."

"Glad you approve," he said dryly. And she still married him after she'd met Uncle George. Gabe shook his head in wonder. When they got home, he was going to have to have a long talk with his uncle about boundaries and guarding his tongue a little better.

"I wouldn't go that far," Uncle George muttered. He scowled and rolled his beer over his blistering forearms.

"Did you use the aloe lotion Jen gave you?"

"Doesn't work." He moved the beer to his other arm.

"You'd think at your age you'd be able to avoid a sunburn."

"I shouldn't have burned. I'm out in the sun plenty playin' golf."

"The sun doesn't reflect off the green like it does the ocean. You know that. Besides, Jenny reminded you to put suntan lotion on before we left."

"What? She's my mother now?"

"Nope. She's just right." He smirked.

Gabe's uncle had been put out at having to fly all the way to Maui for the wedding, so to make it up to him, Gabe paid a small fortune and gave him the fishing trip of a lifetime. While the ladies indulged in a little retail therapy, Gabe chartered a fishing expedition for the men.

He gave Michael, Mike, and Dillon their first fishing lesson, while Uncle George and Ted chased marlins. And Uncle George fried his arms. Gabe wasn't sure he made fishermen of the Campbells, but they seemed to enjoy it well enough, and it was a nice chance for the men to spend a day together.

When the last notes played, Jenny pulled her subdued brother out on the floor. The photographer darted in and around, getting pictures of the bride dancing with her brother and then some shots of the group.

Michael wasn't half-bad. He watched the kid shimmy and move. Geeze, the guy had rhythm. Everybody formed a circle around him, and amid clapping and shouts, Michael threw himself to the floor executing a pretty good version of the Worm that ended with a breakdance twirl.

To his surprise, Ted pulled Mary to the center and twirled her around a bit before pointing to Cindy and Dillon to take center stage. Alex ran over and held out her hand to Uncle George. "Come dance with me, Uncle George."

"Aw, no thanks, Alex. I don't dance."

She tugged on his arm. "You do, too. I've seen you."

"I don't know this song."

"So? It's got a good beat. Come on, Uncle George."

"Uhh, my sunburn's botherin' me. I'll just watch."

Gabe stood to dance with his daughter and let Uncle George off the hook, but then Mike approached. Mike held out a hand to Alex, and jerked his head toward the others on the dance floor. "Come on, Alex. Let's show 'em how it's done."

"Okay." Alex beamed.

"Look like a bunch of fools boppin' around out there. Back in the day that's what we did to get in shape for skiing."

Gabe sat back down and smiled. "They're having fun."

Gabe was grateful to Mike for dancing with Alex. Until this week and seeing Alex and Ted with Mary and Mike, it'd never occurred to him that his kids had been missing out on the grandparent experience. His parents were dead, and Judith's lived in North Dakota and didn't visit often. Dave had an elderly mother living with her sister in Florida, so the kids didn't see her much.

It was good to see the generations together enjoying each other. The Campbells were proving a good find, the whole bunch of them. They were fun and loving, and they seemed to have some connection to his kids.

Uncle George heaved to his feet. I'm gonna go back to my room and get some aspirin."

"Okay. You're coming back, right?"

"Maybe. I'll see how I'm feelin'"

"Come back. It's only nine o'clock. It's my wedding."

"I might turn in. I've got an early flight in the morning, and I still gotta pack."

"All right." He stood and walked Uncle George out.

Uncle George stopped at the door. "See ya at seven-thirty for breakfast?"

Obviously his uncle didn't think that the morning after Gabe's wedding, he might want to sleep in late, or perhaps share a leisurely breakfast alone with his bride before enjoying a little morning loving. Hmm, breakfast with Uncle George or making love to his sweet, sexy wife?

Uncle George looked at him with raised eyebrows, patiently waiting.

"How about nine?"

"Shuttle picks me up at nine."

Forgive me, Jenny. "We'll meet you in the dining room at eight-thirty."

Uncle George grunted and with a nod, turned, and left.

Good God he was a difficult man. Was it aging or having to share him with Jenny that was making his uncle grumpier? Hopefully once they got home, time would settle him down. Now that they'd won Jenny's parents over, he fervently hoped Uncle George wouldn't become a problem.

Chapter 10

Steve Grant parked his silver Mustang convertible in the middle of the garage. Getting out of the car, he twisted right then left, stretching muscles made tight by sitting at his desk for most of the last ten hours. He strolled out of the garage and looked out over the placid, barren lake.

Bright yellow daffodils and pastel tulips Mom planted around the house were in full bloom as decades-old maple and oak trees leafed out. A pair of quacking ducks flew low overhead, gliding into Lake St. Claire. Wouldn't be long before sailboats and water-skiers were out in force.

Steve drew in a deep breath and put his hands on his waist. Maybe he'd go for a run before having a bowl of tomato soup and a grilled cheese sandwich for dinner while watching a little TV. He turned and walked down the driveway toward the mailbox, humming an Elton John classic, "Goodbye Yellow Brick Road," and looking over his yard. Grass needed cutting and edging. Better get on it tomorrow before it got too long. Steve riffled through the junk mail, separating the bills from the letters, relegating the *Sports Illustrated* and *The American Lawyer,* to the back of the pile. He slapped the mailbox closed, then lifted his hand in greeting as his neighbor sailed up their driveway.

Through the budding privet hedge that divided their driveways, he watched the lady remove flat after flat of colorful impatiens, pansies, and snapdragons from her Jeep. Never having actually spoken to them, Steve only knew his neighbors by sight.

They'd bought the cottage house late last summer and immediately began ripping it apart. From the size of the dumpsters and the number of workmen constantly crawling all over the house, they must have gutted the place. Luckily for them, it'd been a late winter, and they'd been able to complete a large addition before the snow arrived.

He'd like to check out the inside, just to satisfy his curiosity about the renovation, he told himself. It had nothing to do with his curiosity about the couple living in it. At first he'd thought they were father and daughter. The guy wore suits and from a distance looked to be in his forties—but could have been older. She was usually dressed in jeans, with her long hair tied back in a perky ponytail or left loose trailing down her back, and could have been his college-aged daughter.

From afar, that's what it looked like, but up close he could see he was wrong. If any daughter gave her father that passionate, lingering kiss, or smiled at him like he was her whole life and fantasy wrapped into one, then someone should've called Social Services on them long ago. Nope, had to be husband and wife.

Steve stopped in front of a couple of dead bushes between their driveways. Grabbing one, he gave it a quick tug and fell back a step when the whole bush, roots and all, dangled in his grasp. Dirt fell in a fine shower, covering his loafers.

"I'd say that one's a goner." Chuckling, she approached, still holding a flat of flowers.

He smiled wryly. "Afraid so."

Putting down the flowers and brushing her hands on her faded jeans, she stretched a hand through the hole where the dead bush had been. "Jenny Harrison."

He threw the bush aside and shook her hand. "Steve Grant."

"Deader than you thought, eh?" she smiled, nodding at the bare bush. Dirt barely clung to the scraggly roots. She giggled. "You looked surprised when it came out so easily."

"I was. I thought I'd have to dig it up."

"Do you live there?" She looked beyond him at his house.

He nodded. "The past few years."

"You're certainly a quiet neighbor. I was beginning to wonder if it was abandoned."

"I haven't been home much. My dad had Alzheimer's. Mom refused to put him in assisted living—so I moved in to help her until he passed."

She frowned. "Sorry for your loss."

"Thanks." He nodded toward her house. "Looks like you're done. How do you like it?"

"We love it." She pointed at the flowers. "Just the finishing touches left."

Over her head, he admired the house. "Did a lot of work. It looks great."

She turned and looked at it. "We had to update most of it and nearly doubled it in size with the additions, but we're happy with the way it turned out." She looked down the driveway to the street where a car pulled in their drive. "Oh, good. Gabe's home."

Her husband approached in a red station wagon. A hot red station wagon; what an oxymoron. Her husband came over, and after a quick kiss, Jenny introduced them.

Hands in trouser pockets, Gabe looked toward Steve's house. "Have you lived here long?"

"Couple of years, right after I got out of school."

Gabe pursed his lips and raised his eyebrows. "Starting pay for new grads has gone up quite a bit since I was in college."

"Law school."

Gabe frowned. "Your name sounds familiar..." He looked to Jenny for help.

She shrugged.

He got that a lot. "I used to play ball for the Tigers."

Gabe's face lightened the way everyone's did when they recognized him. "Pitcher, right?"

"'Til my arm gave out."

"Rotator cuff?"

"Yeah. What do you do for a living?"

"Doctor. General surgeon." Gabe turned and wrapped an arm around his wife's shoulder. "And Jenny's a journalist."

"Is that so?" Steve inclined his head politely. A writer? Great. Just his luck to get a professional spy for a neighbor. The bane of his existence.

"Books?" he asked hopefully.

"No, I freelance. Human interest stuff mostly."

"Great." His stomach growled loudly. "Well, welcome to the neighborhood, and if you need anything, feel free to..." he waved a hand at the hole. "Come on over."

"Thanks." She picked up the flowers, which Gabe took from her as they walked toward the house. Her ponytail whipped her face as she turned around, calling, "You too," as an afterthought.

He forced a smile and flapped his hand in a semblance of a wave.

ം ം ം

Watering can in hand, Jenny generously doused the thriving impatiens and geraniums with blue fertilizer water, then snipped off the dead flowers so new ones would bloom. Surprisingly, Jenny found she enjoyed fussing over her potted flowers, and it turned out she had her mom's green thumb. Who knew?

Before moving in here, Jenny never had the urge to grow anything, but over the six months they'd been married, their new home seemed to bring out her latent nurturing instincts. Jenny'd planted colorful pots of flowers all around the front yard and back patio—even the dock had a welcoming pot of petunias.

She turned at the sound of a car rolling up Steve's long brick driveway. The familiar slim blonde popped out of the car as Steve came out of the house. Barefoot, wearing a worn Princeton T-shirt and frayed blue jean shorts, he looked ready for a relaxing day. He took the toddler and pastel diaper bag from the woman and ruffled the older boy's hair before waving the mother away.

Jenny mixed more of the solution while centering her attention on her neighbor and the kids. The woman dropped the children off almost every weekend, for varying amounts of time. Was Steve divorced? The solution gushed over the top of the watering can, splashing her feet. She turned off the water and crossed to the large planters flanking the porch.

Divorced. Maybe she dumped him when Steve couldn't play ball anymore. That would account for the flash of sadness she glimpsed in his eye when he admitted to Gabe that he used to play. Quitting in the middle of a successful career must have been tough, especially when he'd been forced out by an injury.

It would have been a huge lifestyle change to go from celebrity athlete always in the limelight to lowly first-year law student. There was no shame in being a lawyer—usually—but maybe she'd left him when he chose a less visible career. Interesting. There could be an article in it.

Her attention returned to the empty watering can she held over the overflowing planter. *Oops*, she'd given it all to the one. Hopefully the extra fertilizer wouldn't kill them.

While mixing up some more food for the other flowers, her gaze frequently returned to the roughhousing, screaming, and giggling coming from next door. Annoyed that they so easily distracted her, Jenny finished her yard work and moved inside. Firmly shutting the window to lock out the childish shouts and squeals of laughter, she entered the kitchen and fixed a glass of iced tea.

Jenny tried to work, but from her study over the garage, she could clearly see into his backyard and found herself watching Steve and the children frolic in the wading pool. Steve sprayed the children with the hose as they slid down the plastic slide, screaming at the top of their lungs, floundered in the pool, and then climbed out and raced around to do it all again.

It certainly was quieter when he was living with his parents. Exasperated with her lack of concentration, Jenny resurrected her earplugs and took her laptop to the opposite side of the house to work.

Hours later, she clasped her hands high over her head and then twisted from side to side, stretching stiff muscles. The garage door droned open. Yay, Gabe was home early. Smiling, she shut down the computer and padded into the kitchen. Her welcoming smile faded, and she came to a complete stop near the doorway, when she saw a big dog standing patiently at Gabe's side.

He dropped the leash and came forward to kiss her. "Surprise."

She moved around him to look at the golden retriever. "Who's your friend?"

"Ritz."

"I see." She nodded. "And what's he doing in my kitchen?"

"*She* is a present for you."

"For me?" Eyebrows raised, Jenny looked at him.

"Yup. You said you didn't want kids, but you didn't say anything about dogs. I thought you'd like some company. She might not be as smart as a kid, but she's easier to care for, less expensive, won't talk back, and is far more obedient. She probably eats less, too. Definitely eats less than Alex."

Jenny squatted to pet her silky coat. The dog wagged her tail furiously and licked her face, knocking her backward. Laughing Jenny pushed her away and looked up from her spot on the floor. "You got her for me?"

"I didn't think you'd want to bother with a puppy, so when one of the OR nurses mentioned that the Leader Dogs for the Blind in Rochester placed their drop-out dogs with other people, I put us on the waiting list."

"Without asking me?"

"Wouldn't have been much of a surprise if I had."

"What if I didn't like dogs?"

"Don't be ridiculous. You love animals."

Okay, so she'd give him that; she did like animals. "A dog's a big responsibility. Don't you think we should've discussed it first?"

He frowned. "Really? I thought for sure you'd love her." He stroked her head, cooing, "What's not to love about this sweet little girl?"

They both looked at her with soft, pleading eyes. *Geesh. How's a girl to stay annoyed?* Jenny'd never really thought about owning her own pet since keeping goldfish alive had proved an impossible feat, but a dog was a little hardier than a fish.

"How sweet. You got me a reject."

He grinned. "Only the best for my girl. They kicked her out 'cause she's scared of moving traffic."

"Smart girl." Jenny turned her attention to the dog and ruffled that spot behind her ear all dogs love rubbed.

"She's house broken, passed advanced obedience classes, and even had her teeth cleaned. So what do you think?"

She smiled up at Gabe. "Ya done good, Harrison."

∾ ∾ ∾

Ritz merged into their lives with hardly a ripple, her only fault being that she wanted to be with Jenny constantly. After getting stepped on several times, Ritz learned to be unobtrusive, lying under tables and in corners out of the way. To give her greater freedom and still preserve the open beauty of their yard, they had an underground fence installed around the perimeter of their property.

Not that they worried about her wandering into the street, but they discovered she loved swimming in the lake. The fence worked beautifully, and Ritz quickly learned that she couldn't get within five feet of the lake while wearing her electronic collar. After a few weeks, she didn't mind leaving Jenny's side to chase the ducks and Canadian Geese perpetually parading through the backyard.

One sunny Saturday afternoon, Jenny worked in her office, when Ritz's frenzied barking broke her concentration. The frenetic bark, punctuated by yelping, differed from her usual bird chasing bark.

Jenny went to the window and saw her neighbor's boy racing down the hill in their back yard, chasing his soccer ball. "Chill, Ritz, he's getting his ball."

Ritz continued whining and then started scratching at the door.

"Ritz, no!" She was going to scratch the heck out of the glass if she kept that up. Jenny got up and went in the kitchen. "Knock it off."

Arms wrapped around his soccer ball, the boy wore an exasperated expression as he stood halfway up the hill and looked down behind him. He put a hand on his hip, like she imagined his mother did when she was annoyed, and called out to someone just out of view.

Ritz whined and pawed at the door again.

"Stop it." Jenny frowned and stepped closer to the window.

Oh, no. So that's what had Ritz all in a tizzy. At the base of the hill, toward the far side of the yard, Steve's toddler was chasing four little goslings. Uh oh. A baby goose was never far from her—yup, there was the mom on the dock. The goslings hurried after their mother, but the toddler was closing in fast.

Steve was nowhere in sight.

Jenny unhooked Ritz's electronic collar and yanked the sliding door open. "Get 'em, Ritz!"

Hopefully the charging dog wouldn't give the baby a heart attack, but Jenny was pretty sure Ritz would go for the geese before she'd stop to lick the kids to death. And if the little girl got a scare, too, maybe that wouldn't be such a bad thing either.

"Hey! Leave those babies alone, sweetie," Jenny called out as she trotted down the slope.

The toddler got within a foot of the goslings before the mother goose whirled on her, sprinted back hissing and flapping her wings furiously. Oh, crap. A pissed off goose could hurt the child.

The golden retriever streaked by the little girl and rushed the geese. The furious mother hissed, honked, and lunged at Ritz while her goslings scrambled over the break wall into the water.

"Sophie, come back here," the boy called, as he raced behind Jenny.

The startled child stood frozen, mouth open, wide-eyed watching the frenzied animals. Ritz barked and dodged mama goose, trying to stay away from her sharp, pinching beak.

Jenny scooped up the sweaty, scared little girl. Tears pooled in her eyes, but she seemed too enthralled with the animals to cry. "And what're you doing out here alone?"

The honking goose half-ran and half-flew after Ritz, chasing her across the yard, driving her away from her goslings.

Jenny carried the toddler up the hill. Whistling, she called, "Ritz, come."

Ritz seemed happy to give up her game, and as soon as she turned away, luckily, the mama goose went in search of her babies. Good thing, too. The last thing Jenny wanted to do was to try to outrun a mad goose while carrying twenty-some pounds of kid uphill.

The baby twisted in her arms, pointing over her shoulder. "Duck."

"Goose. No touch. The mama goose will bite you."

"Sophia? Josh?" Her neighbor called from his yard.

"Over here." Jenny carried the baby up the hill. Ritz pranced ahead beside the boy.

Ping-pong paddle in hand, Steve strode through the hedge with Gabe on his heels. "What're you guys doing over here?"

"Getting my soccer ball and playing with the dog." The boy stroked a panting Ritz.

"And rescuing this one from a piss—," Jenny glanced at Josh, "—an angry mama goose." Given that his son was watching them, Jenny reigned in her annoyance when she really wanted to bite

Steve's head off for not watching his kids better. She raised her eyebrows at Steve. "She tried to pet some goslings."

Steve lifted the baby from Jenny's arms. "Thanks." Turning to the toddler, he frowned sternly. "Sophie, you know you can't touch the babies. We talked about that, remember?"

With one chubby arm anchored around his neck, she twisted in his arms, pointing to the dock. "Duck."

He turned to Jenny. "Sorry about that."

"You need to watch your kids better."

"Yeah, they slipped away while... I will."

"If Ritz hadn't been there, that goose could have really hurt her or she could've fallen in the water."

"I know. I'm sorry." He met her annoyed gaze with a soft, contrite expression. "It won't happen again. Though, she can swim."

"She can?" Gabe asked. "How old is she?"

"Two. Josh is four." He turned to the kids. "Josh and Sophie, this is Doctor and Mrs. Harrison."

Josh muttered a greeting.

"Josh and Sophie are my girlfriend's kids. Josh swims pretty well, and Sophie swims well enough to float on her back if she fell in."

The fact that they could swim somewhat mollified Jenny. Shaking off the lingering fright, she inspected her husband, taking in the Ping Pong paddle and white ball in Gabe's hand, his sweaty, flushed face, and his mussed hair. "You look like you're having fun."

"Just a friendly game." He pointed at Steve. "He got a new table and needed a little help putting it together."

"And then you had to try it out."

"Had to break it in," Gabe agreed.

Steve set Sophia down, and the adults watched chubby, short legs pump as she retrieved a basketball from the garage and carried it to the hoop seven and a half feet over her head. Jenny worried the baby would hurt herself with the hard ball that was half her size, but Steve didn't object.

"We'll see. You're going to be jealous. I'll be all hard muscles and buff."

Jenny loved his hard muscles and doubted that he could be much more buff, but if it made him happy, why not?

She ran her hands over strong arms and down his firm, hairy chest. Trailing her arms under his shirt, she circled his warm, bare waist and pulled him close until their stomachs and thighs pressed intimately together.

"And I'm gonna love it. But first...maybe we should conduct a thorough inspection, a sort of before and after, hmm?"

A growl rumbled deep in his throat as he lowered his head for a long, deep kiss that left them both breathless. Jenny slipped her arms around his neck and nuzzled the spot under his jaw where hints of his morning cologne tended to linger.

God, with so little effort, just a simple kiss really, he had her trembling, longing for more. It'd never been this wonderful with any other man—not even during her infatuation with her first love—and she suspected it never could be with anyone else. She rubbed her hips against his arousal in blatant invitation.

"I love the way you think, lady." Suddenly bending and lifting, Gabe scooped her in his arms and carried her into the house.

Jenny's phone started playing the theme song from *Jaws*. She pulled Gabe's head down for another kiss. Gabe pecked her lips and set her on her feet. "Answer your mother."

Jenny slid her phone from her back pocket. "Hey, Mom. What's up?"

"Dad was sharpening the kitchen knives, and he sliced his hand. I've got to run him into the ER for stitches."

Yow. Jenny winced.

"But Michael's got a dance tonight and the parents of the other boys we're carpooling with have already gone out to dinner. Can you drop the boys off at school at eight if we're not back by then?"

"Sure. No problem. Has Michael eaten?"

"No. I was starting dinner."

"No worries. I'll be right over to get him. He can eat with us."

"Thanks. I appreciate it."

"Okay, Bye."

"What's going on?"

"Mom's gotta take Dad to get stitches." Gabe followed Jenny from room to room as she searched the house for her purse. "Michael's going to have dinner with us, and then I'm chauffeuring him and his buddies to a school dance if Mom and Dad aren't back in time."

"What happened to Mike?" Gabe followed her out of the bedroom and downstairs.

"Cut his hand sharpening knives." Could she have left it in her car? Jenny headed for the garage. Not in the front seat. Ah! There it was on the backseat. She picked it up and went inside for the Jeep keys. "If Alex gets home before I get back will you ask her to make a salad?"

"What hospital are they going to?"

"Probably St Francis. That's the one we always use. Why?"

"Hang on a minute. The ER's packed most Saturday nights. Let me make a phone call." Gabe pulled out his phone. "Hey Helen, it's Dr. Harrison. How're you doing tonight? Great. Is it very busy there? Mmm hmm. Okay, well, look. My father-in-law's on his way in with a hand laceration. His name's Mike Campbell. Can you put him in a room, and I'll be there in ten minutes?" He nodded. "Thanks very much. Bye"

Gabe turned to her. "I'm going to run in and take a look. If it's a simple cut, I'll sew him up myself. If it's complicated, I'll call in a plastic surgeon buddy of mine to take care of him."

Jenny frowned. "What about your bike ride?"

Gabe shrugged it off. "Steve will understand. We'll go tomorrow."

"Why would you do that?"

Gabe smiled. "Perk of having a doctor in the family."

"Oh, yeah? What perks do you get from my dad?"

Gabe wrapped his arms around her. "He gave me you. I can't think of a better perk than that."

Chapter 11

Spring and summer flew by in a flurry of work, finishing touches on the house, and settling into married life, and before she knew it, Jenny and Gabe celebrated their one-year anniversary. They'd fallen into a comfortable pattern.

Jenny was glad Gabe continued to get up early to whip around the Pointes with Steve. It was a healthy stress buster that kept her guy in great shape. Gabe came up with the idea of having residents do a rotation at the Donnatelli clinic for credit, so getting that program off the ground kept him extra busy. *Make a great suggestion and you acquire a job. Duly noted.*

Jenny grew accustomed to having Alex with them every other week. Her summer job as lifeguard, college applications, and field hockey practices kept Alex as busy as Jenny and Gabe. Ted happily spent the summer in Ann Arbor working for a professor in the computer science lab.

Jenny settled in nicely at the paper, honing her interviewing skills and budgeting her time so that deadlines no longer filled her with dread. They spent their leisure time playing tennis—often round robin with Steve—enjoying the occasional movie and dinner out, chatting around their new fire pit over a glass of wine, or fiercely competing during game night. Once in a while Jenny joined the men on the golf course, but she didn't play often enough to master the game. She was a beast off the tee, but her short game sucked.

Jenny leaned over her vanity to get closer to the bathroom mirror. She swiped red paint around her cheeks, then freshened the triangle painted on her nose before trading the red for the black makeup pen. She drew a curvy line from the corner of her mouth to her rosy cheeks; first one side, then the other to complete an exaggerated smile. She pulled back to get a broader perspective. Consulting the picture taped to the glass, she drew extravagant bottom eyelashes.

Ritz barked as the doorbell rang and children chorused, "Trick or treat." Gabe answered the door, but she only detected murmuring voices.

Twisting her long hair into a tight bun, Jenny stuffed it under her red yarn wig. She stood and backed up to inspect her costume. Perfect. From the top of her white cap, down the blue dress covered with the classic white smock, to her red and white stripped tights and black Mary Jane shoes, there was no mistaking who she was. Jenny neatened up the bathroom and skipped downstairs.

Jenny loved Halloween. It celebrated the end of her favorite season, in a fun, spooky way. She loved the warm fall colors, the musky scent of dying leaves and smoky fires, and the fun decorations adorning the houses. Some Grosse Pointers got incredibly elaborate and creative. The changing season brought out a nesting instinct in Jenny, and invariably she found herself cleaning house in anticipation of the cold weather driving everybody inside.

Dressed all in black, with cape and mask, Gabe made an imposing figure. The lightsaber and breathing device were his favorite part of the costume. Jenny shook her head. Boys never really grew up. Gabe pulled off the mask and tucked it under his arm.

"Your turn to man the door. Sorry babe, I've gotta run into the ER and check on a patient." He picked up his phone and tucked his wallet in his back pocket.

"Like that?" Jenny nodded at his costume.

"Of course not. I'll leave my lightsaber in the car."

"What about the mask?"

"Did Batman go to work without his mask?"

Jenny bit back a smile and shook her head.

"Spider-Man? Superman? Captain America? Green Hornet? The Lone Ranger—"

"Actually, I'm pretty sure Superman didn't wear a mask."

Gabe scowled. "Okay, the others then."

"They fought criminals. They needed to hide their identities."

"Whatever. I fight disease, repair bullet holes and knife wounds. I save lives, too." Mask and lightsaber in hand, Gabe headed for the garage. "If I have to work on Halloween, what they see is what they get."

Jenny laughed. "All right, Darth Vader."

Jenny stood at the window and watched the taillights disappear down the drive. Having a long driveway tended to discourage trick-or-treaters, since it simply wasn't as efficient as hitting the streets with houses closer together, so Jenny made sure to reward those hearty enough to make the trek with their choice of an assortment of huge candy bars.

So far they'd only had a half-dozen kids come by. Jenny went into the kitchen, opened the fridge doors, and surveyed the contents. *What does Raggedy Ann want for dinner?* The doorbell rang.

"Trick or Treat," high-pitched voices chorused. Ritz barked and ran to the door.

Jenny pulled the door open, then smiled brightly at the three older kids. Somehow Michael had conned Alex and her friend Suzy into bringing him over. "Hi. Come on in."

Michael, dressed as a pirate, bent to pet Ritz and admire her lion costume. "Where'd you get the mane, Jen?"

"She looks like a real lion," Alex said as she followed Michael inside. "I can't believe she leaves that on. Sadie wouldn't."

"Great costume, Maleficent," Jenny said to Alex. Then her smile faded as she took in Suzy's costume. "Oh. My. God. I don't even know what to say."

Jenny stared at Suzy's stomach with mixed feelings of fascination and horror. Suzy wore a tight T-shirt that accented her six-month baby bump. Bloody splotches surrounded baby arms reaching out of her stomach, and she'd attached a miniature pumpkin candy basket to one little hand.

She'd known Alex's best friend was pregnant, but she couldn't decide if the brazen display was brave or stupid. Part of her thought it was hilarious, the other half was horrified.

I am so glad Gabe's not here! He'd be apoplectic.

On an older woman it'd be irreverent, and ghoulish, and funny, but on a pregnant teenager, in conservative Grosse Pointe...it was... Oh my God. Jenny couldn't take her eyes off Suzy's stomach.

"Have your parents...seen...uh, you?" Wide eyed, she tore her gaze from the ghoulish sight to look at Suzy.

"It was her mom's idea," Alex said.

Jenny's jaw dropped open. She knew Suzy's parents had been supportive about her decision to keep the baby, but this...this went beyond support. "Nooo. You're kidding."

"Nope." Suzy wagged her head back and forth.

"Uh... How many houses have you gone to dressed like that?"

Michael poked her. "You are *so* gullible."

"What?" Jenny frowned. "Why?" she looked from one kid to the other.

The girls burst out laughing.

"You should see your face," Suzy giggled.

"It's priceless," Alex grinned.

"*Very* funny. Okay, you got me."

"My parents almost had a heart atta—"

"Your mom thought it was kind of funny," Alex corrected.

"Yeah," Suzy smiled. "But Dad threatened to lock me in my room until I promised to wear this mask," she held up a cat mask, "and come straight home after we came here."

And Jen thought she'd been a difficult teen. Oh, man. She felt sorry for Suzy's parents. She winced. "Did my parents see you when you picked up Michael?"

Alex rolled her eyes. "I wouldn't do that to Grams and Pops." She frowned and looked around. "Where's Dad?"

"But your dad's fair game."

"Well, *yeah*."

Michael came out of the kitchen. "He's not in there."

"He's at work."

"Here." Alex handed Jenny her phone and pulled Michael and Suzy close. "Take our picture."

Jenny raised the iPhone, then lowered it. "No. I'm not going to be an accomplice in tormenting your father—at least not that way."

"*Fine.* I won't send it to him. Just take the picture."

Jenny narrowed her eyes at Alex.

Alex harrumphed and made a face. "I promise."

"Fine." Jenny raised the phone and zoomed in, taking a close-up of the kids from the waist up.

"One more, please," Alex said. Her phone started beeping. "Hurry. I'm running out of battery."

This time Jenny lined it up to the left so Suzy was cut out. She handed back the phone and simultaneously thrust the candy bowl at them to distract Alex from checking the pictures.

The doorbell rang, and Jenny hurried off to hand out more candy to a Tin man, a clown, a witch, and a baby in a stroller dressed up as a pumpkin. Suzy lowered the kitty mask over her face, and the three kids followed the crowd out.

"Where to next?" Jenny asked.

"Back to Suz's house so she can change, then I told Grams and Pops we'd follow Michael and his friends around for an hour or so."

That was nice of Alex to bother with Michael and help her parents out that way. "That's nice of you."

Alex shrugged. "I don't mind."

"What cut of their candy are they giving you?"

"Whatever do you mean?" Alex opened her eyes wide, innocent.

"Been there, done that, Maleficent," she said dryly.

"Two pieces each—her pick," Michael said as they got in Alex's car.

Jenny laughed and waved them off, as another group of kids from the left rushed across their lawn. Jenny duly admired the black cat, witch, and Sponge Bob costumes and held out the candy basket as their parents walked up to the door. The woman had a chunky baby dressed as a pumpkin in one of those slings across her chest. Looked heavy.

"Hi. I'm Dan and this is Wendy. Are your parents home?"

Parents? Jenny frowned. *They think I'm the kid.* Natural enough assumption given her costume. Jenny smiled and held out her hand. "Nice to meet you, I'm Jenny."

They shook her hand. "And the ghost and Sponge Bob are our kids, Penny and Caleb. We're your neighbors three doors down," Wendy said as she rocked side to side. "I've been meaning to stop by before now to meet your parents, but this one," she patted the drooling baby's head, "kept me busier that you'd believe—not that he's a bad baby, but—"

"We were excited to hear the new neighbors had a teenage daughter. Do you babysit much?" her husband interrupted.

"Not at all actually, but my *step-daughter*, Alex, does. You just missed her, but I can give you her number if you'd like."

Wendy frowned. "Step—Oh—Gosh, I'm sorry. I... You just look so young, I assumed..."

"It's okay." Jenny smiled. She swept her hand up and down in front of her. "I *am* dressed as a doll."

"Hey, you kids wait for us," Bob called out as the children ran across the lawn toward Steve's house. "Well, welcome to the neighborhood, we'd better catch up with them."

His wife backed up and with a faint wave hurried after her family.

"Come, Ritz." Jenny returned to the house and shut the door. "Somehow I doubt we're going to be bosom buddies with them." Apparently they were in dire need of a babysitter and had little interest in being neighborly.

Her phone rang. Jenny looked at the number. *Judith.*

"Jenny, it's Judith."

I know. "What's up?"

"Is Alex there? She's not answering her phone."

"Her battery probably died, it was beeping when she was here." She put the candy on the entry table and crossed her arms. "Is there something I can help you with?"

Judith sighed loudly. "How long ago was that? The kids are waiting for her to take them trick-or-treating."

Jenny frowned. It wasn't like Alex to blow off a commitment. Judith wasn't going to like finding out that Alex was with Michael. "Does *she* know that?"

"Not yet. Dave took them out, but they want to go longer and he's not feeling well."

And you told them Alex would do it. And what about you? You could take your own kids trick-or-treating like a normal mom.

"She left about ten minutes ago. They should be at Suzy's house soon."

"Fine. I'll try there."

"Judith, wait. While I have you on the phone I wanted to ask you something. Would it be okay if the kids came over here during the day on Thanksgiving? I know it's your turn to have them for Thanksgiving, but this will be the first holiday dinner we've hosted in our new house and we were hoping the kids could join us. They'd be back by four, in time for your dinner."

"We have the kids for Thanksgiving this year. Gabe had them last year."

"I know, but the house wasn't done, and we went to my parents. This year we're having it here, and we wanted the family together. I thought, maybe, the kids could celebrate at both houses—that's why we moved it up to noon."

"So the kids will eat turkey, stuffing, and pumpkin pie and get back to our house stuffed," Judith said flatly.

"No! I'll remind them to just snack. They'll be plenty hungry when they get to your house."

"No."

"We wanted the whole family together for our first holiday in our new house."

"Touching, but no."

Jenny struggled to hold onto her temper. *Come on; bend a little.* "I...will you think about it?"

"Nothing to think about. We've got the kids Thanksgiving and Christmas Eve, and Gabe gets them Christmas and New Year's. That's the schedule."

God forbid they amend the schedule. "Maybe you could have them for New Years instead?"

"No." *Click.*

Jenny scowled. "Goodbye to you, too." *Bitch.*

Jenny went into the kitchen and poured herself a glass of wine. The doorbell rang. She took a big gulp as she scooped up the candy and rushed to the door.

"Trick or treat." Sophie, dressed as a miniature Elsa, stood in front of her brother, a vampire.

"Hel-lo. Well, Ms. Elsa, you're looking lovely tonight." She pointed at her white gloves. "Glad to see you've got those on so we don't have any accidents." Jenny bent down and wrinkled her nose as if confiding a secret. "Red wine is best served at room temperature, not frozen."

Sophie giggled.

Jenny turned to Josh. "And you, sir, look very dashing and frightening with those fangs, I might add. I hope you've already fed tonight."

Josh nodded as a deep voice out of the dark said, "Well, well, well. I always suspected Raggedy Ann was a lush."

Jenny peered past the bright porch light into the darkness. "Funny, Grant."

"Ohhh," Sophie squealed. "Lion."

Jenny turned to the kids and backed up. "Come on in."

Sophie and Josh ran to the dog and knelt before her, petting her. Ritz bore the attention with her usual good nature and got in a few friendly licks of her own. Steve and Annie stood in her entry, looking around.

Steve had a huge burger in one hand and bag of fries in the other. He swallowed and said, "Where's Darth Vader?"

"Work." She held up her glass. "Wine?"

Steve looked at Annie in question.

"We can't." Annie said. "It's getting late, and they need a bath."

"Have you had dinner?" Steve asked.

Jenny shook her head.

Steve handed his fries to Annie to hold, then split his burger and passed half to Jenny. She considered refusing the food, but it smelled heavenly and Steve knew she loved cheeseburgers.

He pushed it at her. "Take it. You get cranky when you don't eat."

"Thank you." Jenny took a big bite of the burger, closed her eyes and savored the sinful taste of grilled beef and cheese, then quickly swallowed. "What time's the game Sunday?"

"Do we have to watch football *every* Sunday?" Annie pouted. She glanced at the kids. "Only one piece each, you guys."

Steve crammed several fries in his mouth, quickly chewed and swallowed, nodding. "We always get together on game day. It's tradition."

Steve had invited Gabe and her to join his firm's Fantasy Football league, and Jenny was crushing everybody else. It was mostly beginner's luck, but being the only woman made being in the top of the bracket extra sweet. Every Sunday, a bunch of the guys gathered at Buffalo Wild Wings to watch the game.

"I understand if you skip it. After all, it must be humiliating the way my boys are stompin' all over your teams," Jenny said as she polished off the burger. Talking smack was one of the best parts of the league, though the tidy pots for first, second and third places winner were enticing, too.

"Only because you have Peyton Manning."

"And Demaryius Thomas, and Calvin Johnson, and LeSean McCoy—"

Steve snorted

"Don't worry, I'm sure Drew Brees and Andre Johnson will start coming through for you any week now." She smirked. Sipping her wine, she washed down the last mouthful.

"It's hard to get a babysitter on a Sunday, and football is so violent," Annie whined. "Why don't we see a movie instead? There's this new French film that's won all kinds of awards." She frowned and tapped her lip with her manicured index finger. "Now what's it called? It's about a devoted cellist in the Romanian orchestra and how she had to run for her life and goes into hiding when the country was invaded and how she made her way to Canada and became a huge hit there, but then something tragic happens and she's dragged back to Russia—"

"Romania?" Jenny corrected. Jenny raised her brows and cocked her head at Steve, pretty sure he'd rather poke himself in the eye with a hot stick than miss football to watch a foreign film, no matter how many awards it'd won.

"Right. Back to Romania to protect her childhood love–"

The doorbell rang, and Jenny gratefully leapt to answer it rather than listen to Annie's monologue.

"That sounds like something you should see with your sister. I think she'd appreciate it much more than I would," Steve said, as Jenny closed the door on the departing trick-or-treaters.

Annie frowned, "You think?"

"Definitely." He watched Josh and Sophie sort the candy they'd scattered all over the rug. Ritz sat nearby drooling, looking for an opportunity to sneak a piece. "All right guys, put it all back, we've gotta get going."

The kids piled the loot back in their pumpkin buckets under Annie's guidance. Steve looked at Jenny. "Do you guys have plans

December fifth? I've reserved a couple of extra tickets to see *A Christmas Carol.*"

Annie threaded her arm through Steve's. "That's a Friday night. I'm sure they already have plans."

"They might not." Steve looked at Jenny.

"But we were going to take the kids and make a night of it. Remember?"

Steve frowned at her. "We were? It's okay, I haven't bought the tickets yet. I can pick up a few more." His eyes lit. "You know what? I'll see if I can get eight, and then we can bring Alex and Michael, too. It'll be fun."

Annie smiled brightly. "You're so busy. Why don't I take care of that? I'll get the tickets first thing Monday morning."

"You sure? It's no problem."

I bet. And somehow Jenny was sure Annie's luck would run out, and she'd buy the last four tickets. "Uh... I'll have to check with Gabe and the kids first. Why don't you buy yours and then if we can make it, I'll get our tickets."

"We won't sit together then," Steve said.

When they'd seen *Motown: The Musical* a couple of months ago, Annie talked and sang along throughout the whole musical and nearly got them kicked out of the Fisher Theatre. Not sitting together would be a bonus.

"I gotta go potty," Sophie whined and did a little dance at her mom's feet.

"Just a minute, Sugar."

"Now."

"I gotta go, too," Josh said.

Jenny pointed to the restroom. With a hand on each child's back, Annie herded her offspring to the bathroom.

"I'll check with Gabe and the kids and let you know if we can make it." *And don't hold your breath.* Annie didn't want them going any more than Jenny wanted to go. How could Steve be so oblivious?

"It's at the Meadow Brook Theatre," Steve said.

"Got it." She nodded as the trio headed back their way. Sophie's mouth stretched wide in an impressive yawn for such a little thing. Jenny smiled. "Looks like it's bedtime."

They said goodnight and left. Jenny grabbed her jacket, and she and Ritz walked down the driveway to blow out the two jack-o'-lanterns flanking their entrance, then the ones on the front porch. They went inside and turned out the porch light. Hanging up her jacket, she pulled the lion's mane off Ritz and brought her wine into the kitchen as Gabe came through the back door.

"Hey, babe." He moved into the kitchen, put his mask and saber on the counter, then dropped a kiss on her lips.

"What're you doing back so soon? I thought you had to operate."

"They're observing her overnight. If she's not better in the morning, we'll go in." He tugged on her wig. "By the way, did I mention what a doll you are tonight?"

"Ha ha." Jenny pulled the wig off her head and plopped it on the counter. She tugged the hairband from her bun.

Gabe brushed her hands aside, gently unwound her hair, and dug his fingers in. She shivered, and her eyes drifted shut at the tingling feeling his head massage generated. Gabe finger-combed her hair. "What's the matter? Didn't we have any trick-or-treaters?"

"No, that's fine." She leaned into his touch and moved her head around like a cat being stroked. "I'm just annoyed."

"At..."

"Your ex-wife."

"Because..."

She's a bitch? "She's unyielding and mean."

Gabe settled back against the counter, crossed his legs at his ankles, and took the wine glass from her hand. "Be-cause..."

He swirled the wine in the bowl and sniffed it before tasting. Gabe raised his eyebrows and nodded his approval.

"I asked if she might share Alex and Ted with us on Thanksgiving, and she said no."

"It's their turn. We had them last year."

"I *know*, but I explained that it was our first time hosting a holiday dinner in our new house, and that we're having George and my family over, and I promised they'd be back with her by four—in plenty of time for their dinner—and she flat out refused to even consider it." She hesitated, then said, "I even offered to trade her New Year's Day for it, and she said no."

Gabe frowned. "Why would you do that? I don't want to trade New Year's Day. Ted and I watch football together. It's tradition."

"Well, we could make new traditions. Doesn't matter anyway. She said no." Jenny took her glass back, reached for the wine bottle, and poured another half a glass. "This is our first holiday together. I'm making the turkey. I wanted the whole family together."

"I understand, but we have a schedule. It's worked well for over ten years."

"Well, it doesn't work for *me*. All I asked for is a half of a day to make our first Thanksgiving special. I've gone along with everything for a year now. I worked my family around your and Judith's precious schedule, and now I ask for one *tiny* modification, and you guys are totally unyielding." Jenny took a sip of her wine, then frowned. "And, she was totally snotty about it. Like I was this inferior being bugging her. She even hung up on me. It's not fair."

"You're right." Gabe pulled her stiff body into his arms. "It's not fair. You've been very understanding, and I appreciate it." He set her back and sat her on a stool. "Why don't you ask your mom to have Thanksgiving at her house again, and we'll have our first big holiday dinner at Christmas when we have the kids? We can do Christmas brunch and dinner—a twofer."

Jenny frowned. Great. Then Mom would think she couldn't even plan a simple dinner without screwing it up.

"It's all arranged. I can't change things now. I've already bought the turkey." She'd been so excited about cooking her first turkey, she'd bought it as soon as they hit the grocery store.

"You can still cook it and take it to your mom's."

"I bought a new table cloth and Thanksgiving decorations. No, we're having it here. I am not going to let Judith muck up all my family's plans." She paused, then looked hopefully at Gabe. "But, maybe *you* could ask her."

He looked at her out of the corner of his eye and slowly shook his head. "I don't think that's a good idea."

"Please."

He drew in a deep breath.

"Please. She'll listen to you."

"Fine. I'll talk to her, but don't get your hopes up."

Jenny smiled. "I have confidence in you."

"I'm serious. I'll ask, but if she says no, I want you to be okay with it." His serious, steady gray eyes held her gaze. "The kids are growing up and moving on, as it should be. You and me, we're family now. That's part of the reason we got married, right?"

She nodded.

"Don't get me wrong, I want a big family gathering, too, but if Judith sticks to her guns, it'll be fine. We'll still have a good time with your family and Uncle George." Gabe took the wine glass and raised it to his lips.

How about Judith takes George and we get Alex and Ted? Jenny nodded. "Fine. I understand, but I'm betting on your powers of persuasion. After all, you convinced her to let us take the kids out of school to go to Maui."

Gabe quickly swallowed his wine. "For our wedding. That's completely different. And it didn't take anything away from her. Judith works a lot, and that cuts into family time. These holidays mean a lot to her."

Don't stand up for her. Jenny frowned. "It means a lot to me, too."

"I'm just warning you. She's not going to change her mind. I don't want you to be disappointed." He set the wineglass on the counter.

"It sounds like you're on her side."

"Of course not." Gabe stood, came up behind Jenny, and wrapped his arms around her. "I just understand her." He rocked Jenny from side to side and kissed that sensitive spot behind her ear. Jenny shivered. His warm, wine-sweetened breath tickled her ear. Gabe brushed her hair aside and gathered it in one hand to give him unobstructed access to her neck.

"I am *always*." He kissed the sensitive skin below her ear. "On." Kissed a little lower. "Your side."

Gabe ran his lips down the side of her neck. His coarse hair brushed her cheek as Gabe bent over her shoulder. Jenny drew in a deep breath, and her eyes drifted shut as she savored the feeling of his hot mouth at the top of her collarbone.

"And your back." Gabe shifted to the other side and with great care rearranged her hair so he could lavish equal attention to the other side of her neck. "And your front—that's my favorite place."

Jenny kept her eyes closed and purred. Hmm. What had they been talking about? She struggled to focus her clouding mind as Gabe's hands dove beneath her apron. Thanksgiving. The kids. Judith. Suddenly her eyes popped open. Eureka! A way to outwit the almighty Judith. "I could ask the kids."

Gabe stiffened and the questing hands on her breasts stilled. "What do you mean?" His voice was tense.

"I could ask Ted and Alex and let them decide. After all, they're both over eighteen. I bet your custody agreement isn't even legally binding anymore. I could invite them and let them decide." Why hadn't she thought of that before? It was brilliant.

"That's not a good idea." Gabe withdrew his hands and backed up.

"Why not?"

"Don't put them in the middle of this. Don't make Ted and Alex choose." Though his words were gentle, his tone was hard and full of warning. Gabe clenched his jaw and held her gaze with steely narrowed eyes. Cold distance replaced the passion of minutes before.

Jenny recognized the protective reaction; she'd seen that expression on her mother's face often enough. It hadn't occurred to her that letting Ted and Alex choose would put them in the middle, but Gabe was right. It could be awkward for them.

"I wouldn't. I was just thinking out loud."

"Good."

While Jenny understood Gabe's reaction, she couldn't help getting a little defensive that he thought he needed to warn her off. He felt he had to protect his kids from her. She'd *never* do anything to hurt Alex and Ted. He should know that. Didn't he trust her?

Like you have total trust in him? her little voice whispered.

"Never mind. Leave it the way it is," Jenny conceded.

Chapter 12

Thanksgiving and the Christmas holidays taught Jenny several valuable lessons—reminders, really, about boundaries and respect. Gabe had gently, yet clearly reminded Jenny of the boundaries regarding his children and past family.

He had a decades-long established relationship with his ex-wife and an unbreakable bond with his children that Jenny had to respect and tread lightly around. They all were comfortable with the status quo, and Jenny had to introduce change slowly to fit into their world. She'd instinctively known this from the beginning and naively dismissed it, thinking that her relationship with Gabe was all that really mattered.

But comfort and confidence in their marriage had Jenny naturally expanding her reach to include more people in their sphere, and therein lay the conflict and challenge. Especially when her husband reminded her of those boundaries.

Jenny's feelings had been hurt until her conscience reminded her that she had similar intangible borders she fiercely guarded, it was just that Gabe had no idea they even existed.

Like a lie by omission, Jenny protected her family, and she fully intended to continue doing so—marriage would not change that. With that understanding in mind, Jenny regrouped and realigned her holiday expectations, determined to be satisfied and blissfully happy with whomever they had to share them with. As long as she had Gabe by her side, she had everything.

She had everything, but she was happy to use her Christmas gift from Gabe for a spa visit. Not only would she have a massage, but she'd treated herself to a makeup lesson. She needed help to look more sophisticated. Jenny wasn't really a spa girl, but on Alex's recommendation, Gabe had gotten it for her for Christmas, and Jenny intended to make full use of it.

After her lesson and a hundred dollars in Estee Lauder products, Jenny felt confident that there would be no more repeats of the Halloween embarrassment.

They settled into the New Year, and as spring moved toward summer, Gabe and Jenny decided to take up a new activity together, so they bought a speedboat and took water skiing lessons. Didn't take long to find neither of them had much talent at it. Steve did. Surprise. He had been a professional athlete after all. The kids, on the other hand, couldn't get enough of it, and they especially enjoyed tubing.

Secretly, Jenny enjoyed the power of being able to lure her stepchildren and brother over. She wasn't making them choose her and Gabe's house over Judith's, so she couldn't be accused of creating conflict. Once Jenny stumbled onto this side benefit of living on the lake, she convinced Gabe to buy a couple of jet skis for her birthday.

As Memorial Day weekend approached, Jenny waved Gabe and Steve off on their Saturday marathon ride before running off to the grocery store. She selected some fresh French bread, lemons, and asparagus, Alex's favorite vegetable, to go with the salmon. Passing the bakery, she grabbed a lemon meringue pie, another Harrison favorite, before hurrying to the checkout counter. At home, she found Alex's little green Volkswagen Golf blocking the garage. She was early.

Jenny grabbed the paper bags and walked around back to the patio looking for Alex. They should probably give Gabe's kids keys to the house, or maybe give them their own code to the garage door. She still had a key to her parents' house. Then again, though Jenny was fond of Alex and Ted, she wasn't sure she wanted them having free access to her home. At least not yet.

"You're early. I had to run to the store to get a few things."

Alex looked up from the paper she was writing on. "I was leaving Dad a note. Is he with you?"

"No, he's out biking. Is something wrong?" She inclined her head toward the kitchen. "Come on in. I've got to get this stuff in the fridge."

Alex took one of the paper bags and followed Jenny into the house. "I really need to talk to my dad. A bunch of us are going camping up north after graduation and Mom doesn't want me to go—she hasn't said no yet, but she's going to."

They deposited the bags on the counter, and began unpacking. "Why wouldn't she let you go? You're eighteen, you're a responsible kid, you're about to start college and could go away every weekend and your mom wouldn't even know."

Alex lifted her hips to sit on the countertop, fully engrossed in her cause now. "*That's* what I told her. But she said I'm not at college yet, and while I'm living under her roof—yada, yada, yada."

Jenny remembered the rest of the hackneyed speech, wondering if it came from some parenting manual mothers read to pass the time while in labor. "So what's her objection?"

"Greg."

"Boyfriend?"

"We're not exclusive—yet."

Ahh. Jenny's motions slowed as she turned away to put the peanut butter in a cupboard. Suddenly it made more sense. "And Mom doesn't approve?"

"No, she likes Greg."

"Then what's the problem?"

Alex flashed Jenny an incredulous, how-dumb-can-you-be look. "Sex. She's afraid we'll spend the whole weekend having wild sex."

Valid concern. This is where you shut your mouth and mind your own business, Jenny. "Will you?"

Alex rolled her eyes. "There's gonna be a whole bunch of us there."

Uh huh. "Well, I don't know. You could all pair off in your own little tents, for all I know."

Alex's eyebrows rose and she smirked, but not before Jenny glimpsed a flash of interest. *Great Jen, like she doesn't have enough ideas of her own without you giving her more.*

"Yeah, right."

Warning bells chimed loudly in Jenny's head. *Boundaries! You should not be the one having this conversation with her.*

In way over her head, Jenny wasn't prepared to counsel Gabe's daughter on sex, but this was the right time and opportunity. "Have you talked to your mom, or dad, about boyfriends...or sex?"

Alex's eyes widened an instant before the familiar derisive grin shaped her face. "Of course. Every night before bed, my mom and I chat about how hot my boyfriend is and how many different ways we did it that day in the gym after school."

Okay, she'd deserved the sarcastic comeback. Teenagers didn't let their parents in on anything important. A wealth of unwelcome adolescent memories flooded her. Jenny desperately sought a way to end the conversation without turning the teen against her. Alex should talk to her mother.

The way you talked to your mom, her inner voice prodded.

"Maybe you should wait and talk to your dad. He'll be home in an hour."

"About sex? You're kidding, right?" Alex gave her a get-real look. "Dad does *not* want to know. Trust me."

"What about Ted?"

"My *brother*?"

Yeah, dumb suggestion. Gabe was out. Judith was the enemy. That left...shoot—her. Maybe she could pull it off. Maybe Jenny could actually do some good and keep Alex from making an irreversible mistake, without having to bare her soul.

"So..." Jenny said. "Not that it's any of my business, but...have you done it with Greg yet?"

"Not yet," Alex declared airily.

"But he wants to."

Alex rolled her eyes. "What guy doesn't?"

"Have you ever done it?"

"You think I'm an eighteen-year-old virgin?" Her chin shot up.

Now I do, but I'd like to hear you say it. "I don't know. Are you?"

Alex crossed her arms and raised her eyebrows. "Did you have sex with Dad before you married?"

How could she answer that? If she told Alex it was none of her business, she risked alienating her, and if she told her the truth, risked setting a bad example for Gabe's daughter. "I was twenty-six—almost twenty-seven, when I married your dad."

"You're only ten years older than me."

Ten critical years. But she knew Alex wouldn't agree. "I had a college degree and a job. My parents weren't supporting me, and I could've coped with an unplanned pregnancy if I'd had to." She arched an eyebrow. "Can you?"

"Well, yeah," she drawled. "Besides, abortion's always an option."

A lot of teens saw that as an easy out—until they truly had to consider it. She glanced out the window at the driveway. Where was Gabe when she needed him? A parent had to be good at this stuff by the time their kid got to these discussions. Heck she hadn't even had the warm-up talk of where babies come from. But Gabe wasn't here and Alex wanted to talk now.

"Abortion's a major decision," Jenny began tentatively. She blew out a deep breath. "When I was your age, I..."

Alex's eyes widened, and she leaned forward, resting her arms on the counter. "You what?"

"I had to write a paper about abortion. It's actually killing a tiny, innocent baby. Could you really do that?"

"Girls do it all the time. Julie did."

"That doesn't make it right. Could you?"

"Having a baby now ruins your life. Suzy just had her baby, and they won't let her walk at graduation with the rest of us. She has to go to summer school to get her diploma, and her boyfriend dumped her." Alex sank back. "At first, her parents were *really* mad. Now that the baby's here, they're cool. But Suz can't go away to school. She has to go to Wayne State so her mom can babysit. She's really tied down. I'd have an abortion before letting a baby ruin my life."

Jenny's stomach churned at her answer. "It doesn't have to come to that—if you're smart. I can't tell you when you're ready to have sex—nobody can. You have to be ready mentally as well as physically. But I can tell you to be smart and use some kind of birth control. Get on the pill or use condoms—or both. Do some research, use something, and you won't have to worry about an unplanned pregnancy."

Alex stared at the floor while she digested the advice. "My parents are both doctors. They'd find out."

"Then buy condoms." Jenny raised her eyebrow, cautioning, "I'm *not* telling you to have sex. But. If you're going to, at least make sure you're protected. Especially with all the sexually transmitted diseases, you'd be a fool if you didn't make a guy use a condom. Always." Uncomfortable preaching, Jenny quickly put the rest of the groceries away, letting her words sink in.

"So. Do you think Dad will let me go?"

Not a chance. "I don't know. But if you promise to call if there's trouble and give him a list of the other kids going and their folk's phone numbers, he might."

"Would you talk to—"

"Nope."

"Plea—"

"Nope." No *way* she was getting in the middle of that. Nothing could convince her to champion Alex against her parents. Not for a weekend camping trip.

Alex's worried frown broke into a huge smile. She jumped off the counter and gave Jenny a quick hug before backing away. "For a step-mom, you're okay"

Jenny smiled. "You're a lot better than spit up and smelly diapers, too."

"See ya. I've got to talk to Suz and get to work on that list."

"What about dinner?"

"What time?"

"Six-thirty."

"I'll be back." Alex headed for the side door.

"Hey, do you want to play Euchre tonight? I can see if Steve's available to be our fourth."

"Sure." Alex hesitated in the doorway. "Thanks, Jenny."

"You're welcome." *Well*, she smiled, feeling pretty proud of herself. *That went fairly well. Maybe this step parenting stuff isn't so hard after all.*

∾ ∾ ∾

"What the hell did you think you were doing?" Judith demanded.

Gabe's ex-wife stormed their kitchen, slamming the door hard enough to rattle the keys on the key rack. Tall and beanpole thin, Judith's small brown eyes narrowed angrily above thin, pursed lips and a straight, pointy nose. Even the highlighted brown curls cropped close to her head coiled rigid in indignation.

Although she faced both Gabe and Jenny, her glare locked on Jenny, making her long to inch behind Gabe for protection.

"What's the problem, Judith?" Gabe swiped the knife across his bread and laid one slice atop the ham and cheese. He finished making his sandwich as if his ex-wife's explosion was nothing unusual.

"The problem is your child bride," she jabbed a stiff index finger at Jenny.

Gabe rested his hands on the counter and gave Judith his full attention. "Calm down and tell us what happened."

"I found these in Alex's bag." She threw a handful of silver square disks onto the granite countertop.

Staring at the scattered condoms, Jenny's heart dropped to her stomach.

"Alex said that *your* wife told her to use them."

"That's ridiculous. Jenny'd never tell Alex to use condoms."

"Not exactly." Jenny tore her gaze away from the incriminating foil packets and turned to Gabe. "Last week, Alex wanted to ask you about that camping trip, and we got to talking. She told me about Suzy having her baby, and how Alex thought she was stupid to let a baby ruin her life instead of aborting it." She shrugged at Gabe. "I didn't know what to do."

"You *should* have sent her home to talk to her mother," Judith said.

Jenny stiffened and frowned. Though not particularly prepared for that talk, she'd done okay. Judith had no right barging into her home, hurling accusations, and acting like she'd emotionally scarred Alex.

"She didn't *want* to talk to her mother. She thought her *mother* wouldn't listen." Jenny looked at Gabe. "I couldn't let her think abortion was an acceptable way to deal with an unplanned pregnancy, so I told her that if she was smart, she'd avoid the problem altogether by using birth control."

"So you gave my daughter a green light to have sex," Judith said, making it seem like Jenny had bought them a hotel room, undressed them, and put them in bed together with a how-to sex manual.

"Like they need my blessing." She crossed her arms and raised her eyebrows. "How do you know she's not already sexually active?"

"I know," Judith narrowed her eyes.

"You hope. You don't know." Jenny rested her hip against the counter, finally feeling like she had the upper hand. In fact, she almost enjoyed taunting Judith. The almighty Judith was floundering. She *didn't* know if her kid was sexually active, and it was killing her.

Must be hard to having to face you're not perfect.

"I'm her mother; I know."

"She's a teenager. You don't know anything. Her best friend would know, but not you." Tired of sparing with Judith, she turned to Gabe. "Anyway, we talked about the consequences of sex and how to avoid the pitfalls."

"You shouldn't have. You're not her mother," Judith said.

Again. Another mother telling her she'd messed up. Another mother, jealous of Jenny's relationship with her child. Only this time, Jenny felt completely justified in defending herself.

"*You* weren't there. And she asked *me*—not you."

"You've been a part-time parent for all of what? A year and a half? And suddenly you know it all?"

Gabe moved between the women, facing his ex-wife. "Look, Judith. Maybe that isn't exactly the tack we would have taken, but Jenny handled it fine. I don't see that any damage was done."

Wasn't the tack they would have taken? Was Gabe actually siding with his ex?

"You don't?" Judith sputtered. "Your little wife stuck her nose in where it didn't belong and gave our daughter permission to have sex." She turned to Jenny. "Did you explain the different positions? Encourage her to try oral sex? She wouldn't get pregnant giving a blow job, either."

Jenny's eyes widened at Judith's crudity.

"That's enough," Gabe snapped. "Look, we knew this was coming. Teenagers are preoccupied by sex. Jenny did the right thing. Instead of finding condoms you could've found a home pregnancy test. Would you rather that? I wouldn't."

Judith glared, resentment pinching her nostrils. "She *should* have sent her to me. Or you. You're her father."

"She didn't want to talk to us." He put a supportive hand on Jenny's shoulder. "I realize your feelings are hurt, but Jenny's my wife. She's a part of this family now, and you'd better accept it and work with her, like I accepted Dave," Gabe reminded.

Judith's jaw remained rigid, but her malicious tongue quieted. The two maintained eye contact in a silent battle of wills. The standoff lasted one long minute before Judith looked away, muttering between tight lips, "Next time, send her to me."

Jenny would have liked to leave it at that, but heartened by Gabe's support, she wasn't willing to lose the ground she'd gained with her stepdaughter. "I can't promise that. Mothers and daughters often disagree. I'm beginning to think it's the nature of things."

"Don't judge us all by your own troubled relationship with your mother."

Jenny ignored the stab of pain at the truth. "You didn't argue with your mom as a teenager?"

Judith raised her eyebrows. "No."

Liar. All girls clash with their moms at some point. She paused, searching for a compromise. "As long as you don't tell Alex, I'll let you in on all pertinent conversations."

Judith crossed her arms over her chest. "Conversations, *you* deem pertinent."

Well, duh. Jenny tried to marshal some sympathy for the older woman. "Look, you'll just have to trust me. I would never do anything to hurt Alex or Ted."

She turned to Gabe. "What about this camping trip?"

Gabe let out a deep breath. "I think we have to let her go—with strict guidelines, of course. Why don't you call a few of the parents and check the stories out? That might make you feel better."

"I don't like it."

"I don't either. But she's eighteen. She's a good kid. We've got to trust her."

Judith nodded. "Okay. I'm going to call Greg's parents first. They should know about the condoms."

"You can't do that," Jenny jumped in. "It'll make Alex look like a slut seducing their little boy." *Geeze.* Did Judith have an ounce of heart or common sense?

"They should know."

"Before they leave, we'll talk to Greg and Alex," Gabe said. "Greg might feel differently about the whole thing if he knows we know. We'll tell them that we think they're not ready—"

"Then talk about the consequences," Judith interrupted. "Abortion is *not* an option."

"We'll talk about the consequences and leave the decision-making up to them," Gabe finished calmly.

"I don't like it," Judith scowled.

"Me either, but we don't have a lot of good choices."

"It'll have to do." She sighed, then looked at Gabe. "What time do you want us here to help set up for Alex's party?"

Their hosting Alex's graduation party had to be upsetting to Judith, though she'd never said so. When Alex had asked them if she could have her graduation party at their house so she and her friends could water ski and play in the lake, Jenny'd silently cheered.

Gabe frowned at Jenny. "Don't we have something going that morning... Michael's piano recital?"

She shook her head. "That's Sunday. Tennis with Steve. He reserved a court for eight-thirty, but we should be home by ten." She turned to Judith. "Is eleven good for you?"

"Fine. We'll bring the jello, potato salad, and chips. Call if you need anything else."

Yes, ma'am. Jenny resisted the quip and the urge to salute.

"Judith? Try not to worry so much," Jenny offered, then smothered a smile at Judith's tight lips and brief nod.

Judith was dying to tell her to drop dead, but choked back the bitter retort in a supreme effort to get along. Alex's choice had made Judith a guest in Jenny's house so she had to be polite to her.

Jenny bit her bottom lip to cover a triumphant grin.

Chapter 13

The day Alex graduated couldn't have been more beautiful, and the families had been polite when they'd gone out for a celebratory lunch before Alex headed off for the massive round of her friends' graduation parties. While Alex was party hopping, Jenny double-checked her lists. Everything was set.

Jenny was determined to make this party perfect for Alex. This was the first big event she and Gabe had hosted since marrying, and it was her chance to impress both families and friends. It was the perfect opportunity to prove she wasn't a gold digger and could do something nice for Gabe and his daughter. Jenny might not have been able to fit into the family holidays like she'd wanted, but this graduation was all hers. For once, Judith and Mom would be *her* guests, outsiders being invited into Jenny and Gabe's world.

Alex had given her the guest list and suggested menu but was worried her mom would be upset she was breaking with tradition in wanting an assortment of ice cream bars for dessert instead of the big sheet cake. Jenny reassured her that they'd have a spectacular dessert table even Judith couldn't fault.

The morning of the party, on their way back from tennis, she and Gabe picked up a carload of balloons she'd ordered. Jenny lined the driveway with blue, gold, and blue devil mascot balloons. She'd continued the blue/gold color scheme with all the tablecloths and paper plates. Ted looked up from unloading the popcorn machine she rented. "Where do you want this?"

"Patio off to the side near the porch, please. The popcorn, salt, and oil's on the kitchen counter. Thanks." She went in the house, calling out, "Gabe?"

He lifted her wrinkled list. "Eleven o'clock, start the grill and watch out for the pizza guy."

"Do you have the—"

He flapped the envelope of cash she'd clipped to his list back and forth. "Got it."

"Great. Hey, wait." She rushed to the refrigerator and pulled out a veggie platter and platter of fruit kabobs. "Will you put these on the big table on your way out?"

Gabe bent and dropped a quick kiss to her lips, then tucked the envelope in his back pocket and took the trays from her. "Sure."

The buzzer went off, and Jenny grabbed hot pads, and pulled trays of wrapped wieners from the oven. She scooped them on a big dish as Ted came in the sliding door. "Popcorn's poppin'. Where are the bags for them?" He looked over her shoulder. "Mmm, I love those things." He reached out and snatched one from the top.

"Careful. They're hot." Jenny tossed the spatula in the sink. "Bags are on the desk. You can leave them next to the machine." She handed him the dish. "Put this on the table next to the mustard and catsup, please. Oh, and did you plug in the freezer next to the dessert table?"

"Yes, ma'am. First thing this morning like you asked."

"Thank you," she said in a singsong voice.

Jenny went to the refrigerator and pulled out her surprise for Alex, plates of graduation caps Jenny'd made with Reese's cups topped with chocolate squares complete with Sour S'ghetti tassels. Jenny carried them outside, past the dinner table and freezer holding all the ice-cream bars to the dessert table.

She placed the plates on the tiered display in the center of a half a dozen tall glass candleholders full of Skittles, Reese's Pieces, Starbursts, Lemon Drops, mini Milky Ways, Snickers, and

Butterfingers. Off to the side sat a tiny six-inch token graduation cake. Jenny smiled. Perfect.

Alex, Judith and her family arrived right before the guests began to trickle in. Alex's dropped jaw, bugged eyes, delighted squeal, and little jig when she saw the decorations and food spread was the exact reaction Jenny hoped for. She let Gabe serve the adults drinks in the kitchen and give a tour of the house, as she went off to make sure there were cups out and plenty of ice for the sodas.

Shortly, the kids poured in and the music cranked louder. Jenny picked up her camera and moved around the patio and yard capturing lots of candid shots of Alex and her friends. Her camera turned uphill toward her husband at the grill.

Beer in hand, Gabe flipped some burgers while talking to his cousin. Dressed in navy shorts, untucked pink polo shirt, and sandals, he looked relaxed and happy. Jenny framed the shot and clicked.

She threaded her way through clusters of teens, picking up abandoned plates and napkins and tossing them in the garbage can. She pulled the garbage can a little closer to where the kids might see it and use it. She climbed the steps from the yard to the patio and checked the buffet table.

Enough food for the stragglers. Her eyes narrowed in thought. *Maybe a little more pizza.* She lifted the cooler lid. *More soda too.*

Jenny took refuge in the kitchen, happy to escape the swimsuit-clad teenagers swarming her patio and yard. She must be getting old 'cause the music wore on her. She was partial to country, pop, and soft rock, not the rap pounding out of the speakers pulsing the patio.

Would it be totally uncool to ask Alex to change the music to something with identifiable lyrics? Probably. She doubted that Alex liked the music either, but a group of boys had taken control of her iPod a while ago. Since it was Alex's graduation, she could tolerate it a few more hours—if she resurrected her earplugs.

Jenny took a hot pepperoni pizza box from the oven and placed it on top of the case of sodas. She pulled the screen door open with one bare foot. A cute, suntan guy walked around the side of the house, took one look at Jenny, stuffed his phone in his back pocket, and rushed forward.

"Let me help you." He took the case from her.

Jenny lifted the pizza box off the top. "Thanks."

"No problem." He moved with the grace of an athlete. "You want these in here?" he nodded toward the cooler.

"That'd be great."

He dumped all the sodas in the cooler and pushed them to the bottom under the ice. Standing back, he stood feet apart and chest out. He gave her a slow, confident smile and held out his hand. "Greg."

The "not exclusive" Greg? Alex's Greg?

"Jenny," she shook his hand and pulled it back when he held it a second longer than necessary. *I hope not.*

"Looks like a great party." He jerked his head toward the steps. "Wanna dance?"

"No, thanks."

"Aw, come on." He held out his hand.

Jenny shook her head, then looked beyond him to Alex who was coming up the stairs behind him. "Alex will dance with you."

Alex glanced at Jenny, then smiled brightly at Greg. "Hi."

"Hey, congrats." He reached out and hugged Alex. "Great party." He cocked a head. "I didn't know you had a sister."

"I don't. Jenny's my step-mom."

He laughed. "Funny."

"True." Jenny held up her left hand and wiggled the fingers, showing off her engagement ring and wedding band.

The smile wilted from his face. "Oh."

"Uh... I have to check on something in the kitchen. You guys have fun," Jenny spun around and headed for the house.

Oh, no. No. No. No! Stupid boy. How much had Alex heard?

In the kitchen, Jenny gathered three empty pizza boxes and headed for the garbage. Alex came up behind her in the back hallway.

"What'd you say to Greg?" she asked in a low, tight voice.

"Nothing."

She frowned. "Why'd he think you were my sister?"

"I have no idea."

"He asked you to dance."

"I'm sorry. But—"

"This is *my* party, just stay away from my friends." Alex whirled and pushed past Ted.

"Hey!" Ted, carrying a platter of burgers, pulled up short to keep from running into Alex and bumped into Gabe instead. Gabe raised bags of chips and buns high to keep from getting crushed.

Gabe frowned at Alex's disappearing back, then raised his eyebrows at Jenny as if asking what happened. She shook her head and waved him away.

Jenny went into the garage and sank against the door. She banged her head several times. *Stupid. Stupid. Boy.* She blinked back tears. *Damn it!* After another minute, she blew out a deep breath, tossed the boxes in the recycle, and rejoined the party.

She and Gabe spent the next hour feeding the waves of friends that dropped in. Then Gabe captained the boat as the kids took turns tubing. The one bright spot was that Gabe's uncle only stopped by long enough to say hi to Alex and hand her a card and fat check. After a mumbled complaint about the kids and loud music, George had a quick burger on the deck with her parents and then left.

As the afternoon wore on, her mother and father approached, with Michael in tow.

"We're going to head on home now, honey. It was a great party. Thanks for inviting us," her father said.

"You're leaving?"

"The kids don't want us hanging around," her dad said, and then under his breath, "Things are getting a little wild out there."

Jenny laughed. "It's a party, Dad, and they *are* teenagers." She put an arm around Michael's shoulders and turned to her mom.

"Thanks for coming, and for the little refrigerator you got Alex, Mom. She really liked it."

"Well, I know you got a lot of use out of yours." Mary looked around the kitchen. "The house is beautiful, Jenny. You did a wonderful job with it."

"Thanks. Stop by anytime."

Alex popped up beside her mom. "You're not leaving already, are you?"

"It's time the old folks got outta the way," her mom said.

Alex put an arm around Jenny's mom's waist. "You're not old, and you could never be in the way, Grams. You should stay."

Jenny smiled, grateful for the easy rapport between her mom and Gabe's kids—it was an unexpected bonus for them both. Who knew her mother would have taken to being a grandma? At least Jenny had given Mom one good thing—two counting Ted.

Her mom squeezed Alex. "We can't, honey. I've got work to do around the house, Michael's got to practice for tomorrow's recital, and Grandpa's got to pack. He's traveling for the next ten days. Gotta make sure he has clean clothes."

Alex looked at Jenny's dad. "Where're you going this time, Pops?"

"China then Australia."

Alex's eyes grew wide and sparkled. "Can I come? I'll stay out of your way—you'll hardly know I'm there. Please?"

"Me, too," Michael piped up.

"You're still in school, kid," Alex dismissed Michael. "But I'm free until August."

"It's a long flight," Dad said.

"How long?" Michael asked.

"Almost fourteen hours to Beijing, probably about nineteen from Detroit to Sydney."

"Forget it," Michael said. Michael got motion sick and wasn't a fan of long flights.

Alex wasn't so easily deterred. "I don't mind."

Dad's eyes sparkled in amusement at her begging. "How about I bring you a souvenir instead?"

"Baby kangaroo?" Her face lit.

"Something like that."

"Well, at least you should leave Michael. We're about to take the jet skis out and then make s'mores."

Michael turned to Mom. "Can I, Mom?"

Mom looked at Dad.

"Please?"

Dad looked at Jenny. "Jenny's busy enough."

"I don't mind. It's up to you guys," Jenny said. She loved having Michael with them, and with Ted around, he'd be easy to keep track of. Wherever Ted was, Michael wasn't far behind.

"I'll watch him, Pops," Alex said.

Dad looked at Michael. "Did you cut the grass like your mom asked?"

"Yes," he nodded, eyes wide, smile bright.

"And you've got all your homework done?"

His smile faded. "Uhhh..."

"Next time, son." Dad leaned over and kissed Alex on the forehead. "Congratulations, sweetie. We're very proud of you."

"Thanks, Pops. Have a good trip. See ya." With a wave and an irritated glance at Jenny, she went back to her friends.

"Where's Gabe?" Mom asked.

Jenny walked them to the door. "Seeing Judith, Dave, and the kids off. Judith got paged and has to get to the hospital, so Dave's taking the kids home."

Jenny waved goodbye to her parents and Michael. Returning to the patio, she checked the food supply one last time before preparing for her and Gabe to retire to the enclosed patio where they could watch the kids from a distance while enjoying some Pinot Grigio.

They'd promised Alex they'd stay out of the way, as long as things didn't get out of hand. She took out a third glass; maybe Steve would join them for a game of cards. She picked up her phone and texted him. *Up for Spades?*

The back door slammed as Jenny popped the cork on the wine bottle. "Hey, Jenny, check it out," Ted said, awestruck. "Steve got a motorcycle."

"A wha—?" By the time she turned around, Ted was rushing back through the hedge. Boys and their toys. Jenny abandoned the wine, slipped her feet into flip-flops, and joined the men around a gleaming emerald motorcycle.

Ted grilled Steve about the various features, while Gabe stood to the side with his arms crossed, eyes narrowed, and his expression tight and guarded.

"Why a Kawasaki? I always thought Harleys were the top of the line," Ted said.

"I don't like paying for the Harley name, and I wanted a bike that wouldn't need an oil well to maintain it. This Vulcan's a beauty."

"What kind of gas mileage do you get?"

"Fifty-five miles a gallon."

"Wow, that's great." Ted turned shining eyes to his father. "Maybe I should get one to run back and forth to school. It'd save a lot of money in gas."

"Won't matter if you're dead," Gabe said.

Ted sent his dad an impatient look. "Come on, Dad. Motorcycles are safe." He picked up Steve's helmet and put it on. "These helmets are state of the art."

Not the smartest thing he could have done to convince his father.

"Yeah, they're real great. Instead of dying, your brain gets scrambled, and you live like a vegetable for the rest of your life. You're better off dead."

"They're fun," Steve said.

"No doubt. But up against a car or a tree trunk...you don't have a chance."

"You have to be careful," Steve said.

"No amount of careful's going to save your life in an accident." Gabe pointed a finger at the gleaming bike. "They ought to be banned from the road to protect irresponsible fools like you."

"They're no more irresponsible than that gas-guzzling piece of crap Jenny drives." Steve waved at their garage.

"Hey now!" No need to drag her car into this argument.

Gabe shrugged. "At least it's safe."

Steve crossed his arms over his chest, *tsking*. "Socially irresponsible. I'll bet it only gets sixteen miles per gallon, if that, and God only knows what it's doing to the ozone."

"At least it doesn't kill people."

"Indirectly."

Ted removed the helmet and reluctantly handed it back to Steve. "Come on, Dad, don't you think you're overreacting?"

Jenny watched in fascination as Gabe turned on his son. She'd rarely seen him this angry about anything, but his tense body and barely controlled snarl gave evidence to his hot temper.

"No. I'm *not* overreacting. And get that gleam out of your eye, if I *ever* catch you on a motorcycle... I... I..." He stuttered, at loss for words.

Jenny raised an eyebrow at Gabe's unfinished threat. He looked like he was about to send his grown son to his room.

Still struggling to rein in his temper, Gabe's hard eyes swept the two men. "The next time a motorcycle idiot comes into the ER, I'm gonna drag your butts in there and show you what those bloody morons look like. I hope you've got a strong stomach, because it isn't pretty, and there's usually not a whole lot we can do for them."

The group went silent. Steve and Ted contemplated the weeds sprouting in the driveway cement cracks while waiting for Gabe to cool down. Suddenly Steve looked up. Blue eyes twinkling, he looked at Gabe. "Guess that means you don't want to go for a ride?"

Jenny smiled; trust Steve to find a way to alleviate the tense situation while at the same time poke fun at his friend.

Gabe's features lightened as he answered with a pointed negative look.

"I'll go," Ted volunteered.

Gabe's head whipped around to glare at his son.

Ted stared at Steve, ignoring his father.

Steve's glance flickered between angry father and defiant son, temporarily at a loss. Jenny watched Steve carefully, wondering how he'd handle the tight spot Ted put him in.

"Maybe another time, Ted," Steve said.

Jenny breathed a sigh of relief when Ted nodded in agreement, instead of pressing the issue.

Steve looked at Jenny. "How about you? Want to go for a spin? You can wear my helmet." A glossy black helmet dangled from his finger.

"No, she doesn't," Gabe said, before Jenny could decline.

Eyes popping wide, Jenny looked at Gabe. "I can answer for myself."

"Just making sure you came up with the right answer." He raised his eyebrows and stared.

"The *right* answer?" She snatched the helmet from Steve's hands and crammed it on her head, ignoring the way it pressed tightly against her braided hair. "I'd love a ride."

Jenny marched over to the motorcycle. She looked back at Steve. "Come on."

Jenny's anger burned hotter when Steve glanced at Gabe before slowly joining her. "Jenny, I didn't—"

"Let's go," she ground out as she struggled with the helmet strap.

He brushed her hands aside and tightened it. Conscious of Ted's interested look and Gabe's hostile glare, he lowered his voice. "Look, I was kidding. Gabe seems pretty pissed."

"I'm not some simpleton he can order around. Let's go." She grabbed a bit of his knit shirt and turned him toward the bike.

"Okay." Steve swung a leg over the motorcycle and started it.

She climbed on behind him, feeling quite competent, until she realized she didn't know where to put her dangling feet. She leaned to the side away from Gabe, asking, "Feet?"

He turned and pointed down at the pegs. "Hang on and lean with me on the turns."

Jenny nodded and rested her feet on the metal pegs. Squirming around till she was comfortable on the plush leather seat, she lightly rested her hands on Steve's sides and put a circumspect six inches between them. Gabe thought he could make decisions for her, did he? She had two parents; she didn't need another.

Jenny stared at Steve's back, refusing to give Gabe the satisfaction of looking back. The motorcycle rumbled and vibrated between Jenny's legs, then eased forward. The slight bump at the end of the driveway when they turned into the street made Jenny gasp. She lunged forward and clutched Steve's waist until she was plastered along his back.

Love handles would have come in handy about now, but Jenny made do, grabbing fistfuls of shirt and skin, digging her nails in deeply. If she weren't so afraid of falling off, she would've wrapped her legs around his waist too.

Steve yelped and pried one hand open, then patted it reassuringly. She probably looked ridiculous hanging onto Steve like a big cancerous lump on his backside, but she didn't care; she closed her eyes and clung to his solid, warm back.

Surprisingly, after a couple of turns, Jenny relaxed and learned to flow with the movement of the bike. She bravely lifted her head from his back and even managed to lean back enough for air to whistle between them. Another block, and she lowered her hands to Steve's hips, using them for balance more than a safety line.

Jenny smiled and sat a little straighter as their houses came into view. This time she braced herself for the bump at the end of the driveway, so she'd look like a pro biker babe to anybody watching. Ted was nowhere in sight, but Gabe sat on the back stoop.

In Steve's garage, she dismounted, took the helmet off, and handed it to him. "Thanks for the ride."

"Uh huh." He put the helmet on the motorcycle then nodded his head in Gabe's direction. "Want me to talk to him?"

"Naw. See ya later." She walked away.

Steve nodded, then turned his attention back to his bike.

As Jenny approached Gabe, she tried to gauge his mood. Had his anger burned away as hers had? She sat down next to him, thighs touching.

"What're you doing out here by yourself?" Jenny asked.

"Waiting for my wife."

She didn't know what to say to that. She didn't want to apologize, yet it was a stupid thing to fight over.

"Have fun?" he asked in a casual tone.

She wrinkled up her face. "Not really." Jenny paused. "I don't really see the attraction. It's kind of buggy and cold."

"Yeah?"

"I wouldn't have gone in the first place, but I really hate controlling people. Really pisses me off, ya know?" She bumped shoulders with him and looked in his eyes.

"Yeah, I do."

"I don't tell *you* what you may and may not do."

"No, you don't." He wrapped an arm around her shoulders and then rubbed her back. "I'm sorry, Jen. I was out of line. I..." He shrugged. "I don't want you to get hurt."

"I'm *not* one of your kids, and I don't respond well to you treating me as if I were."

"I'm sorry."

"'S alright. Speaking of kids, we should probably check on them."

"They're down by the fire pit making s'mores."

"Never too old for s'mores. Wanna get some wine and watch a movie?"

"Sure." Gabe and Jenny collected the Pinot Grigio, and headed for the study.

"That troublemaker Ted started all this asking for a ride. Steve should have said no," Gabe grumbled as he poured the wine and handed it to Jenny.

"Ted was just yankin' your chain. They both were. Steve would never encourage your kids to defy you," she chided. Her lips curved in a soft smile. "And Ted's a great guy. You did a good job raising him."

Gabe took a sip of his wine, nodding. "He *is* a good kid—they both are." He frowned at Jenny. "By the way, did I overhear Alex telling you to stay away from her friends?"

Jenny cocked her head. "She was miffed. Greg asked me to dance. He thought I was her sister." Jenny giggled. "It can't be easy having a step-mom as young as me."

"Especially when she's beautiful and looks like a teenager. It's surprising Alex doesn't hate you."

She hurled a pillow at him. "It's not like I act like her big sister."

Gabe easily deflected her missile and set his wine down. "Didn't say you did." Grinning, he pulled her across his lap. "As a matter of fact, you're more serious and responsible than I am." He tickled her. "You need to lighten up. Have a little fun, lady."

Shrieking, she squirmed off his lap, and with arms still around his neck, pulled him down to lie on her. She lowered her voice, seductively. "What'd you have in mind, mister?"

He growled deep in his throat. "After these kids go home. I'll show you."

Jenny wriggled out from under him. She unfastened her blouse, button by button, as she backed up to close and lock the door. "Why wait?"

"Hey," Alex popped up behind Jenny.

Jenny jumped and pulled her top together. *Geeze!* "Alex. What's wrong?" She quickly rebuttoned her shirt, then smoothed her hair.

"Nothing." Alex's narrowed gaze went from her dad to Jenny, but then her face cleared as if dismissing a thought. "Will you show us how to do the Electric Slide?"

"Just a minute, young lady," Gabe said, "You owe—"

Jenny raised a hand and flashed a quick frown to quiet him. "*Now* you want me to dance with your friends?" She raised one eyebrow. "You know...that would require me being around your friends."

A gracious person would've brushed off Alex's temper tantrum, but Jenny thought she needed to be called out on it.

Alex shifted her weight from one foot to the other as a blush pinkened her cheeks. "Yeah, I'm sorry I was rude to you earlier. I shouldn't have taken it out on you because Greg was flirting with you."

"I didn't do or say—"

"I know. I heard." She shrugged. "He's a flirt."

"I can't do the Electric Slide to rap."

"The guys are gone. We can put country on."

"Okay, then." Jenny smiled and looped an arm around Alex's waist, before turning back to Gabe. "Coming?"

"You go on. Line dancing's not really my thing."

Chapter 14

Jenny returned to the kitchen, picked up her water bottle, and headed upstairs to work. Karen assigned her to do a series of articles on John Spears and his legacy—one a week. At first, it seemed like a fun assignment and Jenny'd found the history fascinating. But now that she was past the first few introductory articles and needed to get a more in-depth take on what it was like to be in the foster care system, she was stuck.

She'd completed her interviews and had all the material she needed, but now it was time to dig in and get personal, yet remain respectful and productive. This piece had to have the exact right tone. Jenny combed through the history again, hoping for inspiration.

John Spears survived the Detroit foster care system decades ago and never forgot the gift he received. Upon his death, to his heirs' surprise, he left most of his ten million-dollar estate in trust, with proviso that his favorite caseworker at Christ Child House oversee the building of an expansion facility to be called the Woodward House, which would create supervised independent living care for older teens.

He didn't want other children to go through the terrifying experience he had of being cut loose from the system at eighteen. Living without a biological family was tough, but leaving his Christ Child family of seven years before he was ready had been traumatic.

John survived, got a scholarship to University of Michigan, then made his fortune. His bequest was motivated by the desire to help boys like him, those not fortunate enough to be adopted or integrated into a foster family. He wanted kids that were at CCH long-term to have the consistency of being able to stay nearby the staff and kids at CCH. The staff became the long-term kids' family, and family was important.

Three hours and several false starts later, Jenny drove impatient fingers through her hair. She pursed her lips and shoved her laptop away. Scowling, she slouched deep in her chair. Nervous energy drove her from her seat, and she paced her office.

Nothin'.

Her phone chimed with a text from Gabe. Jenny sighed. Quitting time. She headed downstairs to pack food. Maybe the fresh lake breeze would blow this fog from her brain and inspire her.

Ritz chased Canadian geese in the backyard while Jenny carried a cooler with snacks and drinks down to the boat. It was a perfect evening, not too hot and not too muggy. The bug zapper helped keep the mosquitoes at bay with a comforting *bzzt* as each insect flew toward the white light death. She stowed the food on board and returned to the dock. Sitting, she dangled her bare legs over the edge and leaned against a post.

Stop obsessing, Jen. Think about something else; you're trying too hard. Think about...Michael's tennis match. He and his partner played pretty well yesterday.

She had enjoyed cheering Michael on at his match. He'd spent the earlier part of his summer vacation attending an intensive camp that prepared him well for junior league competition. Learning to operate and care for their boat and jet skis, Alex's graduation party, and work, kept Jenny busy without much time left over for Michael, and she'd missed him—more than she'd ever have thought.

Yeah, she'd had fun watching the match until one of the parents asked Jenny which one of the boys was her boyfriend. Dumb ass.

Jenny looked up as Steve approached. Dressed in a gray pinstripe suit and a solid blue tie that matched his bright eyes, he looked the part of the handsome lawyer. Steve wore the suits with natural nonchalance, but only because it was expected, not because he enjoyed the formal clothes.

"Sorry I'm late. Got stuck in traffic. Give me a few minutes to change, and I'll be ready to go."

"Take your time. Gabe's stuck at the clinic. He won't be home for another half an hour."

"You're looking thoughtful. Everything okay?" Steve shrugged out of his suit coat and draped it over the dock post. He unbuttoned his white dress shirt cuffs, and with quick, efficient twists of the wrist, had both sleeves rolled halfway up tanned forearms.

He lowered himself to the wood, disregarding potential damage to his expensive slacks. Resting a forearm on one bent knee, he squinted into the fading sun. The breeze rustled his blond hair, giving him an attractive, mussed look.

All he needed was to loosen his tie, and he'd make a great cover shot for some men's magazine.

"Contemplating life, I guess. It's been a rotten week," she confessed.

"It's only Tuesday."

She paused, raised her dark sunglasses, and gave him a long sideways look. "*Really* rotten."

"Want to talk?"

Pulling her knees up to her chest, Jenny drew her windbreaker around her bare legs to shelter them against the cooling breeze. She squinted, then lowered her glasses against the bright setting sun. "Why does it seem like you *always* take three steps backward after you're so excited about making two steps forward?"

"That's a rhetorical question, right?"

"Everything's become so complicated. I've made so many mistakes."

"Haven't we all?"

Jenny looked away, shaking her head. "Not like this. When I was younger, I kept taking steps backward. Very big steps backward." She paused, wondering how much to trust him with.

"Then Gabe came along, and we fell in love. My mom thought it was a huge mistake because he's older, and she thought I was too impulsive and immature for marriage and parenting. But I loved him, and marrying Gabe was my shot—my chance to fix everything and leap forward. Now it looks like she's right. Not about Gabe," she quickly amended. "He's the best thing in my life."

She looked out over the water, letting loving feelings of Gabe warm her. Her voice lowered, taking on a reverent tone. "He's a wonderful person, compassionate and giving. As a husband, he's perfect. Kind and sensitive, and funny, and sexy," she trailed off, embarrassed about sounding like a teenager with a massive crush. She studied her white shoelaces. "Anyway, we'd be great if people would just let us."

"Who has a problem with it?"

"Who doesn't?"

"Me."

She smiled. Steve was sweet and a loyal friend. Maybe it was his nature, but Steve inspired people to talk about themselves. *You sensed he'd respect your privacy and keep your secret.*

"Besides you?" Jenny asked. "Gabe's uncle tried to trick me into drawing up a prenup, Alex was furious with me when she caught her crush flirting with me, and things with my mother are still tenuous." She sighed. "It's so slow gaining her confidence. I'm probably being overly sensitive, but, it's exhausting keeping my guard up, feeling like I'm being judged constantly by everybody."

"What about your dad?"

"Dad's always there for me." She struggled to find the words, yet needed to say them, as if admitting this great flaw was the first step in finding a solution. "At first when people mistook me for Gabe's daughter, I laughed it off, thinking they're just dumb." She frowned and looked down. Voice lowered, she huskily confessed, "But it's getting harder."

"Why?"

"It happens *all* the time. Yesterday, at Michael's tennis match...one of the moms asked which of the boys was my boyfriend."

Steve turned away and choked back a chuckle.

"Go ahead. Laugh. Somebody might as well enjoy my humiliation."

"So? You're beautiful, and you look young. It's hardly the end of the world."

She wrinkled her nose. "I'm not beautiful, but thank you. Last weekend when we took Alex and Ted out for dinner, I got carded. Then bartender wanted to know what my 'dad' wanted to drink."

"Uh..."

Steve's speechlessness was comforting; he was beginning to get it. "Yeah. It's just with Gabe's kids there, it was embarrassing." She frowned. "And that annoys me, too. Why should I care? I shouldn't. But I do."

"You care 'cause it hurts," Steve explained. "It's implied criticism."

"So what? I'm a grown woman. Sticks and stones." She smiled wryly, then shrugged and tilted her head.

"Yeah, well, names *do* hurt. What does Gabe think?"

"It doesn't bother him, but he's so easygoing about stuff like that."

"Then don't let it bother you. Just because you're a young stepmother doesn't mean you're a bad one."

She groaned and washed a hand over her face. "I'm bad, too. Instead of sending Alex to her mother to talk about sex and birth control, I gave her my opinion." She told him all about the fiasco.

"Then I spent the past few days interviewing kids in the foster care system, and that rammed home exactly how shallow I am."

Though their lives were light-years more challenging than Jenny's, she'd known the pain of feeling like a failure, of being an outsider looking in, of wanting the chance to belong. She knew the panic of having to face an adult situation long before adulthood and experiencing that without the support of loving family would have been exponentially harder. Jenny had dented and bruised herself, but these kids had been damaged through no fault of their own.

"You're hardly shallow, Jen."

"Oh, comparatively, I am." She nodded. "I have to do a piece on the foster care system and it's killing me. These kids, abused and/or neglected by their families, are ripped away from everything they know to try and give them a better life, but their needs are so great and so complicated."

She looked at Steve.

"There are *fourteen thousand* kids in Michigan foster care. That's crazy. Through no fault of their own, their childhood has become a nightmare of loss, neglect, abuse, inconsistency, lack of love..." She scowled. "And not enough people care or help. These children are *not* disposable human beings. They deserve a second chance with a loving family. They deserve a mulligan."

Jenny'd been granted several mulligans in her twenty-eight years, and look at her now. Happily married, good job, beautiful home, plenty of food to eat... She'd come a long way in the past few years, all due to forgiveness, love, patience and persistence—but mostly love. Gabe's love.

"I agree. Those kids do deserve help, and your article will draw attention to their need. You should feel proud of that."

"Hopefully. If I ever get it done."

"You will. As for you...I wish I had some words of wisdom, but I don't. Things may seem grim, but you're lucky." The breeze ruffled his hair as he looked out over the lake, then turned to her. "You and Gabe have a great relationship. All this other stuff is just stuff. But what you and Gabe have is special."

Steve shook his head, smiling wistfully. "Those other things, the parenting thing, people doubting you—that's their problem. Don't let them project their issues onto you and ruin what you have with Gabe. Just be true to yourself and Gabe, and everything will work out."

Just be true to yourself and Gabe. If only Steve knew what a fraud she really was. Would he judge her too, or would he understand? As a lawyer, he had to be able to see both sides of an issue. Even if he didn't agree with her decision, she doubted he'd ridicule her for it. Steve was pretty open-minded.

Jenny brushed the hair from her eyes, and stared at Steve. He was usually fun and entertaining. This prophetic, philosophic counsel was a new side to him. "That's pretty sage advice, counselor. How'd you get to be so wise?"

He pursed his lips and looked at her, allowing her to see the pain shadowed in his honest blue eyes. "The hard way—by paying too much attention to what others thought."

"When you stopped playing ball?"

He nodded. "Then, too."

"It must have been tough, going from being idolized to a regular person overnight." Jenny pushed her sunglasses up on the top of her head so she could better see his expression in the waning light.

"It's an adjustment." Steve stared at a rusty buoy bobbing gently in the pewter water. "I really loved playing ball, ya know? I knew it wouldn't last forever, which was why I finished college."

He plucked at his perfectly creased pant leg. "But somehow, I'd always expected the decision to quit would be mine. Being sidelined by an injury never occurred to me. I mean, it was baseball, not football or hockey. I worked out regularly with a trainer specifically to avoid this type of injury. I played ball for six years. Between spring training and the season, I'd never stayed in one place for more than a couple of months. With no time to prepare for retirement, I was a fish out of water."

"So what happened? After you retired, did people hound you?"

He nodded. "At first I refused to talk about it. I tried to disappear, but reporters dogged me, digging. Once I'd been accepted to law school, I agreed to do this one article to satisfy curiosity."

"And?"

"It was a disaster." He sighed. "The reporter made a joke of it, implying that I'd bought my way in, insinuating that a jock could never cut it in law school and certainly not in a profession requiring no knowledge of sports. She intimated I wanted to become an entertainment attorney to use my contacts. She turned the piece into a joke." He shook his head, as if still feeling the sting of embarrassment years later. "It was humiliating."

"You didn't insist on approving the piece first?"

He shook his head. "Dumb, huh?"

"But now you're working for one of the most prestigious firms in the Detroit area."

"And fighting to prove myself every day." He grunted. "The truth is they took me in to use my name. They parade me out in front of important clients like cheap entertainment. I never get assigned the interesting cases."

Though he spoke matter-of-factly with a hint of resentment, Jenny knew the situation hurt. Steve was a smart guy and hardworking; he deserved to be taken seriously.

He glanced sideways at her, then went back to inspecting the wood splinter he'd ripped off the dock. "Know what I'm doing now?"

She shook her head.

"Cite checking an article one of the partners wrote about civil procedure. I don't think there could *possibly* be more boring work." He paused, immersed in the disappointment. "But that's okay. I can be patient. Soon, the right case will come along, and I'll have my chance."

"I'm sure you will. Meanwhile..." She hesitated, trying to broach the subject without destroying his trust. "If you wanted, I could write a favorable article about you. I could cover your baseball career, your sudden forced retirement, and your successful career change. We could publicize your graduating from Michigan, with honors, and your coup of obtaining a job with a top law firm."

Steve's head whipped up to stare at her. "How'd you know I graduated with honors?"

"Whoa there." Jenny leaned back, away from the suspicion flashing in his eyes. "Because I know you and your determination. I wouldn't be surprised if you'd been the valedictorian—if they even have such a thing in law school."

Relaxing, he cracked a smile that showed a deep dimple in his left cheek. "Number two."

"See? An article like that would vindicate you, and I'd give you total editorial control."

Steve's smile evaporated. "I don't think so. Not yet, at least. Maybe once I have a few wins under my belt."

She shrugged, trying not to show her disappointment. "Whenever you're ready."

"I appreciate the offer."

"Even though I'm the enemy?" Jenny joked.

He chuckled. "Even so."

Ritz nudged in between them, poking and licking Jenny's arm. "What? Is it time for dinner?"

"While you feed her, I'm going to get changed." Steve stood, brushed off his pants, and offered Jenny a hand up.

She took the proffered help and then released his hand. Brushing her loose hair away from her face. "Thanks for listening. Can I ask you something?" She smiled. "Off the record."

"Sure."

"So you've been with Annie awhile now. What's the deal?"

"No deal. Her divorce has only been final for a few months and having young kids complicates thing. We're taking it slow." Steve retrieved his suit coat and with a hooked index finger, he tossed it over one shoulder.

Molasses slow. She and Gabe married six months after they'd met. *When it's right, you know it.* "If things with Annie don't work out, I might know somebody at work—"

"No, thanks." Dropping a heavy hand on her shoulder, he turned her and started walking toward the house, gently pushing her up the hill as an older brother might help her along after counseling his kid sister. "My sisters are always trying to set me up. I don't have time for that now. I'm too busy cite-checking life-altering articles."

At least he still had a sense of humor and could laugh at himself. "Okay. But that soul mate you're waiting for doesn't always come at a convenient time, you know."

Steve paused by the hedge and stared at her as if considering, then shook his head and turned away. "See ya in ten."

ↄↄↄ

Finding a soul mate doesn't always come at a convenient time. As if he needed that warning. Steve got a beer and headed upstairs. Timing wasn't exactly his specialty. In fact, he expected his love would find him at the most inopportune, inconvenient moment possible—that was if he was lucky enough to ever find what Gabe and Jenny had.

He and Annie probably didn't have it. Wasn't true love something that hit ya, and you knew it on a gut level?

Annie wasn't the love of his life, and he suspected she felt the same. But they were compatible, and he really enjoyed her kids. Sophia and Josh had wormed a place deep in his heart, which was probably why he let the relationship with their mother coast on. He and Annie understood each other and were good in bed, but they didn't have that magical mating of souls that Jenny and Gabe had.

He wanted it, but maybe magic wasn't meant for everybody.

Steve stripped out of his suit and tossed it on the chair in his room. At first he'd been curious—and ungenerous, he admitted— about Jenny and Gabe, but that was before he got to know them.

Their relationship was clearly no sweet young thing looking for a sugar daddy or surrogate father, and he sincerely doubted that Gabe married Jenny in a deluded attempt to recapture his youth. He was only in his early forties and clearly cherished his wife.

What's not to love? Kind and generous, Jenny possessed an innocent, charming quality about her—yet could be assertive when she needed to be. He found it hard to believe that anyone wouldn't like Jenny. So she dressed in jeans, went around barefoot, and wore her long hair in a ponytail? Looking younger than her age wasn't a crime.

Steve changed into jeans and a polo shirt.

He gave Jen credit for even trying to help her stepdaughter. If it'd been him, he probably would have avoided that minefield altogether and sent Alex to her parents for answers about sex. But Jenny cared. Being a good stepmother was important to her. Steve admired her for it, and he could certainly identify with her need to prove herself.

Convenient or inconvenient, he hoped to someday find a woman like Jenny Harrison. He wanted someone to look at him the way she looked at Gabe, like life was special because he was there to share it. But deep down, he doubted he'd ever experience that kind of love. For now, he had to concentrate on proving to everybody, himself included, that he could hack it as an attorney.

Steve remembered how Jenny's small hand and quick, shy smile had sent a surprising warmth shooting through him earlier on the dock when he'd helped her to her feet. He wanted that kind of magic all the time. Some day.

∾ ∾ ∾

"Why can't we go to the barber?" Michael asked, as Jenny pumped quarters into the Village parking meter.

"Stop whining. Mom said to take you here." She hurried down the sidewalk, but her brother lagged behind. Hands crammed deep in his cargo short pockets, he lumbered along. "Michael, let's go."

"Come on Jen, don't make me go to that old-lady place. Dad takes me to the barber."

"Dad's not here." And Mom had asked Jenny to take Michael to get his haircut. She'd put up with his mop of hair for half the summer but insisted he get it cut before starting high school. Though it was weeks before school started, tennis practice began next week, and Mom figured shorter hair would be cooler.

Michael came to a halt. "Chez Lou Lou? Lou Lou? You've *got* to be kidding? I'm not goin' in there."

It was a fancy name, but Mom raved about the place her long-time hairdresser had moved to. Jenny put a hand to his shoulder and nudged him forward. "Let's go. We're late."

"Barber's cheaper," Michael wheedled, pushing back against her hand. "I won't tell. She'll never know."

Jenny held open the salon door. She and Mom had been getting along well lately and she finally trusted Jenny to be alone with Michael again. No way she was crossing Mom over a haircut. "She already paid. Get in here."

Michael passed by her, took one look at the sparkling chandeliers, chic black-and-white triptych of the Eiffel Tower, and half-dozen chatting women, pivoted and bolted for the street.

Really, Mom? What were you thinking?

Michael collided with a couple of girls on their way in. The three sprang apart and took stock.

"'Scuse m– Oh, hi, Michael," the pretty blonde said.

"Katie. Sorry." He flashed her a shy smile and looked at the ground. A flush climbed Michael's neck.

"Do you go here?" She smiled widely. "This place is awesome."

"Uh..."

"Isn't this where Cam got his Bieber, cut?" the brunette asked Katie. "Not that I *like* Justin Bieber, but Cameron is *totally* hot."

"I think so." She glanced at Michael and shifted her weight from one foot to another. "Guess we'll see you at orientation."

"Uh. Yeah." Michael backed out of the way and let them pass. He pursed his lips, drew in a deep breath, and followed them in.

Jenny suppressed a smile. *Way to go, kid.*

Cindy looked up from the clumps of hair she was sweeping. "Hi, guys. Have a seat. I'll be right with you."

Jenny sat down on the black plush sofa next to the girls. She wouldn't have pegged this as Mom's type of place. The black and white decor and chandeliers were elegant and modern, but she'd expected to hear more sophisticated or French music, yet somehow the soft upbeat hip tunes worked too. Funny that it appealed to Mom. Jenny picked up the latest *People* Magazine.

"I thought we were late?" Michael muttered, while dropping into the corner chair.

Jenny's hand froze over the opening pages as she shot him a warning glance. Cindy was a nice lady; she'd been Mom's stylist since they moved back from San Diego, and Jenny didn't want her feelings hurt because of Michael's pissy attitude.

Wiping his hands on his shorts, Michael studied the glossy white floor tiles. He looked out the window, then began biting his cuticles, all the while assiduously avoiding looking in the girls' direction.

With a warm smile, Cindy came over and put her hands on her trim hips. "How's married life, Jenny? Your mom sure dotes on those grandkids. We love her pictures of Alex and..." She squinted and frowned. "Teddy? Ted?"

"Ted." Jenny said. "Yeah, they're pretty crazy about her, too."

"That Alex is a beauty."

"She is. How's your baby? Isn't he about two now?"

"He's three—and adorable. Thanks for asking." She turned to Michael. "Ready, Michael?"

Michael glanced at the girls at the far end of the room where they were consulting with a stylist. With a brief nod, he followed Cindy to her station.

Jenny smothered a grin. *The things we do for love.*

Jenny thumbed through the magazine, scanning the latest batch of celebrity pictures, when she hesitated on a two-page spread of before-and-after shots of celebrity haircuts. There were several comparison shots of Katie Holmes—she was beautiful with or without long hair, but it seemed hardly a fair comparison when in the pics of her after the haircut she had makeup on and before she seemed more natural.

Reese Witherspoon was the exception who didn't really look very different with shorter hair, but Jenny unquestionably preferred her as a blonde. She winced at Nicole Kidman's short haircut shots. Nicole looked okay with a bob, but Jenny definitely liked her better with longer hair. Jennifer Lawrence and Gwyneth Paltrow, too.

Wow. Halle Berry and Victoria Beckham totally rocked a really short pixie cut. She scanned the photos on the next page with envy. Selena Gomez, Taylor Swift, and Jennifer Aniston were gorgeous no matter how they wore their hair.

Miley...well...too bad she hadn't stopped before sliding into ridiculous, where she tried to shock everybody by every means possible. Now Julianne Hough was classy. Julianne'd always been Jenny's girl-crush. She'd loved her Dancing with the Stars-long sexy hair, but looking at Julianne's gorgeous layered bob—"

A shadow fell over the magazine, and Jenny looked up at one of the stylists, who craned her head sideways to look at the magazine. "I hear she's dating Brooks Laich now. I kind of liked her with Ryan Seacrest. They were cute together."

"Yeah, but Ryan can't really compare to those hockey player pecs and biceps."

She chuckled. "True. Do you need help?"

"No, I'm just wait—" She glimpsed Julianne's happy face, cocked her head sideways and looked up. "Well, maybe..."

She trotted upstairs. "Gabe?"

Jenny pulled her cell from her pocket, then paused. Maybe he was down by the boat. She skipped downstairs and headed for the patio doors, when she saw him cleaning off the grill. "Gabe?"

"Hi, babe. I saw the steaks thawing so thought I'd get the grill rea—" Gabe turned around, and his mouth dropped open.

"Surprise." Jenny threw her arms wide, then pirouetted so her hair whipped around her face. "What do you think?"

Gabe snapped his mouth shut and stepped closer, peering. "Oh. My God. *What* did you do?"

"I got my hair cut."

"What did you *do*?" He moved closer, circling her, staring.

"I got my hair cut. Do you like it?"

"Oh my God, you cut your hair."

She nodded. Smiling, she tucked a lock behind her ear. "Isn't it great? It's like Julianne Hough's."

"You cut your hair."

She frowned. "Stop saying that."

"Why?"

"Because it's annoying."

"No, why'd you cut it?"

"I wanted to."

Gabe lifted the back of her hair. "It's a wig, right? It's a joke?"

Jenny slapped his hand away. "*No*, it's not a wig. I cut my hair and donated it to Locks of Love."

"But why?"

"I wanted to." Her face fell. "Don't you like it?"

"I... It's different."

"You hate it," she said flatly.

"Nooo, I...it's a surprise." He examined her closer. "You look so much..."

"So much what?" she narrowed one eye and cocked her head in warning.

"I don't know. Older. Different. What do you think?"

"I love it. It's so much lighter and gonna be easier to care for, and I think it makes me look chic." *Older. Sophisticated.*

"If you love it, then I love it." Gabe pulled Jenny close and locked his arms around her waist. Then he leaned back and tipped his head this way and that, inspecting her face and hair. He frowned. "You look so different. Like someone else. It's almost like I'm having an affair."

Jenny chuckled. *Looked like someone else?* That might be a slight exaggeration, but a move in the right direction. This could very well be the perfect thing she needed to help her. "Well, knock yourself out, and let's make all your fantasies come true, 'cause this is the only affair you're ever likely to have."

"Fantasy affair? More like a nightmare." Gabe shuddered, then pulled her close and rested his cheek on her head. "Pleasing the woman I have keeps me busy enough."

Jenny grinned. *Good.*

ख ख ख

Gabe kissed Jenny on the cheek and watched her burrow deeper under the flowered covers until all that showed were a few wispy clumps of hair. How could she breathe, let alone sleep, like that? Strange woman.

Gabe put Ritz's electronic collar on her, grabbed his black helmet from the hook, and tapped the garage door opener. Rolling his bike into the drive, the early morning mugginess sent him back inside to add ice cubes to his water bottle. Damn, it had to be the hottest August on record. He went back outside.

"Ready?" Steve stood in the drive petting Ritz.

Gabe nodded and mounted his bike. Tail wagging, Ritz trotted behind them down the drive as far as her electronic collar would let her go. They turned onto the near deserted street.

"Gonna be hot today," Steve said.

"And humid."

"There's a cold front moving in."

"Can't wait."

Gabe loved these morning workouts. Steve was a good companion, and he knew how far to push them to keep testing their tired muscles. In the beginning, he suspected Steve held back a bit until he'd gotten in shape, but now Gabe held his own.

Steve was a smart, interesting guy even if he did disagree with Gabe, sometimes just for the hell of it. Typical lawyer. An hour ride to warm his muscles and wake him up, followed by a hot shower, was a great way to start the day. Making love with his wife was the only thing to top it.

They peddled south on Lakeshore Drive in silence, passing the Pier, St. Paul's church, and before long they approached the War Memorial. Suddenly Gabe downshifted and sprinted past Fisher, pumping furiously until his thighs burned. He coasted a bit, but before long Steve zipped by, and he was hustling to catch up.

They rode side by side awhile before Steve glanced sideways at him. "So what's with Jenny?"

"What do you mean?" He dropped back behind Steve as they entered a busier area, then moved back up beside him when traffic allowed.

"Short hair. Heels. Makeup."

Gabe shrugged. "She wanted a change."

"That's not a change, it's a transformation. Like a fat person losing a hundred pounds."

"Don't let Jen catch you callin' her fat." Gabe looked over his shoulder before crossing the street and heading for Three Mile Drive Park.

Steve followed. "What's wrong with the way she looked?"

"Nothin'. She wanted to try out a new look." What else could it be? Why would someone change her looks so drastically? "Well...the kids and their friends have been around a lot this summer. Jen probably wanted to look her age."

"She'll never look her age."

Sweat trickled down Gabe's temple and onto his shoulder. "Alex got a little ticked at her graduation party when the guy she's had a crush on thought Jenny was her sister."

Steve flashed him a quick glance before adjusting his gears. "Jenny's a beautiful lady."

"Yeah, well, Alex didn't like her heartthrob eyeing her stepmom."

"Understandable."

"Jen laughed it off, but I think she was embarrassed." Longing for the cool shade up ahead, Gabe dropped back and took his bottle out. He squirted water in his mouth and held it there for a minute before swallowing. He replaced the water and hurried to catch up with Steve.

"Bingo. *That's* why she butchered her hair."

"She didn't 'butcher' it. It's way shorter. Took me awhile to get used to it, but it looks nice. She looks older."

"She looks older. That's it."

"Said it was cooler. And she wanted a more stylish look for work," he huffed.

"Did it work?"

Gabe sighed as they rolled into the shade by the park, savoring the break before they turned around and really worked on the six-mile race home. "Hell, I don't know. She'd be gorgeous in a brown paper bag."

Hands on his hips, Steve coasted, resting for their return sprint. "Did you tell her that?"

"What?"

"That she's beautiful. That it's not her age that attracts men." Steve raised a shoulder to wipe his dripping face. "It's her. A sophisticated haircut and preppy clothes isn't going to make men stop admiring her."

"It's stupid."

"Not to her." Steve sloshed water around his mouth before spitting it out. He raised an eyebrow as if considering something before looking away. "Comments about her being so much younger than you upset her."

Steve studied their surroundings with extra attention, as if the conversation made him uncomfortable. Why now? He'd never hesitated to voice his opinion before.

"How do you know?"

Steve swallowed and capped the water. Still not looking at him, he pushed away from the curb, saying over his shoulder, "She told me."

How come she never told me? Was she embarrassed, or maybe she feared he thought she encouraged men? Naw, that was stupid. If it were important, his Jenny would have confided in him. They shared everything important. Steve must be reading too much into some off-handed remark she'd made.

"She'll get over it."

Steve abruptly swerved to the side. Gabe flew on by him, then circled back wondering if he'd gotten a flat, but Steve stood straddling his bike. When Gabe approached, Steve clenched his jaw and looked away a minute before pinning him with an angry scowl. "She's not going to just 'get over it'. She needs your reassurance."

Wow. Steve's anger, an almost palpable thing, hung between them in the humid morning air. How come? A slice of jealousy cut through Gabe. "Why don't *you* reassure her, since you seem to know so much about my wife?"

Steve gave him a look of pure disgust. His lips tightened then released, repeatedly, as if trying to decide to say something, or not. Eyebrows pinched together so they nearly met, Steve glared at him.

"She doesn't want my reassurance, you idiot. It's *your* opinion that matters to her. For some reason she's convinced the sun rises and sets by your sorry ass. It's *you* she's desperate to please, not me." Steve hopped on his bike and rode away, leaving Gabe to trail behind.

Were things really that difficult for Jenny? She had lopped off a good foot of hair. And her new clothes were stodgy. He frowned. Maybe she was going through some crisis, and he'd missed the signs.

Steve was right; something weird was going on with her—not that he'd ever admit it to the other man. He pulled up next to Steve. "I'll talk to her."

"Soon." Steve smirked, all traces of his former anger gone. "Before she gets a buzz cut, starts wearing horn-rimmed glasses and granny smocks." Checking traffic, he turned in a big arc. Steve arched a brow. "Ready?"

Gabe raced after Steve, finally catching him. "How come you know so much about women?"

"Sisters," he huffed. "Three. Seattle. Cincinnati. And Raleigh. Thank God. Couldn't handle it if they lived in state."

They picked up the pace until neither had breath to talk, and the rush hour traffic wouldn't allow them to ride side by side. Zooming into their respective driveways, they exchanged waves before heading to shower.

"Hey, Gabe," Steve called out from his garage. "Tell Jen I'll do the interview. Have her text me."

"Will do." Gabe shut the garage door and headed inside.

Jenny almost ran into Gabe as she left their bedroom. He put a hand on her shoulders to avoid the collision

"Hey, babe," she said. Eyes widening, she backed away. "Boy are you sweaty." She wrinkled her nose and waved a hand in front of her face. "And stinky."

"Before I forget, Steve said to text him. He'll give you the interview."

Her eyes lit up, and she smiled. "Really? Why? What changed?"

"No idea. Don't look a gift horse in the mouth." Gabe looked at Jenny. "Have an interview today?"

"Nope. Working at home."

"So why're you dressed like that?" He waved a hand at her khaki slacks, white oxford shirt, and brown loafers. And she had makeup on—not just lipstick but stuff on her eyes, too.

That wasn't Jenny. When working at home, his Jenny wore soft, faded jeans and a T-shirt. Or shorts and a tank top if it was hot like today. And more often than not she was barefoot. She was a free, unpretentious woman, not this neat, preppy mannequin.

"Like what?" She frowned and looked down at her outfit.

"Why don't you have shorts on? It's already hot."

"Alex and some friends are dropping by to take the boat out one last time."

Steve was right. This whole new look was meant to impress his kids. Gabe frowned and yanked his T-shirt up to wipe his dripping face. "She's seen your legs before."

Jenny avoided his eye and tucked her hair behind one ear. "You'd better get going. You're gonna be late."

He gripped her shoulder and drew her into the bedroom. Nudging her down onto the neatly made bed, he sat next to her. "Jen, you've got to stop this."

"What?"

"Trying to look older. It's not you."

She frowned and studied the floor. "I don't know what you mean."

"Yes, you do." Gabe took her chin in his hand and turned her toward him. "I love you. I love the way you dress—used to dress. I like looking at your legs. You've got great legs. Don't hide them—especially in ninety-degree weather. If you're doing all this 'cause you want a change, fine. But I want you to be happy. I want you to be *you*, not somebody older or more sophisticated to impress other people."

Her pale eyes clouded with worry and she fingered the ends of her hair. "You don't like my hair?"

He smiled warmly and gently tugged a few strands, then settled his hand comfortably around her neck. "I *love* your hair. But I'd love you bald, too. The important thing is do you like it?"

She nodded.

"Good. But you can't like these pants, especially on a hot day like today. Change into something comfortable. I miss the old Jenny Harrison."

Slight lines flickered between her eyebrows when she cleared her throat and gulped. She turned moist eyes to him. "Even if she looks young enough to be your daughter?"

God damn those gossiping idiots.

Gabe slowly shook his head. Cupping her face, he looked deeply into her expressive eyes. "I love you.

Chapter 16

Jenny tuned out the baseball game George and Gabe watched in the family room. Two quick raps sounded at the back door as Steve opened it. "Jenny?"

Waving her feathery tail, Ritz trotted past Steve and approached Jenny.

"Come on in." Jenny finished pouring her drink, then hefted the bottle. "Wine?"

"No, thanks. I'm on my way out. Ritz was wandering around my front yard."

Jenny looked at Ritz's furry neck; Gabe had forgotten to put her e-collar on. "Sorry. Thanks for returning her."

"No problem." Steve backed out of the kitchen. "See ya."

Jenny took a sip of wine, and then hurried to the back door. "Hey Grant?"

Steve paused next to his running car and looked back.

"Have you guys decided who's having the pick party for this year's Fantasy teams?"

"No, but you're not invited," he said. "Gabe's in, but you're out. Guys didn't like losing to a girl."

"What? Really?" She frowned, let down. Jenny's team had come in second—largely due to Peyton Manning having another phenomenal year—and won three hundred dollars, but she didn't think the others were sore about it. "Andrew won, not me."

"Just kidding." He grinned. "Picks are weekend before Labor Day. Want to host?"

"Sure."

"'Kay. See you later." He swung into his car.

Jenny waved as he drove away.

Back in the kitchen, she mulled over her disturbing interview with a foster care coordinator while dicing red and green peppers. Jenny mechanically washed and sliced the yellow onions, and then covered them with plastic wrap to keep from crying.

Her editor wanted this next piece to be a more broad-range look at the foster care experience than the residential program Christ Child offered, but how could Jenny effectively present the issues burdening the foster care system in a way guaranteed to get readers' attention and sympathy without exploiting the children?

There were plenty of heartbreaking stories she could tell, but she hated the way most of the agencies presented the children on their websites, like puppies up for adoption. It seemed degrading to Jenny; hopefully the kids didn't feel that way.

And she'd been obsessing over people thinking she was too young for Gabe or that she was a gold digger. In light of the struggles these children faced, Jenny was reminded again to be thankful for her many blessings.

She propped one bare foot on the other as she diced the chicken. No more ugly clothes or wearing makeup at home. She flipped her hair away from her neck. She was gifted with good health, a loving husband, great friends and family, beautiful home, great job—she was so very fortunate, and now it was time to show her appreciation and give back.

Jenny flicked water droplets to test the oil in the wok. With it being hot enough to spit the water back, Jenny tossed in the chicken slices and efficiently moved them around with two wooden spoons to keep them from burning.

The bell dinged on the rice cooker. Jenny added vegetables to the sautéed chicken, then sprinkled them with garlic salt, pepper, ginger, and a little soy sauce.

"George? Gabe? Five minutes."

After they dished up, Jenny glanced at Gabe's uncle. "What're you up to these days, George?"

"Keeping busy. This weekend my buddy Bob Limber's gonna show me a new fishing hole. Claims it's his secret spot."

"Judge Limber has time for fishing?" Gabe asked.

"Yeah, even though he's a hoity-toity judge, he makes time. You should have seen him in the old days—smooth. Surprised he didn't go into politics. He talked our way out of more than a few messes, I'll tell you."

George took a fork full of food, quickly chewed, and swallowed. "Anyhow, I'm still golfing three days a week, and then there's my garden to finish cleanin' up, and Will, the guy I sold the shop to, wants some help. He's opening a new branch and needs advice setting it up and stuff."

Maybe there was hope for George after all; it wasn't like him to help anyone out of the goodness of his heart. Everything was a deal with George, whether the person knew it or not. "That's nice of you," Jenny said.

George shrugged. "He's payin' me."

Of course he is.

"Mmmm, this is great, Jenny, just great." He munched appreciatively. "Adele never did stir-fry. Had to go out for that. By the way, we could use a fourth on Saturday. Tee time's eight." He looked at Gabe. "You interested?"

"Sorry, can't." Gabe scooped a forkful of rice and then stabbed a broccoli floret.

"Why not?"

"Gotta get a new car. Jenny's Jeep keeps leaking oil all over the garage."

"So, get it fixed."

"I'd rather she had a more reliable car."

George harrumphed and went to the kitchen for seconds.

They ate quietly for a few minutes. Jenny chewed slowly, thinking about her morning visit with the social worker Emily.

Jenny'd tagged along on a home visit where, ultimately, Emily had to recommend CPS remove an infant from the care of her drug-addicted mother.

The poor ten-month-old's arms were covered with bruises that her mother said came from falling down, and blisters covering her small bum went light years beyond Jenny's comprehension of diaper rash. The little mite sat, sucking her fist, staring at them through dull eyes during the entire interview.

Jenny sighed and took a sip of her wine. Good thing she'd gotten to interview Steve in the afternoon. His success story and photo session had been a welcome break that helped restore her equilibrium. After outlining it, she could see Steve's story was going to practically write itself. She'd be able to finish it tomorrow and have it ready for his approval shortly thereafter. Jenny sighed. Too bad her assigned story wasn't that simple.

"Jenny?" Gabe sounded muffled, like he was speaking from some distant place. "What're you thinking about?" he asked. "You're scowling."

She blinked at Gabe. "I...nothing. Just a rough day."

"How?"

"Research for the Woodward Home," Jenny said for George's benefit. "I've been doing a series of articles on this new extension of the Christ Child House and the whole foster care system."

"What a waste of time." George reached for another roll.

"Why do you say that?" Jenny asked.

"There shouldn't be any need for foster care. What is it, they take kids away from druggies and hookers, and then give them back when the parents are, so-called 'rehabilitated'? Stupid. They need ta' take the kids away forever." He shoved his food around the plate with abrupt motions.

"I'm sure it's a little more complicated than that," Gabe said.

"Sometimes they do," Jenny said, "but they still need foster homes for them."

"Put 'em with the kids' families. That's what family's for."

"What if they don't have family? Or the family can't take them?" Jenny asked.

George didn't look up from his plate, didn't slow in his eating. "They gotta take them."

Is that how you felt when Gabe needed a home? Did you only take him out of obligation? She longed to peek at Gabe to see his reaction to his uncle's careless words but didn't. She didn't want to make Gabe feel bad at his uncle's insensitivity.

"What if they can't? Somebody has to take care of those poor kids. And the kids aren't only from drug-addicted parents. Some kids are simply neglected, abused, or runaways avoiding the sickness at home. Society has a responsibility to these kids. It's not their fault they're born to a bad set of parents."

"So besides financial problems, what's the foster system's greatest challenge?" Gabe asked.

"They're in a crisis now because of lack of quality foster families. Studies have shown that foster families work best for these kids, but there's a critical lack of volunteers—especially for the older children."

"No wonder. Who wants to open their home to those screwed-up kids? Raising teenagers is hard enough without takin' on that extra problem," George observed matter-of-factly.

Jenny scowled at George. What a horrible thing to say. "I'm glad not everybody feels that way. Not all the kids have deep emotional problems either, George. In fact, you'd be a great foster father."

"Me?" He raised his eyes from his plate and stopped chewing. "Are you nuts?"

"No. Think about it. You raised Gabe, so you're experienced. You're semi-retired, which would give you more time to devote to a child. You're good with kids. You could adopt an older child. I interviewed three sweethearts just dying to be a part of a forever family."

"Without any emotional problems, eh?" His fork hovered over the plate, while he squinted at her through one eye and raised the other eyebrow.

"They might have a few issues, but they're getting counseling—on the State. You wouldn't have to pay for a thing. There's this one ten-year-old who's been there for three years."

"Why? What's the matter with him?"

Interesting that George assumed it was a boy. Maybe he was more open to the idea than she'd given him credit.

"His mother's a prostitute. Tommy took to the streets when he was only eight 'cause he hated what she did, especially after one of her johns tried to fondle him."

"And he's not too screwed up?" George snorted. He returned his attention to his meal and speared a hunk of sautéed chicken.

Well, who wouldn't be? But Tommy was a good kid who deserves a chance. "He has some anger," she allowed, "but he's getting help. He's a bright kid—really smart. With a family to love him, he'd thrive—I know he would."

"What about his relatives?"

"No idea who the father is. His maternal grandma's caring for his half-brother and sister. The grandma gave him over to child services; she claimed she couldn't afford him and the other two, but the caseworker suspects she did it to get him away from neighborhood gangs. He's a great kid, George. You should meet him."

"No, thanks."

"Just think about it."

"If this kid's so great, why don't *you* take him?" George challenged.

He voiced the question that'd been tickling Jenny's subconscious all afternoon. She wanted to help and felt she was in a position to do so. After nearly two years of marriage, she and Gabe were in a great place. Jenny'd carved a niche out in the family, and work was in a good flow. Life was pretty great. Maybe now was the time for them to take on more.

And how could you ask people to do what you weren't willing to do yourself? She turned to Gabe, thoughtful. He'd been surprisingly silent during this whole discussion. "Gabe? Would you want to meet Tommy?"

"Are you nuts?" George exploded. "I was kidding. It's not like picking a puppy from a pet store. You can't just send these kids back if it doesn't work out."

Hmm, maybe George wasn't as callous as he appeared.

Gabe watched her carefully, wary. "Are you serious?"

She slowly nodded. She hadn't really considered it in such concrete terms, but why not? Together they could save one kid. And Tommy was a terrific kid. And if that worked well, perhaps they could unburden his grandmother and adopt Tommy's brother and sister too. Children should be with their siblings. They could give three children a great home. Hope built within her. "Yeah, I guess I am."

Gabe swallowed his bite and took a sip of water. He stared at her. "I'm not sure you've given this a lot of thought. It'd be a huge commitment of time and energy."

"I know."

"Jenny, you're a remarkably generous person. It's what makes your work so good. You care, passionately."

Her heart dropped at his cautious tone. He was working his way up to a no. "But..."

He reached across the table for her hand. "But maybe you care too much. We can't get personally involved with every cause that comes along. Eventually it'll drain us. Think about it. This is the first time in three days we've been able to share dinner. Where would we find the time to integrate a child into our lives?"

Hope deflated, leaving her feeling defensive and combative. She pulled her hand away. "What if we had our own? I mean I know we're not going to, but what if I got pregnant?"

"God, Jen, that's totally different."

"Why?"

"Why?" Gabe echoed, incredulous. "It's *our* kid. Our child. Besides, it'd be a baby—not a child with a long history of emotional problems."

"Okay, what if it was born sickly," she shot back. "Say it had...spina bifida, or, cystic fibrosis, or, or, I don't know, some other serious problem. What then?"

He frowned. "Then we'd deal with it. It'd be our child, our responsibility. We'd cope."

"Because it would be our *responsibility*?"

He shrugged. "Well...yes."

She stared at him, softly asking, "But we can't cope with a stranger's child that's been discarded and desperately needs us?"

He was willing to take on the stress of a dying child because it belonged to them, but not Tommy, a sweet boy who only needed a stable, loving family and a little time and patience? Where was the logic in that? Tommy was a few years younger than Michael, but just as self-sufficient. A boy that age wouldn't place many demands on Gabe's time—mostly hers—and she could handle it.

He'd be in school six hours a day while she worked, and then he'd have after school activities that she'd drive him to, and then in the evenings, he'd be busy with homework leaving her and Gabe free. Maybe if Gabe met Tommy, he'd see that it'd be like having Michael around. He liked Michael.

Gabe bridged his fingers, deep in thought, before sadly shaking his head. "Taking care of our own sick child is dealing with fate. There's nothing we could have done to avoid that stress. Committing to foster care would be like shooting ourselves in the foot. It's just stupid."

"Stupid?" Jenny raised her eyebrows and leveled a cold stare at him. *Being foster parents would be stupid? She was stupid? Why not impulsive, too? Mom would probably agree.*

Or not. Her mother was very protective of children. She just might side with Jenny on this one.

"I'm already working at the clinic two days a week, and they could use me full time." Gabe said. "If using the clinic as a training ground for residents didn't create so much goodwill with the hospital administration, my partners would've kicked me out of the practice long ago. Between our careers, the clinic, the resident program, and the kids visiting, we spend little enough time alone together as it is.

"I like having the freedom to grab a few free hours when we can. We need that time." He sighed and took her hand. "Look. I'm sorry, Jen. I'd like to help. But we can't get involved with every tragedy you write about."

"Finally, someone with some sense," George said, making Jenny wish they'd had this conversation in private. "No kids—your own or other people's. Now *that's* smart."

"But that's not to say I don't agree that *you'd* make a great foster parent Uncle George," Gabe said. "You should think about it."

"*Me?*" George raised his eyebrows and grunted. "Where can I send a check?"

Chapter 17

Fall set in unusually early this year with the cold causing trees to shed their leaves in a bright array of browns, reds, oranges, and yellows, mid-September. Ted and Alex had been back at school for three weeks, and life settled down into a predictable pattern.

Saturday morning, Jenny raked the leaves while Ritz either watched or raced through the huge piles she made. She swiped the bangs out of her eyes; she needed some bobby pins. Her hair had grown out already, making a respectable ponytail, but if she was going to keep the bangs, she needed to get them trimmed. They were driving her nuts. Fifteen minutes later, bangs pinned back, Jenny leaned against her rake and surveyed the yard.

She didn't mind raking but despised bagging them, which was why a half-dozen piles heaped like enormous bright anthills littered the front lawn. When there were no renegade leaves left to corral, Jenny decided she needed a lemonade break before bagging. Maybe by the time she finished, Gabe would be back from the hospital and could help her.

She brightened. Maaaybe, she could pay Michael to bag them. He always needed money and it'd give her a good excuse to spend a little time with him. She'd call Mom if Gabe didn't show up soon.

Once inside, Jenny decided it was close to lunch and she should eat before bagging. Then, the dishwasher needed emptying, and the dog pen cleaning, and...then she ran out of legitimate procrastinating jobs. She picked up her phone and called home, but nobody answered. She dialed her mom's cell, scowling when it went to voicemail. "Nobody's ever around when you need them."

Well, that left...her. Dang. Jenny dragged an empty garbage can and a roll of large black plastic bags down the driveway just as Alex pulled in.

Saved. A good stepmother would put her child's needs first. She'd be willing to forgo finishing this job, if she had to. Or she could get Alex to help. She snorted. *Fat chance.*

Jenny tied the bag shut and blew stray strands of hair from her face before greeting her stepdaughter with a big smile and a hug. "Hey, you. What're you doing here?"

"Came home for the weekend."

Suzy got out of the backseat with a baby perched on her hip. He looked so bundled up, Jenny doubted he could even wave his little arm. "Hi, Mrs. Harrison," Suzy said as she approached.

"Hi, Suzy."

"Suz wants me to go shopping with her, but the baby needs a nap." Alex slanted Jenny a sly look. "You wouldn't want to babysit for a few hours, would you?"

Not particularly.

"He'll probably sleep the whole time. Please, Mrs. Harrison?" Suzy begged.

Be responsible for that little guy? Jenny looked from the pleading faces to the drooling baby. "I haven't babysat in years."

"He's really good. He hardly ever cries, and I have an extra bottle in case he wakes up early—which he won't. He always takes a long afternoon nap."

"I don't know," she drew out, looking out over the yard. The leaves. Pasting a regretful look on her face, she turned to them.

"We'll finish the leaves for you before we go," Alex blurted out. "Besides, it's good practice for when you and Dad have a baby."

We're having a baby? News to me. Defeated, Jenny held out her arms, half hoping the baby would reject her.

For one long minute the baby stiffened in her arms. He studied her through solemn hazel eyes, then yawned widely, laid his head on her chest, tucked under her chin. Stuffing his pacifier in his mouth, he sighed.

"See. I told you he was tired," Suzy said.

Okay, she could do this. She might not want kids, but she was certainly capable of babysitting one little guy for an afternoon. How hard could it be? She'd put him down someplace safe out of Ritz's reach for a nap... "I don't have anywhere for him to sleep."

"How about Steve?" Alex asked. "I've seen Sophia sleeping in a Pack 'n Play under the tree."

"Pack 'n Play?" She frowned at Alex. "How do you even know what that is?"

"Suzy."

Of course. "Okay. I'll ask Steve if we can borrow his playpen, while you two get to work."

At least she'd get the dang leaves done. Crossing through the hedge, the baby's mouth moved against her neck as he sucked his pacifier. His weight felt strangely comforting in her arms. She knocked on Steve's back door and tried to push it open but couldn't juggle the baby and door. Jabbing the doorbell, she tried to peer through the glass, wondering what was taking so long.

Opening the door, Steve pushed a pencil behind one ear, folded arms across his chest, and leaned against the door jam. A slow, broad smile lit his face. "Congratulations. I didn't even know you were pregnant."

She pushed by him. "Funny, Grant. Do you have a playpen I can borrow?"

He ducked his head to get a better look at the sleepy baby. "Cute kid. What's his name?"

"I don't know. I'm doing Alex a favor."

"Getting in practice?"

"Why does everyone keep saying that? We're *not* having kids."

Steve frowned. "Why not?"

She shifted the baby in her arms. Now was not the time to go into that. This kid was getting heavy, and he was slobbering all over her neck. "Do you have a playpen or not?"

"Sure, Annie leaves one here. I'll get it."

The baby heaved a big sigh, and the pacifier fell out of his slack mouth, hitting her arm before the floor. With one hand, she smoothed his downy blond hair and shifted him to see if he was still asleep.

She studied his little bud lips, fat cheeks, and down-swept lashes, remembering Michael at this age. He looked so adorable; she couldn't help pressing a kiss on his smooth forehead that felt as soft as it looked. He must have just had a bath because he smelled of baby shampoo and sweet baby.

Steve returned, carrying a rectangular thing with a handle.

He took in the sleeping baby and automatically bent to pick up the pacifier.

"Great." She nodded at the folded package. "That's a playpen?"

He passed her and held the door open. "Come on, I'll set it up for you."

He assembled the playpen in the study. Suzy brought in the baby's supplies and settled him in it with his favorite soft blankie and stuffed monkey. She popped a bottle in the refrigerator, showed Jenny where diapers and extra outfits were located in the backpack diaper bag, and left her instructions as if she were an old pro at leaving her baby, then breezed out the door.

Shell shocked, Jenny caught up with the girls as they piled in Suzy's car. "What time will you be back?"

"A couple of hours."

Okay. Two hours wasn't that long. "Staying for dinner?"

"Nope, but thanks. Mom's taking us out."

Of course she was. How come Judith got the fun part and she got stuck babysitting? Judith was probably working. *I guess heart surgery trumps yard work and babysitting duty.* Jenny swung around. "What's his name?"

"Adam."

"Okay. Have fun, girls." Jenny waved them away. Turning, she caught sight of Steve crossing back through the hedge. "Hey! Steve, wait. Where're you going?"

Frantic to catch him, Jenny sprinted forward, tripped over Ritz, and went careening into him. Clutching his shoulder, she nearly knocked Steve off his feet to avoid putting her full weight on the yelping, scrambling dog. He grabbed her by the waist, plastering her against him before getting a solid grip and firmly righting her.

"Sorry." Trying to sound nonchalant, she asked. "Soooo. Where're you going?"

"Home."

"What're you doing?"

"Work."

"Oh." She seized on an idea to bring him back over to her house and the sleeping baby. "I was going to make cookies. Want some?"

"No, thanks."

"How about a beer? I could make some of that hot artichoke dip you like."

He frowned. "It's only two, Jen. What's the problem?"

"Nothing. No problem. Why would there be a problem? I...just felt like company."

"Sorry, I've gotta get back to work." He turned and left.

Well, she huffed; he couldn't get away fast enough. Feeling slightly rejected, Jenny walked back inside, careful not to let the door slam. Was Steve mad at her? All she'd wanted was a little company. It wasn't like she asked him to babysit for her. She wasn't a total novice with babies. She'd cared for Michael. A decade ago.

Maybe the baby would sleep the whole time the girls were gone. She tiptoed into the study and found Ritz stretched out in front of the playpen. The dog lifted her head and slapped her tail on the carpet in greeting but didn't get up. Jenny muted her cell and unplugged the house phone so its ringing wouldn't waken Adam.

She tried to write, but couldn't focus on her article. It must be lack of practice that had her hovering over him. But he was so dang cute. Jenny finally gave up trying to work and settled in next to the playpen.

After a long hour, Ritz bounded to the garage door, barking her loud, welcome home woof. Jenny chased her, whispering, "Ritz, *be quiet*. No bark!" Jenny grabbed her muzzle and held it shut. "Shh! You're gonna wake the baby."

Darn. The baby couldn't possibly have slept through that racket. Jenny hurried back to the study where he lay whimpering, looking around at the strange room through wide, curious eyes.

Ritz trotted back into the study, ears cocked, tilting her golden head as if trying to understand this new little creature. Jenny lifted him and gently patted his back. She glared at the dog. "See what you did? Big mouth."

Gabe found them, gave her a kiss, then braced a hand on the baby's back and smiled. "Who's this?"

"Adam, Suzy's baby. Alex stopped by for a visit, and somehow I got stuck babysitting."

"The yard looks great."

"Had to get something out of the deal." She reached into the diaper bag, pulled out a fresh diaper, and handed both it and the baby to Gabe. "Here, change him while I warm his bottle, please."

Gabe backed away and shook his head. "No thanks, I've changed more than my share of diapers, but I'll warm the bottle for you."

Jenny stuck her tongue out. She followed Gabe to the kitchen and spread the baby's blanket on the kitchen table and changed his dirty diaper. Gabe took the bottle out of the fridge and put it in the microwave for ten seconds. When the timer chimed, he took the bottle out, shook it before dribbling some milk on his wrist to check the temperature. He popped it back in the microwave for a few seconds.

Taking advantage of Gabe's empty hands, Jenny thrust the clean baby at him. If she needed practice for the children they weren't going to have, so did he. "Hang on to him while I take this to the garbage. I don't want it smelling up the house."

Or maybe he didn't. Jenny came back inside to find Gabe handling Adam like a pro. He bounced the little guy on his lap while telling Jenny about his day, all the while smiling and looking at the baby, letting him think Gabe was talking to him. *That must be how he was with Ted as a baby.*

And the baby responded to Gabe, too, as if they'd always been great buddies instead of strangers. Were all babies that amiable? Jenny scrubbed her hands, dried them, then retrieved his bottle from the microwave. She tested on her wrist like Gabe had. Lukewarm. Good enough.

Bottle in hand, Jenny watched Gabe entertain the infant until Adam noticed his food and nearly lunged out of Gabe's arms in an attempt to get his meal. Intrigued by Gabe and the baby, she handed him the bottle. He settled Adam in his lap and tucked the soft cloth diaper she gave him under the baby's full chin like an expert.

Arms folded across her chest, she leaned against the doorjamb. "You really changed Alex and Ted's diapers?"

"Sure. Judith and I both worked. We had a nanny during the day, but at night I gave the kids baths while Judith did the dishes."

Of course. Gabe would have been an involved father—even before it was commonplace. Jenny sat at the table and watched. Gabe took the bottle from the baby, sat him up and patted his back. After a loud belch that had to have felt good, he settled him on her lap for the rest of his feeding. "Your turn."

Jenny tucked the baby in the crook of her arm as Gabe had done, slipped the napkin under his chin, and held on as dimpled miniature hands grabbed the bottle and crammed it in his mouth.

There was a perfunctory knock at the back door, and Steve let himself in. "Hey, Gabe. You came back to rescue her?"

"Did she need rescuing?"

Steve watched her feed the baby with an intense look on his face. Jenny checked the bottle to make sure the baby wasn't sucking air.

Nope, she was doing it right. So why was Steve staring at her as if she was performing the most fascinating feat? She returned his look with raised eyebrows.

He smiled. "See, nothing to it." Then turned to Gabe. "She was nervous about babysitting, so I took a break to check on her."

"Nervous?" Gabe looked at Jenny.

"I don't do this all the time like he does," she grumbled.

"It's like riding a bike. Babies don't change."

Steve stretched his rigid neck muscles. He obviously wasn't needed here. "Everything looks under control." Gabe was home and Jenny was preoccupied with the baby. "I've got to get back to work."

"Got something interesting?" Gabe asked.

"Not really, but it's my own case. See ya." Steve waved over his shoulder as he left.

Once in his house, Steve let out a deep breath and fell into the leather recliner. He stared out the window into the darkening evening. A light snapped on in the Harrison kitchen. Jenny entered the room, and Gabe followed with the baby.

Gabe took a stool and sat the baby on the counter, while she took a brown glass bottle, probably a beer, out of the refrigerator. Jenny looked at man and child with an indulgent, tender look, even he could identify from this distance. She kissed Gabe, and then handed him the drink.

Stomach churning, Steve swiveled away from the touching domestic scene to frown at his cold empty room. He should've stayed away. She'd been fine without him. Gabe helped her. But he'd been drawn across the driveway by a strange undeniable force he'd been afraid to even suspect was Jenny.

No, it couldn't be her. Jenny was, Jenny. One of his best friend's wives. His bud; Jenny. Who he'd always thought of as a little sister. This sudden nervousness and compulsion, to be with her was stupid—and annoying.

He'd tried to work but ended up watching the clock for fifty-six endless minutes. His instinct was to stay the hell away from her until these weird feelings passed, but that was stupid. It was *Jenny*, for God's sake.

Angry at his preoccupation, he'd decided to test himself by going back over there. He had to be imagining things. He didn't have feelings for Jenny—not intimate feelings. That was ridiculous. But he did.

Standing there, staring at her cuddling the baby on her lap, he must have looked like an idiot. Corny as could be, the image of her and the baby reminded him of pictures he'd seen of Madonna and child.

When Annie held her kids, he never got these melting feelings, making him want to hold both woman and child close to protect them. Why *Jenny*? Damn it. She was no Virgin Mary, yet she possessed a goodness and innocence that entranced him. Damn. There was nothing innocent about these new feelings for Jenny.

Are you fucking kidding me? Why her? Not her. He bolted out of the chair. With clenched fists, he paced from the kitchen, back to the fireplace in the family room.

Earlier when she fell into him, she'd felt so soft and good in his hands the few seconds before he'd pushed her away.

She tripped on the dog, you fool. You shouldn't have even had her in your arms, and you certainly shouldn't have liked it.

But he did. Damn him to hell, he *had* liked it.

He sat and leaned forward to brace his head between stiff arms. His fingers curled into his hair, pulling hard. *Fuck. Fuck. Fuck!*

It had to be a mistake. He couldn't love Jenny—not like that. He was *not* in love with Jennifer Harrison. But the more he repeated the mantra, the more his stomach churned and his heart burned in denial.

Damn. How'd this happen? When'd it happen? He couldn't pinpoint a single event, and no matter how hard he tried, he couldn't erase the memory of her body pressed against his and his ready response to her. He wanted her.

You jerk. Douchebag. She's your fucking friend's wife. What's wrong with you?

Luckily, Jenny hadn't seemed to notice anything had changed. That would've been the ultimate humiliation, for her to realize his infatuation. Worse yet, if Gabe noticed; what a mess that would be.

He looked back out the window into the Harrison kitchen, searching for Gabe, as if Gabe could have suddenly sensed Steve's lust for his wife and was crossing the drive to pummel the hell out of him. He almost wished for it. He deserved a good beating.

Alex and her friend walked toward the side door, with Jenny and Gabe trailing behind. Gabe stood on the landing with his arms wrapped around Jenny, warming her, while seeing his daughter and her friend off.

Wife, daughter, son. Gabe had it all. Ritz chased the car, barking. Gabe even had a dog.

Steve could get a dog. But he could *not* get Jenny.

He'd just have to get over her. Jenny was married to his friend, and there was no way he'd ever betray a friend. He wasn't that guy, and there was no way he'd ever put a woman in that position.

Okay. Okay. Not a big deal. Don't panic. She's off limits, and that's the end of it. Whatever you thought you felt, you didn't. You don't love Jenny; she's your friend. It's that simple.

Annie's single. She's available. She's sexy and sweet, and you love her kids. Work a little harder there, dude. She might be a good match for you. Introduce her to Mom and see what she thinks. Dinner. Great idea. Yeah. He sat back and wiped sweaty palms on his jean-clad thighs. *I got this.*

He'd been a professional athlete. He had willpower. He could do this.

He *would* do it. He was *not* that guy.

Chapter 18

"You look gorgeous tonight, Jen." Gabe's eyes narrowed on her face, thoughtful. "I like what you did with your hair."

Jenny hooked her high heels on her bar stool as the waitress slid napkins across the glossy table for Gabe's beer and her wine and glass of water.

"Thanks." Jenny was discovering a few remnant benefits of her earlier I-gotta-look-older craziness. Learning how to properly apply makeup came in handy when she felt like dressing up and wowing her hubby.

Tonight Jenny switched from her subtle brown eye shadow to a more obvious purple that brought out the blue in her eyes. She'd been back to the hairdresser to trim her bangs but decided to let her hair grow out for the winter. The layers had grown long enough for her to be able to braid the sides and pull the rest up in a loose top knot, allowing a few wisps to trail down.

She wore a dark sweater dress that comfortably hugged her curves and hit mid-thigh, showing off a good portion of leg. Though Jenny wasn't as pleased with her choice in footwear as she was her dress, makeup, and hair. No doubt these pretty red pumps made her legs look good, but dang, wearing them was like walking around on tiptoes.

"So what are we celebrating?"

Jenny took a sip of her cabernet. "Steve won his wrongful death suit case. And I'm celebrating turning in the last foster care article." She sighed and put the wine glass down. "I'm so glad it's done."

"I bet. You put a lot into that series."

Jenny nodded, then sighed. She was pleased with her final efforts, but the experience still left her feeling raw. She wanted to help, but Gabe was right. First it'd be Tommy, and then another, and another. There'd be no end 'cause Jenny wouldn't be able to turn away a single child in need. Where would she draw the line? How?

Three giggling girls huddle talking as they passed, bumped Jenny's back. "Oh, sorry," the redhead threw over her shoulder as they headed for the bar.

"No worries," Jenny said to her retreating back.

Gabe put a hand around her shoulders and leaned close. "Jen, I'm sorry we couldn't help."

"I know." She fiddled with the paper napkin under her wine glass. "I tried to come up with a way to make it work, but we can't. To do it right, we'd have to give up my job or yours at the clinic, or our time together. Helping these kids would be a full-time job."

And I'm too selfish to give up my career and stress our marriage.

She looked at him with raised eyebrows. "But we would've been good at it."

"We would've been *great*." He pulled her close, hugging her.

Jenny sighed, wishing she could erase her memories of Tommy sitting alone on his bed in the small room he shared with another foster child, a two-year-old baby boy. No computer, models, books, baseball mitts, or stuffed animals cluttered his space. He didn't have any—space or possessions. Even the clothes he wore were cast-offs.

"They're so damn needy and lovable."

"Your articles will help. You're such a passionate writer, readers won't be able to help feeling your frustration, concern, and affection for these kids. You'll reach a lot of potential foster parents who will have the time and patience to help them." His face brightened. "Instead of helping one boy, you'll be saving, maybe dozens. That's quite an accomplishment, lady." He brushed his warm hand over her back.

"I suppose." She looked at her watch. "Do you see Steve? It's not like him to be late."

Jenny wiggled her feet in the restricting shoes and considered kicking them off, but perched barefooted on this high stool, with her red pumps lying on the ground beneath her would be gauche.

Gabe put down his beer, leaned forward, then sat up straight to peer around the packed bar. "He just walked in."

She looked at the door to where Steve scanned the crowd. "I'll get him." Jenny eased off the stool, turned, and collided with a solid body. Something bounced off her chest and fell onto the floor.

"Oh, Lord. I'm sorry." A lady pressed an infant that looked to be a little younger than Adam to her chest as she tried to catch the diaper bag sliding down her arm.

"My fault. Are you okay?" Jenny caught the handle and resettled it on the mom's shoulder. The little girl, dressed in the cutest little white romper with tiny rosebuds all over it, stared at her through huge violet eyes. A matching rosebud headband encircled her tiny head.

Jenny reached down and picked up the pacifier. She dipped it in her unused water glass. The baby's face split into a heart-melting smile Jenny couldn't possibly ignore.

She smiled, cooing, "Hi sweetie."

The baby's grin widened, then she noticed her pacifier and she started kicking and reached for Jenny's hand. Jenny handed it to her, expecting to have to pick it up off the floor again, but the little mite popped it into her mouth, tucked her head beneath her mom's chin, and studied Jenny as the pacifier wiggled up and down.

"Thank you so much," the mom said. "Guess this wasn't the smartest place to meet my husband."

"Probably not," Jenny grinned. "She's a cutie. How old?"

"Ten months—I know she looks younger; she's small for her age."

"Well she's adorable." Turning, Jenny saw Steve walking toward them, so she slipped back onto her stool.

∾ ∾ ∾

Steve wove his way through the crowd to the table where Gabe and Jenny sat huddled together. Their heads nearly touched in an effort to hear each other in the noisy bar. Gabe had one arm casually draped across Jenny's back in a light embrace. Steve suppressed twinges of resentment. The man had a right to put his arm around his wife. *And you had no business even noticing, let alone feeling irritated.*

As they spotted him, Jenny's face lit in a welcoming smile that soothed his ego. Gabe stood and slapped him on the back. "Hey, congratulations."

"Thanks." Steve ordered a gin and tonic from a passing waitress, then sat at the small round table. Pulling closer, his knee knocked Jenny's thigh an instant before he jerked his leg away. "Sorry."

Jenny grinned. "So tell us. Were the bosses impressed? This makes two in a row. They had to be happy about that."

He nodded and thanked the waitress for his drink. Taking a fortifying sip of the tangy cocktail, he pursed his lips and grinned. "They're not offering to make me a partner yet, but they were pleased."

Jenny raised her glass. "May this be the beginning of many more successes."

"Many more," Gabe agreed as they clinked glasses. "So now maybe you'll have time to go out on the boat with us? You and Annie."

Steve glanced at Jenny. "Maybe. Annie gets sea sick."

"Has she tried a Scopolamine patch? Ted's had great results with that," Gabe said.

"Probably. Her ex's family owns Fischer's Marina. He's in all the big races. You'd think she'd have tried everything."

"I've got some at the house. She can give it a try."

"Or you can come without her," Jenny said. "It's not like we've got many more days left." Jenny looked beyond his shoulder. "But not 'til you review your article again. After I edit it one last time—," she looked to the right, then after a few seconds...back at him, "—to, um...include your latest coup."

Steve followed her gaze to a waitress moving through the crowded room with difficulty. Her black apron only covered the front of her large, rounded belly, and she wove through standing people and close-set tables with a ready hand out, like a running back evading a tackle. He watched her twist sideways to put drinks on the table because she couldn't fit in the space between people.

Face flushed, the waitress took frequent deep breaths and arched her back, clearly uncomfortable, but she still managed a warm smile for her customers. *Tough way to make a living, especially when pregnant.*

He turned to Jenny. "Know her?"

Jenny tore her gaze away from the waitress to frown at him. "Who?"

"The waitress."

"No. You?"

"No." *But I haven't been staring at her, following her every move.* "But I'll have another drink when she comes this way. Your piece was great; don't change a thing. Where'd you get the shot of me and the kids?" he asked. Jenny'd included a picture of him roughhousing on the lawn with Josh and Sophie.

"I took it one afternoon from my study with my new telephoto lens. I should have been working." She slid him a stern glance. "But I have this neighbor who creates quite a disturbance every now and then."

"You never showed it to me."

"I was saving it as evidence in case I ever need to get you evicted," she teased. "Actually, I wasn't sure you'd want to use it. You'll have every single mother within a fifty-mile radius hunting you down now that they know you're good daddy material."

"Like that's not going to happen once your article's out?" Gabe asked. "Handsome, successful, baseball jock, forced into early retirement makes good as a lawyer," Gabe recapped.

Great. Just what I need.

"That's okay. I'll protect him." Annie materialized at Steve's side. Her short print skirt and peach tank top showed off a dark tan acquired from hours spent in the pool with the kids. Her blonde-streaked curly hair was a bit damp from a recent shower, and she smelled fresh and clean as she leaned on his shoulder.

"Hey, you made it. I wasn't sure you got my message." Steve stood, gave Annie a quick kiss before settling her on his stool next to Jenny and taking the seat next to Gabe. Hopefully Annie's presence would dispel this new restlessness he felt around his friends.

"Ryan was late *again*. My ex—" She glanced at Gabe and Jenny. "I swear he does it on purpose. Stuffs the kids with popcorn and ice cream and gets them all wound up and then hands them back to me. I don't know what I was thinking having kids with that man when he's still a kid himself." She blew out a deep breath, then smiled brightly. "So what'd I miss?"

Ryan was a convenient excuse. From what Steve could tell, the guy was okay. Annie was chronically late for everything.

"We were talking about Jenny's article on me." Steve turned to Gabe. "What'd you think of it?"

Gabe smiled proudly and rubbed his wife's neck. "One of her best. *People Magazine's* expressed some interest, too. It'd be a huge boost to Jen's career if they actually bought it."

Eyebrows raised, he turned to Jenny drawing out the title, "*People*? Not bad, kid."

"That's great, Jenny." Annie leaned close and put a hand high on his thigh. "I could use a margarita, sweetie."

Jenny's gaze followed Annie's hand before shooting him a meaningful glance that made him feel like a teenager caught with his pants down.

"*I* see you as the cover story," Jenny said with mock superiority, then laughed. "Don't know if *People* sees it as cover material, but I do."

Steve covered Annie's hand and moved it to his knee. Twisting on his stool, he signaled the waitress. "Dream big. Never hurts."

"That's what I've been telling her," Gabe said.

Jenny leaned forward. "Would you do a cover shoot, if they asked?"

He narrowed his eyes and looked sideways at her. He'd had his share of photo sessions while playing ball—not his favorite thing to do.

"Come *on*. It's *People*," Jenny wheedled.

"Of course he'll do it." Annie moved closer and trailed her fingers through the hair at the nape of his neck. "It'd be fun. Who wouldn't love all the attention?"

Me. He'd had enough press attention to last a lifetime. "You'd owe me."

"Fine." Jenny laughed. "I'll owe you."

Steve shifted in his seat, uncomfortable at Annie's uncharacteristic public display of affection. Behind Annie's back Jenny smirked, but when he stared at her, she widened her eyes in innocence and nodded at the approaching waitress. "Margarita."

Their waitress came by, bumping into Jenny's back with her distended stomach. "Excuse me."

Jenny smiled. "'S all right. When're you due?"

"Six weeks. I usually don't work the bar—too crowded for me to get around with this big belly." She patted her stomach. "But we're really short staffed tonight. Can I get you anything else? An appetizer?" She looked around the table.

"I'm fine," Jenny said.

"How about some calamari?" Annie asked, leaning into him.

Steve shifted away. What was with her? If Annie leaned any closer, she'd be sitting in his lap. Annie wasn't the demonstrative type, so why was she constantly pawing him tonight?

The pager vibrated, dancing on the table as red lights chased around the square.

Thank you, God. "Table's ready." He turned to Gabe. "Take the girls in. I'll get this."

Thankfully, Gabe didn't argue. Paying for drinks was a small price to pay for getting a break from the women. Steve handed his credit card to the waitress as he watched the trio thread their way through the bar. Annie was in the lead, naturally. Jenny lagged behind—probably the heels slowing her down, but damn they were worth it. Showed off her shapely long legs to perfection.

His gaze immediately shifted to Annie's tight skirt. He'd always been more a butt man. Steve signed the receipt, picked up Annie's drink and went into the restaurant. Gabe and the girls were in a booth to the right.

"One margarita on the rocks, no salt." Just like she liked it. Steve slid into the seat next to Annie.

"Thanks, sweetie."

"Hey, have you been to the Village lately and seen the great back-to-school display Annie made for the Gymboree windows?" Steve asked Jenny and Gabe.

They shook their heads.

Steve smiled and rubbed Annie's back. "Tell them about it. It's really great."

"Really? What'd you do?" Jenny asked.

"Nothing groundbreaking, really."

"She's being modest. She put backpacks on the older kid mannequins—displaying their new backpack line, then had them pushing a double stroller with babies as if they were walking to school." He smiled at Annie. "You packed a lot of product into that scene."

Gabe and Jenny exchanged a quick look like they didn't know what to say.

"I put another little girl skipping off to the side. Took me forever to figure out how to get that pose," Annie said.

"I'll bet," Jenny said.

"It's harder than you'd think," Annie agreed.

The conversation fell into an awkward silence. Gabe opened his menu. "So what're you all going to have?"

After they ordered dinner, Annie regaled them with stories of Josh's first week at first grade, then complained about unreasonable patrons she'd had to put up with, then went on about a fashion show she was organizing for some women's league. Steve tuned her out and let his mind wander to the football games this weekend. It was the beginning of the season, and he had a pretty good line-up this year. He had a real shot at winning for once.

"OMG—you should totally do it." Annie clutched his arm. "Please?"

Steve looked sideway and took a sip of his gin and tonic. "Do what?"

"Model for my fashion show."

Steve swallowed hard, to keep from spewing his drink all over the table. "You're kidding, right?"

"Please? It would be *such* a draw if we could advertise that the Tiger's pitcher, Steve Grant, would be modeling for us. Oh my God, what a coup." She clapped her hands, gleeful.

"Ex-pitcher and no."

"You all right over there?" Jenny asked, her eyes twinkling.

He scowled, sending her a promise of retribution. Jenny didn't even have the decency to attempt to conceal her amusement. At least Gabe hid a smile while he finished his beer.

"Plea—" Annie begged.

"Not a chance."

"But it's for charity," she whined.

"No." He shook his head. "Why don't you ask Jenny?"

Annie frowned and wrinkled her nose. "We've got plenty of women."

"Then Gabe. He's a well-respected surgeon and philanthropist."

"But not a model," Gabe said. "No, thanks. I'll write a check."

Nodding, Steve looked back at Annie. "Me, too. I'll make a donation."

"We'll see," Annie said.

The waitress efficiently cleared the table. "Anybody save room for dessert?"

"I'm stuffed," Jenny said.

"None for me either." Annie put a hand on Steve's arm and gave him a coy look. "Not if I want to fit into that darling little dress I got for next week."

"Have whatever you want, you look amazing," Steve said.

"Awww, you're such a sweetheart." She turned to Jenny, gushing. "What a charmer."

Jenny opened her mouth, then closed it, probably biting back a sarcastic quip. "He's something, all right."

"Just the bill, please," Gabe said.

While Gabe got their coats, Annie had the valet get her car. Steve tipped the valet and, conscious of Gabe and Jenny waiting for him, gave Annie a lingering kiss and a promise to call her tomorrow.

He rejoined Jenny and Gabe, and together they walked down the street to where they'd parked their cars. "That was fun."

"Uh huh," Jenny said.

Steve walked past his Mustang to accompany them to Gabe's wagon. "I'm not going to be able to make Sunday's game, but Andrew, Don, Claire and Dan, Liam and Anne will be there."

"What? Why?" Jenny asked.

"I've got this thing with Annie."

"Modeling?" Jenny's eyes grew wide. "You're going to a *fashion show* instead of football?"

"*No.*" He reared his head back. "God, no. I promised Annie I'd go to a friend's wedding with her. Ryan's going to be there, and she thought it'd be awkward to show up without a date, so I said I'd go."

"Who gets married on a Sunday afternoon?"

"Jen, let it go." Gabe opened the car door and handed Jenny inside. He rounded the car. "Have fun."

Steve waved them off and turned toward his car. *I'm sure going to try.*

Chapter 19

Monday morning blahs, that's what this was, on Wednesday. Jenny had gotten up, fed Ritz, and let her out while her coffee was brewing, then booted up her computer. She'd dressed, checked her email, then fixed coffee, the way she liked it with a generous splash of chocolate caramel creamer and returned to her desk.

She sat in her swivel chair and sipped coffee, while twirling in slow circles. Maybe she'd play hooky today and read a book. She hadn't done that in...ever. Or maybe it'd be warm enough for her to take the boat out. Perhaps that would help drive away this strange funk.

This morning, she was listless and totally unmotivated to do anything. It didn't make sense; she should be on the top of the world. Her fantasy team had won Sunday, maintaining her spot at the top of the division—God bless Peyton Manning, and though it'd stolen a chunk of her soul, Karen claimed it showed and was so pleased with Jenny's last foster article that she finagled a bonus for her from the powers that be.

Alex loved the care package she'd sent her and jabbered on and on about how much she was enjoying college. Michael stopped by the house after tennis practice most days for a snack and a visit before Mom picked him up. Life was good.

She had everything she'd ever dreamed of and more, but something was off. The feeling was so illogical, almost as if it were hormonal; but PMS had never felt like this; not quite irritable, but not her usual happy self either. Her mind skipped from one thought to the next, and she had this constant nagging sense she was forgetting something, like when she misplaced something. What was wrong with her?

Maybe I'm getting sick.

Jenny went downstairs, put her coffee cup in the sink, then meandered down to the dock. A sharp breeze blew her hair across her face. Hmm... It was past her shoulders in the back. Time for a haircut. No, she liked the comforting warmth, but she also liked it being shorter in the front. Oh, for God's sake, she couldn't even make up her mind about that.

Jenny plunked down on a large boulder near the dock. Their speedboat hung over the water looking lonely and empty. Over the summer, the kids had used it constantly, but with them back at school and winter approaching, it didn't get much use. Perhaps that was the difference. She'd gotten used to Alex and Ted coming and going and she missed them.

Could this be loneliness?

Being an integral part of the Donnatelli clinic, Gabe worked all kinds of weird hours, coordinating the resident rotation at the clinic. Some nights she ate alone three nights in a row. And Jenny hardly saw Steve at all anymore. Now that he'd proved himself at work, interesting cases kept him occupied.

Gabe's birthday was later this week, and they'd be together then. She'd planned a special dinner with all his favorite foods and a night of games if he wanted. Jenny sighed, it stank that Alex and Ted wouldn't be here for their dad's birthday, but at least Steve promised to come. Even better, Annie couldn't; she had a previous engagement.

Jenny knew Gabe was going to love the Fit Bit she'd gotten him—actually, she'd gotten four of them, one for herself, Alex, Ted, and Gabe. It synced up with their computers, so once they "friended" each other, they could share their daily stats and see how many steps they took each day. It was a perfect family activity these competitive Harrisons could enjoy doing together even while they were apart. Alex had loved the idea, hopefully Gabe will too.

Jenny stroked Ritz's soft long coat and sighed. "Guess it's you and me today, girl. And this mood."

When Jenny was out and about, she did observe one interesting phenomenon—pregnant women were everywhere. You'd think it had been a long hard winter when people had had nothing better to do than make babies. That, and little children. They were everywhere. But curiously enough, not next door so much.

Jenny glanced at Steve's quiet house. It'd been weeks since she'd seen Josh and Sophie next door. Shortly before they'd watched little Adam—the cutie.

Seemed silly now to think that watching the baby for a few brief hours had made her so nervous; she'd done fine. More than fine, she'd actually enjoyed it. Adam had only been with them one afternoon, but he'd felt good in her arms, a custom-made fit.

His little weight molded to her, and he'd smelled so dang sweet. Jenny pictured Gabe and baby as clearly as if it'd been yesterday. He'd been good with Adam, handling him so naturally. Wonder what he'd been like with Alex and Ted.

She smiled at the thought of Gabe cradling their child, and later, rolling around on the grass, wrestling with him the way Steve did with Annie's kids. Her hand froze halfway down Ritz's back.

Oh my God. I want a baby.

Her mouth dropped open. A baby? Really?

We should have a baby.

The thought didn't create a nervous lump in the pit of her stomach as it would have a year ago; it was okay. Better than okay, exciting. Her lips curved into a soft smile as Jenny pulled her knees to her chest and wrapped her arms around them. A baby. Really? The thought flitting around her brain, settled in her heart. Why not?

What would Gabe say? She'd told him she never wanted children, and he'd agreed. Hadn't he? Though they'd really never talked about it, she'd always said she didn't want children, and Gabe never contradicted her. Traitorous warmth squeezed her heart. He had Ted and Alex; he didn't want more. But she did.

Maybe she was hormonal and this longing would go away. Or maybe she was lonely. Yes, that could be it. Maybe the ache weakening her empty arms could be filled with lots of hugs for Michael. If she spent more time with her brother, this longing would disappear. It had to go away. She couldn't betray Gabe that way. He'd be blindsided.

She pictured him coming home from work one day. She'd give him a big kiss, saying, "Hi, honey, I'm so glad you're home. You know... I've been thinking... I've changed my mind. I'd like to have a baby after all. Can we have one? Please?"

He'd look at her with stunned, confused eyes, then glance toward the kitchen, asking, "What about dinner?" Poor love. She couldn't do that to him. Gabe deserved better. This baby fever would go away. Maybe it *was* just weird PMS.

Which would be cured by pregnancy, a little voice inside her whispered.

∾ ∾ ∾

Gabe settled back in the chair and spread the Sunday news before him. This was his first full day off in ten days, and it felt good to get up, go for his ride, shower and then crawl back into bed and make love to his wife instead of rushing off to work. Now *that* was the way to start a day.

Jenny buzzed around the kitchen, pulling food out of the fridge, preheating the oven, and emptying the dishwasher all to the soft background music of Frank Sinatra. Gabe spread the Sunday news out before him and sipped his coffee.

Handing him a tall glass of orange juice and champagne, Jen pushed his paper aside and sat in his lap.

"Mimosas. What're we celebrating?"

"Spending one whole entire day together." She tapped her flute against his and took a sip.

He would drink to that. The tangy, orange juice was sweet yet refreshing.

"You've been working so hard, I'm beginning to feel neglected—or suspicious." She raised an eyebrow. "Are you having an affair?"

Gabe set his glass on the table and pulled back to bring her face into focus. "And where would I find the energy for that?"

"Just making sure. I'd almost rather it be another woman; hard to compete with the adrenaline rush of saving lives."

Jenny seemed to be joking, but... He slipped a hand beneath her blouse to caress the soft skin above her jeans. Hair loose, barefoot and in jeans and makeup-free, the woman he fell in love with was back, yet something was off. She wasn't her usual carefree self.

He brushed the hair back from her temple and tucked it behind one ear. "You have no competition and saving lives isn't half the rush of making love with you."

Jenny flashed a smile. "Pretty words. But it'd be more convincing if you spent more time with me and less time at the other." She scowled and pushed off his lap. "Don't mind me, I'm being a clingy, whiny baby."

Gabe cocked his head. Jenny, clingy and whiny? Since when?

He watched her chop onions and mushrooms for their omelet. Uncle George's comment about doing whatever it took to keep this wife ran through his head. He hadn't pulled out his A game in a while—or his B game. In fact, he'd been so enamored with his project at the clinic that he'd pretty much put his marriage on the back burner.

It'd been months since he'd brought Jen flowers or even called her between cases just to hear her voice and see how her day was going. Or taken her out for ice cream. Once they'd moved into the house, Jenny'd taken over the grocery shopping, the cooking, been around for Alex, running the house... She'd freed him up from so many things that when his idea for including the Residents in the clinic had come along, he'd fallen back into old work habits.

Sure, they'd had to work through a few adjustment issues, but they'd figured it out and Jenny'd made a place for herself in the family. He watched her over the newspaper. She was feeling neglected, but was that all it was?

Jenny draped slices of bacon on a tray and popped it in the oven. She loved her career and was finally getting the recognition she deserved, but her job was flexible. His program was fairly well established. Perhaps it was time for him to delegate more. What'd he been thinking? With both Alex and Ted off at college, they should take advantage of the freedom. Maybe travel more.

Uncle George was right—which was an odd thought in itself. Taking advice from Uncle George about women. Hmm. Then again, Uncle George had had a great marriage. He might have been gruff and unyielding with other people, but he'd adored Aunt Adele and she him. Now that Gabe thought about it, they'd spent their marriage spoiling each other. And they'd been happy, pretty much to the day she died.

Jenny's phone tweeted. She dried her hands and picked up her phone. "Figures. Pshht." She tossed her phone onto the newspaper and cracked eggs into a bowl.

"What?"

"Steve's canceling on football again."

Gabe frowned. "He didn't say anything this morning."

In fact, Steve had been pretty quiet on their morning rides. Gabe assumed he was preoccupied with work, but maybe it was women trouble. He'd been spending a lot more time at work and with Annie. Jenny cracked the last egg and threw the shell into the sink.

Maybe you should, too—spend more time with Jenny.

"Who knows? Maybe princess Annie came up with a new job for him."

"You're still pissed about my birthday."

"Ya think?" She gave him the same, "well, duh," look he'd seen on the kids' faces.

"He canceled at the last minute and refused to say why. What could've possibly come up that he wouldn't have told us? A quickie with her?" Jenny beat the eggs until they were frothy and poured them into the skillet.

"Maybe he's in love."

Jenny rolled her eyes. "He's not in love with that twit. If anything, he's in lust."

Gabe glanced down at the paper, then lifted it to get a better look. A slow smile stretched his face. And then he began to chuckle.

"Must be. This is too good." He laughed harder. "This is great. Look." Gabe folded the page back and turned the paper around for her to see.

"Oh. My. God." Jenny covered her mouth, then came closer and took the paper from him. "Serves him right." Jenny slowly nodded. "I know *exactly* what to do with this."

The mischievous light in her eyes had him cocking his head. What could she possibly be thinking? What revenge was that beautiful brain plotting? Gabe pulled the paper back and tilted it toward the window to take another look. Yup, it was Steve all right. Standing on a fashion runway, driver in hand, he posed, modeling a golf outfit, complete with plaid pants and old-fashioned cap.

Gabe turned the page and chuckled. "Oh my God, you've got to be kidding." He laughed.

"What?"

"Whatever you were thinking about doing to Steve couldn't possibly be worse than this."

Spatula in hand, Jenny came closer. "What?"

"Did you read the caption? Not only did she dress him up like...like...*that* and make him parade around, but she auctioned him off, too!"

The picture on the next page showed Steve between two older women, with their arms linked through his, and Steve wearing the fakest smile Gabe'd ever seen. "Oh my God that's great. Jen, he's been punished enough." He held the paper up to her. "Look at that expression. It's priceless."

Jenny came over and laughed.

No wonder Steve had been so quiet and morose lately. Women trouble, in triplicate—Annie and his two new cougar lady friends. "I wonder if he's missing this afternoon to go on his date."

"A daytime date? No way." She pointed the spatula at the pictures. "For what they probably paid for him, they'll want a night on the town. Probably want to go clubbing, too, to show him off. Good." She nodded and went back to the stove. "He deserves it."

"No. Wearing that outfit was punishment enough. This is above and beyond." Gabe shook his head. *Poor dumb bastard.*

After brunch, Gabe did the dishes and cleaned the kitchen. Then they settled on the enclosed porch, where he gave Jenny a foot massage while they did the crossword puzzle together. The porch had been more a concession to Jen than anything he'd wanted, but now it was his favorite room in the house.

It got great light, yet the shade of a huge oak tree they'd worked hard to avoid damaging while building the addition kept it from getting too hot. Perched above the yard and lake, they had a wonderful view of the water, yet they'd landscaped it with large, colorful bushes to give them plenty of privacy. The gas fireplace was the finishing touch to create a cozy, comfortable room. Gabe had insisted upon the flat screen TV, yet they didn't often use it.

When they finished the puzzle, Jenny left to run errands. Gabe took advantage of this rare time alone to read the thriller Alex got him for his birthday, but within ten minutes, he drifted off to sleep.

Gabe jerked awake to Ritz's barking. Squinting, he sat up. "You need to go out, girl?"

He opened the sliding door and Ritz bolted out to chase the geese waddling through the yard. He lifted his wrist to look at the time. One-thirty? Shoot, they were going to be late. Moving through the dining room, he called out, "Jen? Ready to go?"

Jenny came downstairs wearing her lucky number eighteen Manning jersey. "Yup. Andrew texted me. They've got our table."

"Great." As they pulled out of the driveway, he glanced at Steve's house and hit the brake. His jaw dropped at the huge poster covering a large chunk of Steve's garage door. Gabe leaned forward and then slowly accelerated down the driveway, gawking at Jenny's handiwork.

"On every tree too?"

"And across his entire front fence," she said with a satisfied grin.

"Oh, shit."

Jenny had taken the photos in the paper and blown them up to varying size posters and plastered them all over Steve's property. His garage door. His front door. The tree trunks. The fence. Gabe pulled out into the street. The fire hydrant.

Holy shit, she doesn't mess around.

Gabe made a mental note to double the size of those flowers and have them delivered first thing in the morning.

∾ ∾ ∾

Failure. You are an undisciplined, weak-willed woman, Jenny Harrison.

Jenny sat on the back patio, rocking back and forth in the metal chair, like a kid rhythmically banging her head against a wall.

The longing for a child had become an obsession with Jenny over the past month. She'd tried, truly tried, to push the fixation to the back of her mind, determined not to selfishly change the rules of their marriage just because she decided she needed Gabe's baby to complete her. But she'd had little success.

Thoughts of a baby assaulted Jenny's defensive mental wall, hammering away until it cracked, allowing recollections and feelings to trickle to her consciousness, until her wall crumbled then burst, flooding every waking moment with thoughts of pregnancy and aching loss.

A baby now was right. They could do it. She could fill the hole in her heart with a new little soul, if Gabe was willing. Uneasiness prickled her conscience. He'd been supportive when she hadn't wanted children. He was happy with their life the way it was. He'd been adamant they couldn't foster children—would he find the energy and time for their child if she asked? How could she ask?

Jenny's gaze wandered next door. Steve was a man. He was Gabe's friend. He might be able to give her valuable insight into Gabe's reaction to changing her mind. He might know a good way to broach the subject and persuade Gabe.

He was a lawyer; manipulating—Jenny frowned, poor word choice. She didn't want to manipulate Gabe; she wanted to approach the discussion the best way possible to optimize her chances of a successful outcome. That was better. Getting people to agree with him was Steve's job. And he was good at it.

Slowly rising, Jenny wiped moist hands down her jeans, slipped her feet into her flip-flops, and crossed through the hedge. She had at least a half an hour before Gabe was due home. Plenty of time for a consultation. She knocked on Steve's door, and then turned the knob to let herself in.

"Hey, Grant? You home?"

No answer. Jenny padded through the silent house. "Steve?"

He was home; she'd seen him come in about an hour ago. Jenny passed the guest room on the way to the garage, thinking he might be working on his motorcycle, when she abruptly backed up and entered the bedroom. There she found Steve sprawled barefoot, face down across the bed.

His cheeks were flushed with sleep and his features relaxed. He lay with one big hand fisted beneath his chin and one bent leg pulled up toward his chest. Jenny sighed. *Not going to get any answers today.* Turning to leave the room, she jumped at the sound of his sleepy drawl.

"What d'ya want, Jen?" He rolled to the side of the bed, scratched his head, then rubbed the sleep from his eyes.

"I...it can wait," she fumbled, feeling awkward. "Go back to sleep."

He glanced at his watch. "Can't. Got to be at Annie's in an hour."

She backed out of the room as he stood. Barefoot, jeans, and wearing a worn navy polo shirt, Steve suddenly seemed intimidating. This was a bad idea, like her mere presence with him in this bedroom was a step over a line she didn't want to cross.

"Okay. Well...we can catch up later. Have fun tonight," she tossed over her shoulder as she rushed down the hall to the kitchen.

Steve hurried after her and grabbed her wrist, just long enough to halt her flight and make her face him. "Wait a minute. What's your hurry?"

"Ah..." Jenny shifted her weight from one leg to another. She folded her arms.

All of a sudden, this feels weird. I know things have been strained between us lately—not exactly sure why, I guess you're mad I don't like Annie, but I need a friend. I've got a problem and that's what we do. I whine to you, and you come up with some sage brotherly advice to make me feel better. But this isn't going to work. Something's wrong. It doesn't feel right and I can't talk to you—not about this. And that makes me so unbelievably sad. I've gotta get out of here.

The words raced through her head in a giant whirlwind, yet she just couldn't get them out. Jenny ducked her head and batted her eyes against hot tears.

Steve waited patiently, and she wished he'd look at something—anything—besides her. His waiting for an answer made her feel like a particularly ugly bug under a microscope, and it was hard to come up with a credible lie under such intense scrutiny. Finally she couldn't take it anymore.

"I want a baby," she blurted.

Well, that was tactful. Jenny peeked at him, sure he must be as shocked as she by her bald declaration.

Steve leaned back against the counter and crossed his legs at his ankles. Though he controlled his expression, he couldn't conceal the glint of amusement twinkling in his eyes. "Isn't that something Gabe should help you with?"

"That's the problem; I don't know how to tell him. I've never wanted kids. Before we got married, I told him I didn't want children."

"And now you do?"

Wincing, Jenny raised her head and nodded. "I know it's not fair, but I've been obsessed with it for months. I tried to talk myself out of it." She lifted slim shoulders. "But I still want a baby."

"So have it." This was her big problem? Wanting children seemed a natural marital progression, not cause for the misery lining Jenny's face.

"I told him I *didn't* want kids. It's not fair to change the rules now."

"Then don't."

"But I *want* a baby."

"So why're you telling me?" He tried to temper the impatience in his voice, but seriously, what did she expect him to do about it? "Gabe's the one you should be talking to."

"I can't. He doesn't want more children."

"You don't know that." Although Steve suspected she was right. His buddy was pretty happy with life the way it was; Gabe probably wouldn't welcome a change—especially not one of this magnitude. But he might. He adored Jenny, and if it was that important to her, he'd probably be willing to start over again. "Talk to him. Make him understand how important it is to you."

"I can't. He'd never understand."

"Why not?"

She scowled and looked away. "Because he thinks I'm good. I... Oh, forget it, you wouldn't understand." She turned away and rushed toward the door.

Oh, no. Not tears. Jenny never cried. Damn it.

Steve clenched his jaw. Her issue was personal; he didn't want to get involved. But she was upset. Jenny was his friend, and she'd come to him for help. She didn't know that her problem was scoring his heart, like dozens of painful paper cuts.

The woman he loved wanted to celebrate her love for another man, her husband and his best friend, by having his baby. She wanted to create a beautiful new life with her husband. It shouldn't hurt so much, but it did. It felt like somebody smashed his chest with a three-hundred pound sledgehammer and then left it over his heart to crush him. And she had no idea.

Taking a deep breath, Steve forced air into his lungs to push aside his pain and caught Jenny at the door. He wrapped a brotherly arm around her shoulders and redirected her toward the couch in the family room.

"What wouldn't I understand? I know you're not perfect, but what's your big faux pas?"

"You can't tell anybody. Not another living soul."

He held up his right hand as if being sworn in. "I swear."

She studied him carefully, frowning as she sized him up. "When I was fourteen, I got pregnant. Michael's my adopted brother—and my son."

Chapter 20

"Oh."

Brilliant response, numbnut. But Steve seemed incapable of anything more coherent. As faux pas go, that was a pretty good one. Jenny, a teenage mother? At fourteen? She'd always seemed so innocent and unworldly.

"Yeah, 'oh'." She rolled her eyes. "I was so naïve. Ridiculously young and stupid. Contrary to popular belief, you *can* get pregnant the first time—even doing it standing up in a lake."

Steve slowly nodded. "Good to know."

"Yeah. My mom and I may have had some issues, but it's *entirely* my fault. She sacrificed..." Jenny pursed her lips and slowly nodded. "She sacrificed a lot for me and Michael. My 'accident' screwed up the whole family's life for three years—at least.

"I mean, they'd always wanted more kids, but not enough to adopt when Mom couldn't get pregnant after me. So she threw herself into raising me and her career. She was in line for VP of HR at Merrill Lynch, but she gave it up because of me." She pursed her lips.

"So when I was ten weeks pregnant, Dad got a sudden transfer to San Diego. Mom found renters for our house, and we moved. She homeschooled me and when Michael was born, they adopted him, and voilà, I had a baby brother. It was two more years before Dad could get us transferred back."

Holy shit. Stuff like that only happened in the movies, not real life. How'd they pulled off a deception like that? "Not even the family knows? Your aunts and uncles?"

Jenny shook her head. "They thought Mom didn't let anybody know about her pregnancy because she was embarrassed and worried about having a healthy baby at her age—if she could even carry him to term." Jenny shrugged. "It made sense to them."

"What about the father?"

"Not in the picture. He and his parents wanted me to have an abortion."

"That must have been hard."

She shrugged. "Not really. Made the adoption easy."

Pregnant at fourteen and abandoned by the asshole boyfriend. Then she had the isolation of being homeschooled in San Diego before moving back. Geeze. "Must've been lonely. None of your friends knew?"

"Nope. Not friends, not family." She hesitated. "I didn't have any real friends. My situation was hardly conducive to making friends. We moved back to Grosse Pointe the middle of my senior year. Mom and Dad enrolled me in Liggett to finish out my senior year, hoping I'd make some friends and have a fresh start.

"It *was* a relief not having to worry about facing Michael's birth dad—luckily he'd been older than me and graduated the year before. But making friends when all the other kids had been bonded since pre-school and then everybody was going away to college..." she trailed away. Jenny looked at him and smiled. "It was hard, but it turned out okay."

Hard was an understatement. Interesting the lengths Jenny's family went to hide the truth. Children born out of wedlock were hardly unusual anymore. But all the subterfuge was necessary given that her parents adopted Jenny's baby, he conceded. That was hardly commonplace. No wonder Jen didn't have a lot of female friends.

"And Gabe doesn't know?"

"Of course not!" Her eyes widened in alarm. "And you can't tell him. He wouldn't understand." She leaned in, pleading. "I was a kid. It was a mistake. I mean, it *wasn't* a mistake 'cause Michael's a wonderful kid, but the pregnancy was a mistake. And abortion was out of the question. But Gabe would *not* understand."

Steve didn't know what Gabe would think of the story. Jenny was so sweet and bighearted. She was remarkably innocent for having endured such a life-altering experience. Why hadn't it made her cynical, bitter, or at least wary of men?

"I'm sure he didn't think you were a virgin when you married."

"No, but he wouldn't think that I'd been a teenage mother who gave my baby up for adoption, either." She sighed. "For a compassionate guy, and a doctor, Gabe's surprisingly intolerant of moral transgressions and lies—even lies of omission."

Steve sighed and sank down on the couch next to her. What a mess.

"It was hard pretending to be Michael's big sister, at least in the beginning." She blew out a deep breath. "God, turning him over to my mother in the hospital was the hardest thing I've ever done. I loved him before he was even born, but it was best for both of us.

"The only way I could deal with it was to convince myself that he *really* was my adopted brother. I never *ever* let myself think of him any other way or I would've gone crazy. But I remember what it was like to be pregnant. I remember Michael's first few days."

She frowned at him, tears thickening her voice. "I want that again. I can care for a baby now. I have a husband, and we could be a family. I want to be a mom, a real mother this time, but how can I convince Gabe without telling him about Michael?"

Steve hurt for the pain Jenny'd endured, yet was proud of her amazing, selfless love for her child. She'd put her baby's welfare first, an incredible feat for a teenager—for any woman. Why shouldn't she share this with Gabe?

Gabe was a good man. He was her husband. He loved Jenny. After hearing her story, Gabe couldn't help but think she deserved a baby. Besides, Gabe should know something this intimate about his wife. If she were his wife, Steve would want to know.

Steve looked sideways at her and held her teary gaze. "Tell him the truth. He'll understand."

"That I've been promiscuous and lived a lie for the past fourteen years?" She pursed her lips and shook her head. "I don't think so." She sniffled.

"He loves you."

"He *won't* understand. Gabe values my innocence and honesty," she said bitterly. "He'd hate me for not telling him sooner. Wouldn't you?"

"Me? I..."

I'd take you anyway I could get you.

Actually, a part of him felt a bit relieved that Jenny wasn't so damned perfect. It brought her down off that pedestal he and Gabe placed her on. Sure, he'd been shocked at first, but everyone made stupid mistakes as teenagers. Just not everyone had living reminders. And not everyone was strong enough to make it come out right.

"Does Michael know?"

"No." She shook her head. "I'm not sure he ever will."

He frowned. "He has a right to know. I'd want to know."

"Why? It's not like he's suffered any. He's had good parents, and I got to love him and watch him grow up. What'd be the point in telling him?"

"He has a right to know. It's his heritage. And he might want to look up his biological father one day."

"There's nothing to gain and everything to lose. He'd hate us. He'd feel betrayed. Think about it, the three most important people in his life have been keeping a secret of this magnitude from him, lying to him on a daily basis." She paused and bit her bottom lip. "We'll probably tell him when he's older, maybe when he's married and has a wife to love and support him.

"Maybe then he can understand and sympathize with the situation, and realize that we did what was best for him, and me—for all of us. But it's not just up to me. My parents have to agree."

That game plan made sense, too. "It's really none of my business, Jenny, but you should tell Gabe. He has a right to know, too."

"I *can't*. It's not my secret, it involves my whole family." She looked at him, pleading for understanding.

"You told me."

"Only so you'd help me find a way to convince Gabe."

Steve stiffened. His sympathy evaporated in that wounding instant. Jenny told him so he'd help her, not because she'd been compelled to share something that personal. His gut burned with jealous angst. He wanted to tell her that if Gabe didn't want to have a baby with her, she should leave him, and Steve would do his damnedest to get her pregnant—and love every second of it.

But she loved her husband. She loved Gabe, not him. Seemed they both had guilty secrets they'd never tell. Maybe she was doing the right thing with Michael after all. But damn, what she was asking of him wasn't fair. How could he get over her when she wanted his help with things like this?

"I don't know, Jen. I still think you should tell him."

"I can't." She turned away. "You're no help."

He stood up to put some distance between them, then turned toward her. "Well, what do you expect? I'm not a marriage counselor."

"I *thought* that as a man and Gabe's friend, you might have an idea about how to approach this."

"Well, you didn't like my idea, so you're on your own."

"Aren't you the snippy one?" Jenny stood.

"Look, I'm sorry I can't help you." He shoved a hand through his hair and looked at his watch. "Crap. And now I'm going to be late getting to Annie's"

"So?" She shrugged. "She's always late whenever we do anything."

Obviously, Jenny thought nothing of burdening him with her marital problems and then dismissing his concern about being late for a commitment. Granted, he knew she didn't like Annie, but still it rankled that she could so easily brush aside something that mattered to him.

Jealous and angry, Steve wanted to hurt her as she'd unwittingly hurt him. "I thought it'd be nice to shave and get cleaned up before I propose to her."

Jenny crossed her arms over her chest and cocked her head to the side. "Propose what?"

"What do men usually propose, Jen?"

"Sleeping together."

"Funny."

Her eyes opened wide as comprehension quickly followed by disbelief, set in. "You're going to marry her?"

Her shock was satisfying—in a sick sort of way. "She has something to say about it, but that's the general idea."

"Well, I hope you're getting a prenup."

He put a hand on his hip. "Like you did?"

Her mouth dropped open before she snapped it shut and crossed her arms and raised her chin. "That's different."

Steve hardened his heart against the hurt in her eyes at being compared to Annie. It wasn't really fair; he knew Jenny didn't care about money, certainly not like Annie did. But he needed her to back off. "It is?"

"Completely. You both have assets to protect, and Gabe and I were in love. You don't love Annie any more than she loves you."

"Oh really?" Jenny was really rattled. In light of the story she'd told him, her counseling him was pretty ironic. "So now you're an expert on love?"

"Anybody can see you're not in love. She's using you. She likes your money and status as an attorney. She uses you as a substitute father for her kids. And as for you..." Jenny frowned and put a glossy fingernail between her front teeth. "I'm not sure what you see in her besides her looks. Maybe she's good in bed," she muttered, almost to herself.

Steve's arms dropped to his side as his amusement flashed back to anger. "What?"

"She doesn't appreciate you. You can do so much better. Don't settle." Jenny moved closer and ran a hand down his arm in comfort, but her touch scorched his skin.

He yanked his arm away and took a step backward. He wasn't a charity case deserving her pity.

"You'll find the right woman. You have to be patient," Jenny said.

Be patient? Steve wanted to howl in frustration. He'd already found somebody, but he didn't think Jenny'd appreciate finding out who he loved the most, who he lusted after, who had stolen his soul.

Jaw locked shut, he took Jenny by the arm and marched her out the door before he said something to ruin both their lives.

Convincing Gabe to have a baby was her greatest worry—if she only knew. If she discovered the feelings he hid from her and battled daily for months on end, she'd know the meaning of problems. Complications. Guilt. She couldn't handle it. Hell, he couldn't handle it. Marriage to Annie *was* the answer.

Annie was beautiful, responsive, a good mother, and she wanted him. Steve could work with that. He had to try harder. And he needed more space from Jenny.

On the porch, Steve released her arm. "Go home, Jenny. Talk to your husband."

Jenny stubbornly stood her ground. "You don't really want to marry her. It'd be a big mistake."

Steve looked over her head, down the driveway to where Gabe pulled in. She wanted *his* baby. She wanted *him*.

Steve's resolve hardened. "Then it's my mistake."

He shut the door before she could argue further. Resting his forehead against the hard wood door, Steve closed his eyes. Maybe marriage to Annie was what it'd take to loosen Jenny's grip on his heart. Maybe then he could stop hating himself and learn to be happy again.

❧ ❧ ❧

Jenny slowly walked across the driveway. Steve was pretty testy for a guy about to propose to the woman he'd wanted to share his life with. He'd bitten her head off just because she pointed out the folly of marrying Annie. She'd done what any good friend would do.

Jenny passed through the hedge and crossed to where Gabe waited by his car.

Gabe smiled, hugged her close, and kissed the crown of her head. "What's up? You look like you've lost your best friend."

I may have. Jenny frowned. "Steve kicked me out of his house."

"What'd you do?"

Jenny pulled out of his arms and glared at him. "Why do you assume *I* did something?"

Smarter than to answer that, Gabe patiently waited for her answer.

"Steve's going to propose to Annie." Bewildered, a sense of loss swamped Jenny, replacing her earlier disbelief and anger. Like she'd thrown up before being hustled onto a tilt-a-whirl.

"And this is a tragedy, because..." Taking her hand, Gabe walked her around the house to the privacy of their backyard.

She scowled at him. *Really? You have to ask?*

"It's *Annie*. He doesn't love her, and she doesn't love him. She's just using him as a daddy for her children, she's stupid and shallow, and she's got a big ass. They're not right for each other." Jenny wound down.

"That's your mother talking."

Jenny's head whipped up and her eyes narrowed in battle. "What?" she drew out in a low voice.

"Sorry, but you're acting like your mother. Don't you think you're being a little presumptuous judging them unsuitable? Just because *you* don't like Annie, doesn't mean she's not right for Steve."

"I don't hate her," Jenny mumbled, as she dropped into a metal bouncy chair.

Gabe crossed his arms over his stomach and laughed loud and deep. "Oh, yes you do. Admit it; you'd be thrilled if you never had to lay eyes on her again. Annie's a little superficial, and self-centered, but she's not *that* bad."

"She's a... a... a—"

Gabe's smiled faded. "Careful, you're starting to sound jealous."

She deflated and looked at Gabe. "You're right; I do hate her. She just doesn't fit." Jenny thought about how to explain it. "You, me, and Steve...we have fun together. We get along great. We like the same games, same restaurants, same taste in movies, football, tennis... We're like the three Musketeers. There was no fourth Musketeer."

Everything would change—was already changing.

"We can make room, if she's who he wants."

"But she's loud. And she's *always* late. And she dresses him to look like an idiot. And—"

Gabe laughed. "I agree, Annie's annoying. But apparently Steve sees something in her we don't. Besides, we were bound to pick up a fourth Musketeer someday."

But not her.

"Fine." Jenny deflated, then brightened. "He can marry somebody else—anybody else."

Gabe chuckled. "That's big of you, honey."

"I think so," Jenny allowed with an arrogant, regal tone.

Gabe sat down and put a sympathetic hand on her knee. "He doesn't need your blessing."

Jenny sighed. "I *know*. You're right." They sat quiet for a minute, then Jenny looked at Gabe. "This is what I get for minding my own business and not fixing him up with one of my co-workers."

"You're right, honey, it's all about you."

"Maybe he won't *actually* do it. Maybe he said that to get a rise out of me." She leaped forward. "You think? To get back at me for the posters?"

"Oh, no." He shook his head. "I think he'll do it."

She pouted. "Big help you are."

Gabe grinned. "Always here for you, babe."

Chapter 21

Friday morning, dressed in her nightshirt, pink cotton robe, and slippers, Jenny padded down the asphalt driveway. She yawned and squinted at the rising sun peeking through the trees. She wasn't usually up this early, but she'd been so tired last night she'd fallen asleep on the couch at eight o'clock while reading, waiting for Gabe to get back from the hospital.

She and Gabe hadn't seen much of each other lately, so it'd been hard to find the right time to broach her delicate topic. Picking up the *Detroit Free Press*, Jenny turned back toward the house.

Maybe she'd surprise Gabe with his favorite meal; it'd been awhile since they'd had a romantic dinner. After mellowed by a great fish dinner and a few glasses of Pinot, having a baby might sound like a good idea to him.

She'd take a nice bubble bath, put on a sexy little dress, spritz some Chanel Chance in a few strategic areas... She smiled. Perfect. It'd been too long since they'd had a romantic evening. Or maybe she'd get a few candles to scatter around the hot tub. Oh! And some sweet-smelling roses. A little champagne and chocolate in the hot tub under the stars... Jenny shivered. This was going to be an amazing night.

Steve walked his bike through the hedge, looking disgustingly alert and cheerful. "Gabe ready?"

"In a minute. He overslept."

"He's been putting in a lot of hours."

Jenny ruffled her mussed hair and yawned. Boy, she needed a cup of coffee. "He's pretty stressed. Hey, do you have any ideas for some cool new bike doodads that he might like? Our anniversary's coming up and I wanted to get him a fun new toy to take his mind off work."

"You could get him a cardiac monitor for training, or Capognola pedals—those are really nice."

She eyed his bike carefully, taking in all his toys, then her gaze landed on his shiny blue helmet. "How about a new helmet? Yours looks much lighter than his, and with all those holes it has to be cooler."

He cocked his head to the side, a doubtful look crossing his face. "Good luck. He loves that artifact of his."

"Maybe if I find something not too bright and garish, he'll give it up," she mused.

Hair sticking up, Gabe pulled his shirt down as he rushed into the garage. "Be right there."

"Water," Steve called out.

Gabe pivoted and headed back inside.

"Hurry up. I got a date," Steve yelled.

Jenny arched an eyebrow. "Doing something fun?"

"Annie and I are heading up north for the weekend."

"The kids will like that."

"Just us. Her mom's watching Sophie and Josh."

She tucked the newspaper under her arm. "Wedding planning?"

"Not yet. I'm working on a special proposal."

"Uh huh." Sure he was. A good friend would ask about his "special" proposal. Guess she wasn't that good of a friend.

"I wish you'd make more of an effort to get to know her. Annie likes you."

"Uh huh," she muttered. He expected her to be gracious before coffee? Now that was simply asking too much.

He laughed. "Give her another chance. I'm sure you'll come to like her."

Fat chance.

"What're you doing today?" he asked.

"Working. Then I thought I'd cook my husband a nice romantic meal."

"I'll think about you slaving away while I'm relaxing in the great outdoors with my girl." He looked beyond her to Gabe. "Ready?"

∾ ∾ ∾

Hours later, Jenny sat at her computer researching quaint bed and breakfast places, when her mom texted her.

Mom: *If you've got coffee, I'll share my doughnuts.*

Jenny: *Front door's open.*

Mom knew Jenny could always be bribed with doughnuts. *Wonder what she wants.*

Mom: *Be there in fifteen.*

Jenny made a fresh pot of coffee and took two mugs out of the cabinet as the front door opened. Ritz charged the entryway, beside herself with joy that they had company. She whined, yipped, and wiggled under Mom's attention.

Jenny wrinkled her face as she took the box of doughnuts Mom handed her. "It's disgusting. You'd think that dog never got any attention."

"Poor, ignored pup." Mom gave Ritz a final pat, then followed Jenny into the kitchen where she washed her hands. Jenny arranged the doughnuts on a glass plate. Sugar, glazed, and Bavarian cream, all her favorites. And then there were the devil's food chocolate ones, too.

Oh my God. She closed her eyes to savor the sweet smell of doughnuts and coffee. Was there anything better? Almost orgasmic.

Jenny handed Mom a mug and pushed the creamer across the granite for her to help herself as she rounded the counter and took a stool. She blew on her coffee and then took a sip.

"Fresh doughnuts? Has to be a bribe." She raised her eyebrows and looked sideways at her mom. "What'd you volunteer me for this time?"

The last time Mom brought her doughnuts, she'd volunteered Jenny to pet sit for a neighbor's two cats and guinea pig for two weeks.

"No bribe. Okay, a little bribe, but first, we're celebrating. To you." She held up a sugar doughnut, and Jenny tapped her Bavarian cream against it, as if clinking glasses.

"Me? Why?"

"Michael says *People Magazine* bought your story on Steve."

"Yeah, they did. It'll be in the January issue." She took a bite.

"That's great. I'm so proud of you." She looked at Jenny. "Why didn't you tell us?"

Jenny shrugged. "I didn't want to brag. It's not like I'm a kid running to Mommy and Daddy with a good report card."

"You're never too old to celebrate accomplishments. Families share the highs and the lows. We celebrate Dad's promotions; we want to share in your good news, too. Next time, it'd be nice if you told us and we didn't have to find out secondhand."

"Okay." That Mom assumed there would be a next time pleased Jenny.

"While we're on the topic of successes... I have to tell you, you've really surprised me these past couple of years. You were right, and I was wrong. You and Gabe are perfect for each other." Eyes wide and smiling, she shook her head. "It seems that Gabe truly was the impetus you needed to grow up. You've blossomed into a responsible, successful young woman, and I'm so proud of you I could burst."

"Aw, thanks, Mom." Jenny smiled, slipped off the stool, and gave her a big hug. She'd worked hard and waited a long time to hear that.

"You're a successful journalist, and then you've made this lovely house a home, for not only you and Gabe, but Alex and Ted, and all of us. Anybody who walks in the front door feels welcome and comfortable, and that's because of you." Mom poked a stiff finger her way. "And somehow you managed to still be available for Alex and Ted."

"Yeah, I know it's the grandkids that really turned you around," Jenny teased to lighten the mood. Mom was starting to go a little overboard on the accolades.

She smiled softly. "I do love those kids. And Gabe. He's been nothing but welcoming and caring to us—and his going in to stitch up Dad that Saturday was above and beyond. But best of all, he clearly cherishes you. And that's what matters most to me." She pursed her lips. "You chose well, honey."

"Thank you." Jenny's eyes narrowed on her mom. "Now back to the bribe. What'd you sign me up for this time?" She winced. "Please, not some fundraising committee at Michael's school. I *hate* fundraisers."

"I didn't volunteer you for anything. But it does have to do with Michael."

Mom polished off her doughnut, and wiped her hands on a napkin. She took a long drink of coffee, put down the mug, and looked at Jenny. "Dad has to go to Ireland for a week next month for business, and I want to go with him and make a vacation out of it."

"That sounds like fun. You should totally do it."

"Can Michael stay with you?"

She blinked. "You want Michael to stay with us? For a week?"

Granted, he'd be in school, but Jenny'd have to drive him to school and pick him up, then get him to after-school events, make sure he did his homework, feed him, monitor his social time, make sure he didn't stay up all night playing video games...for a week.

"Or two." Mom winced. "Maybe three? Would you mind very much? Dad and I haven't been away alone for years, and our fortieth anniversary's coming up, and I've always wanted to see Ir—"

"Go!" Jenny grinned. "*Of course*, we'll watch him. Go. Have fun."

"You should ask Gabe first."

Jenny waved a dismissing hand. "He'll be fine with it. Gabe loves having Michael around."

"You're sure?" Mom's face relaxed in relief and excitement shone in her eyes.

"Positive. But are you?" Mom really trusted her to take care of Michael for weeks? Jenny hesitated to bring up bad memories, but she didn't want any miscommunication, either. "If you're going out of the country, we'll need some sort of guardianship papers so we can authorize medical treatment for him or whatever, in an emergency."

Mom nodded and smiled. "I think between you and Gabe, you're more than qualified to handle any emergency that might come up."

"Okay, then. Make those reservations." Jenny beamed.

They chatted for another fifteen minutes about Ireland, the trip, and the distant relatives Mom wanted to look up, and then she rushed off to pick Michael up and plan their vacation.

Jenny rinsed out their mugs and put the rest of the doughnuts in a baggie. If Mom thought she was responsible enough to care for Michael while she was out of the county, she must be trustworthy enough to have her own kids. Maybe this was just another cosmic kick in the butt to have a baby.

Cosmic kick in the butt? She picked up her phone and opened the calendar app. Three days late. Three days was nothing. She'd been late before. Could be stress. Could be she marked the wrong day. Could be anything.

∾ ∾ ∾

Later that day, Gabe rounded the corner and entered the surgical waiting room. Ignoring the quiet news broadcasting from the flat-screen TV and the groups of quietly chatting people and the elderly man reading a book in the corner, he quickly located Caroline Timons.

"Mrs. Timons?" Gabe lowered himself into the chair next to the plump, middle-aged blonde, and faced her. "Peter's surgery went fine. I'm confident we removed the entire tumor. You should be aware that I did accidentally nick some healthy bowel. However, I inserted a couple of stitches and repaired it right away so there shouldn't be any residual ill effects.

"He received prophylactic antibiotics during surgery, so I don't anticipate any extra risk of complications from the additional sutures, but we'll be watching him carefully for any post-op infection, just to be sure.

"Peter's in the recovery room now. He'll probably be there for..." Gabe looked at the wall clock. "Another hour or so before they move him up to his room. You can get his room number from the aid." He nodded toward the volunteer at the desk. "Do you have any questions?"

"That's great news." She smiled softly. "Thank you so much, Dr. Harrison. Will he be in a lot of pain?"

"He shouldn't be. They've given him something for the pain in the recovery room and I've written an order for pain meds. He should be comfortable. We've also inserted a tube down his nose into his stomach, to help prevent bloating, nausea, and vomiting, which we'll remove in a day or so after normal bowel activity returns."

"When will he be ready to go home?"

"About three or four days. Peter's in pretty good shape, so it'll probably be closer to three." Gabe stood. "If you have any questions or concerns the nurses can't answer, you have my office number, right?"

"Yes." Caroline stood and gathered her purse and magazines. "Thank you."

He nodded. "You're welcome." Gabe whipped off his surgical cap as he strode down the hall, heading for the dressing room. He quickly showered and dressed.

With another couple, Gabe might worry about being sued for admitting making that slight mistake. Technically, he hadn't had to tell them and chances were they'd never have known. His attorney would probably consider him a fool for admitting it, worrying the patient would be looking for any reason to pin a lawsuit on him, but Gabe felt they had the right to know, and he'd been pissed at himself for being so clumsy.

Gabe nodded to an acquaintance and held the door open for him as he made his way toward the parking lot. He wasn't God. Mistakes happened, and as errors went, this one was really almost a non-event, but it still irritated him. Though he'd had a crappy morning at the clinic, he was usually good at compartmentalizing his feelings and not bringing a bad mood into the OR.

Gabe shoved the side door open, stepped onto the sidewalk, and headed for the doctor's parking garage. Maple leaves liberally littered the asphalt, and there was a bite in the air. Gabe lifted his face to the fading evening light. He drew in a deep breath and exhaled. He might actually get home early tonight.

Gabe fished the Samsung from his pocket as he entered the shady garage. His foot caught on some uneven concrete and he lunged forward. He bobbled the phone between his hands while struggling to regain his balance. The phone hit the cement face down. *Crack!*

Oh, no. No. No! Gabe bent and picked up the phone. He closed his eyes and pursed his lips. The way this day was going, there was no way he could luck out, was there? He turned the phone over in his palm. Slowly, he opened his eyes. Dozens of splintering cracks spider-webbed the screen. Crap.

Maybe he'd just cracked the glass. He swiped an index finger across the screen. Nothing. He depressed the power button on the side. Black.

"Come on," he muttered. He tried the power again. "Oh, come *on*." He turned the phone over, peeled it out of its case and removed the battery, then reinstalled it. Still dead. "God*damnit*." He side-armed the phone against the concrete wall.

The *thunk* echoed loudly in the garage, but the Samsung didn't spray into satisfying pieces. Gabe clenched his hands on his hips and glared at the useless cell lying on the concrete floor. *Screw it.* He blew out a deep breath, took a step toward his car, then pivoted and stalked over and picked up the dented cell. He'd need to try and transfer the data to a new phone.

Could this day get any worse?

Gabe closed his eyes and took a calming breath before approaching his car. He circled the station wagon expecting to find a flat tire, but it all looked good. He turned on the ignition—half a tank of gas. Seemed safe. Pulling away from the parking lot Gabe headed for the Verizon store. There went his early night, but he needed a damned phone.

He picked up the phone to call Jen to give her a heads-up he'd be late, glanced at the screen and threw it on the seat. It bounced off the seat, ricocheted off the door, and fell to the floor.

Careful you idiot. The way your day is going, you're lucky it didn't break the window.

As he drove down Harper, Gabe's stomach growled loudly. He searched the console looking for a power bar. None. *Of course.*

He passed Canton Express. Chinese? They hadn't had Chinese in a while. He pulled into the Verizon parking lot, relieved to find no wait. Of course not, everybody else was home eating dinner. Gabe got a sales representative right away, bought a new Samsung and then his luck ran out; it was going to take twenty minutes to transfer the data, if they could coax the old phone to life long enough to access the data.

Okay. Gabe walked down the strip mall into Canton Express, ordered hot and sour soup and a Three Ingredients special for himself, and General Tso's Chicken for Jenny, then added an order of combo Lo Mein. Jen always liked Lo Mein. Hopefully she hadn't made dinner yet. He considered asking to use the restaurant's phone to make sure, but the smells made his mouth water.

Most nights, Jen didn't count on him for dinner unless he called her to let her know he'd be home. He hadn't called today. He checked his watch. Seven o'clock. He wouldn't be home before seven-thirty at the earliest. Jen had probably eaten a salad.

It'd been years since he'd had this much bad luck in a single day. Thank God his kids were grown and out of his house. No diapers to change, baths to give, no homework to supervise or kids making demands of him. After this hellacious day, all Gabe wanted was a little Chinese food, to cuddle his wife, and an early bed. Was that too much to ask for?

~ ~ ~

Jenny paced to the window for the sixth time in the past fifteen minutes. She looked down the empty driveway. "Where the heck is he?"

At six o'clock, she'd called the clinic, only to find that he'd left in the early afternoon to go to the hospital. A three o'clock surgery couldn't last this long, could it? And when it did run long, Gabe always had a nurse call to warn her. He was very considerate that way.

Jenny called his cell but got no answer. He must have run out of battery. She made a note to get him a car charger. Certain Gabe must be on his way home, at six-thirty, she started the rice and tossed the salad. She knew not to put the salmon in the oven until Gabe pulled in the driveway.

Jenny wandered the kitchen, alternately looking out the window down the driveway then back to the stove to stir the rice. She opened the Pinot to let it breathe, straightened a crooked fork, and flipped a knife so the blade faced the plate. Crossing back to the window, she tugged at her shirt that seemed overly tight. Had she shrunk it in the wash or had she gained a few pounds?

At seven, the rice was in grave danger of drying out. Jenny called Gabe's cell again, but it went straight to voicemail. She sent him a quick text. Just as she pushed send, his station wagon zipped up the driveway.

Tail wagging, Ritz trotted to the back door. Jenny hurried to the oven and popped the salmon in. This late, he'd undoubtedly be starving. As the garage door *thunked* shut, she smiled. "There you are. I was getting wor—"

Arms full of a large paper bag, Gabe stomped through the garage door.

Her smiled faded. "You brought home dinner?"

He placed the bag on the counter, took in her dress and makeup, and frowned. "Please tell me we aren't late to some event I've forgotten."

"No." She shook her head. "We didn't have plans. What's wrong?"

He sighed and went to the fridge for a beer. "I've had a bitch of a day. I picked up Chinese food for din—"

He glanced at the table set for two, took in the flowers and china. "You made dinner."

Jenny moved forward. "It's okay, it'll keep."

He looked at the stove at the pot of rice and the oven, then dropped onto a stool. "Damn it. I'm sorry. I thought you would've eaten something earlier. I couldn't call, my–"

"It's fine." Jenny circled his shoulders and kissed his forehead. "I love Chinese food. What'd you get me?"

"But you went to all this trouble." He threw a hand out.

Jenny squeezed his shoulders and pressed her fingers along his shoulder blades, squeezing hard against the stiff muscles. Poor baby. He was so tight. "Stop. It's fine."

Gabe groaned and dropped his head forward. "That feels so good."

Jenny dug deeper, then pushed her thumb up his neck, first one side, then the other. "You're so tense. What happened today?"

She stopped her massage long enough for Gabe to take a long pull of his beer. She glanced at the pot of dried-out rice. Big deal, two dollars of rice down the drain.

Gabe took another gulp of beer. "It was ridiculously terrible. A disaster. Almost comical really." He tilted his beer sideways. "But not really."

"A *disaster?*" Jenny moved around him and sat on the other stool.

"When my alarm didn't go off this morning, I should have stayed in bed. You know how much I hate being late."

"That's hardly a tragedy. Steve didn't mind."

"That was just the beginning. It started at the clinic. Stupid kids. Should just sterilize half of them."

Jenny pulled back. "That seems a bit drastic."

"Not really." He rolled the beer bottle between his palms. "This girl came into the clinic this morning. Amy Riley. Just as I was heading out to lunch, Amy shows up at the clinic, running a fever and in premature labor—with her one- and three-year-olds in tow." He paused, looking at her. "And she's sixteen with full blown gonorrhea."

Jenny winced. *What a mess.* "Is she okay?"

"Oh, *she'll* be fine. A few days in the hospital pushing IV antibiotics will fix her up." A little muscle in his tight jaw pulsed. "The baby died, but the mother will be fine—and probably still fertile, unfortunately." He stood and jammed his hands deep in his pant pockets. "I couldn't save the baby."

"Oh, I'm sorry, honey."

"It was a boy." He leaned back against the wall. "A perfect little boy, born too soon. Because of her." He closed his eyes for a second, then opened them. "It's not right. He was an innocent."

"Maybe she needs counseling." *Maybe she just made one incredibly big mistake.*

His face wrinkled in a give-me-a-break look. "She had her first baby at thirteen, Jen. She's had counseling. She has a long history of noncompliant prenatal treatment. She smokes pot and lives with her mother on welfare. She needs to be sterilized."

"That's a little harsh." *I had Michael at fourteen. Accidental pregnancies happen all the time.* "If they're on welfare, how do you know she wasn't having sex for money to buy food?"

Jenny eased off the stool and handed Gabe his beer. As he took a sip, she moved over to the chair in front of the desk and pulled her sweater down to completely cover the pink First Response Pregnancy kit. Not the time. He'd freak.

"Tell that to her dead son. If she were turning tricks, she'd use birth control. She's had counseling and access to birth control. Nope, she's simply an irresponsible child. What chance do those other two kids of hers have? Being raised by an ignorant girl incapable of doing anything but spreading her legs?"

He poked at the mail on the desk. "I called Social Services. I know the foster situation, but even orphanages would give these kids a better chance than with that girl."

Jenny came up behind him, squeezed his rigid shoulders and guided him back to the counter. "Let's have dinner. You'll feel better with some food in you."

She popped the top on another beer and handed it to him. "Maybe you should step back a bit—get some perspective. Just because this girl's promiscuous, doesn't mean she's a bad mother who deserves to lose her children."

The timer went off, and Jenny took the salmon out of the oven and left it on the stove to cool. Good thing they liked leftovers.

Gabe stopped pacing the kitchen and sat in a chair at the table. "She's a kid coping with babies by herself. They don't even have the same father, for cripe's sake. What kind of life can she give them? I've been there. I was twelve when Aunt Adele died, and then it was only me and Uncle George. Just me and a bitter man trying to cope with his grief. It was hard, Jen. Damn hard."

He arched a brow at her. "And that's coping *with* the benefit of money and education. It's not fair to the kids. I'm not complaining for myself. I'll always be grateful Uncle George took me in, but it's far from an ideal childhood." Gabe set his empty bottle down with extra force.

Jenny took the containers out of the paper bag and reached for dinner plates.

"Then this afternoon during my bowel resection, I dropped a scalpel and nicked the bowel—after, of course, I backed into a nurse and knocked a pack of sterile instruments out of her hands."

"Oh, no." She covered her mouth to hide a smile.

Gabe pursed his lips and shook his head. "No, wait. It gets better." He reached into his pocket and tossed his old phone onto the table. Jenny moved closer to inspect the destroyed screen.

"What happened?" Holy cow, had he sat on it?

"I dropped it in the parking lot." He finished off the first beer and reached for the fresh one.

"Does it still work?"

"Don't be silly."

She thought not but hoped it might. "It's okay, I'll take it to Verizon tomorrow—"

"Already done. That's why I'm so late. Why I picked up the dinner. I got that," he nodded at the containers on the counter, "while waiting for them to load stuff onto the new phone."

"Oh, babe." Jenny sat on his lap and hugged Gabe close. "I'm sorry." Stroking his head, she tried to absorb his frustration and pain. "Now you're going to have to reheat your dinner, too."

He squeezed her back. "That might be the best thing that happened to me today. I just want to eat dinner and go to bed."

They stayed that way, holding one another, each lost in troubled thoughts. Jenny hadn't realized that Gabe's childhood had been that difficult. He always talked matter-of-factly about losing his parents and living with George. She'd thought he'd been happy with George.

Given his past, how would Gabe feel about bringing a baby into the world now? They could make a perfect family to erase his painful childhood. Clearly *now* wasn't the time to broach the subject, but it might be the perfect healing prescription for her love.

But then, if she was already pregnant, what were the chances he'd believe it was an accident? Didn't seem likely, as they'd always used birth control.

And he could *never* find out about Michael—that was for sure. He'd made his views on teenage pregnancy crystal clear. She glanced at the chair and her sweater covering the pregnancy kit. Had to get that hidden, for sure. One glance at that would send Gabe around the bend.

Powerless to know how to help him, Jenny pulled Gabe closer, pressing a kiss into his soft hair. "Poor baby."

She felt his rigid body relax, little by little. Easing away, she scanned his face before placing a hand on his cheek and pressing a light kiss to his lips. "I love you."

Gabe's only response was to pull her closer again and hold on tight.

After a few minutes, she moved away and looked at him. "You've been working too hard. What d'ya say we go away for the weekend? Just you and me. No pager. Turn the cells off. Just us."

He frowned. "I'm pretty busy right now."

"You're *always* busy. You haven't had any time off since we took the kids to Mexico for spring break."

"What'd you have in mind?"

"I'm doing a piece on bed and breakfasts, and have a phone interview scheduled with this place in Saugatuck. Why don't I do it in person instead? We could make a long weekend of it. Go away for our anniversary. That gives you a week's notice. Think of how relaxing it'd be. Say yes."

It'd give Jenny time to see if she really was pregnant. If she was...their lives would be totally turned on end, but at least telling Gabe on a romantic getaway when he was relaxed would set the atmosphere for a productive discussion where they'd figure things out together.

She was no longer an irresponsible, dependent teenager. Jenny had a great job, lovely home, and a loving husband. Like Mom said, she and Gabe made a great team. If she *were* pregnant, they'd figure it out, together.

Her biggest hurdle would be convincing him she hadn't accidentally on purpose gotten pregnant. But she'd have a week to work on that. *If* she was pregnant. If not, it was still the perfect time to bring up the subject of having a baby—but she wasn't going to tell him about Michael. There was no need, and she had no doubt he would not understand.

He thought for a moment, and then stared at her through serious eyes. "Yes."

"Great." Jenny smiled and hugged him close. "This is exactly what you need—we need. You'll see."

∽ The End ∽

Thank you for taking time to read Just Beginning. *If you enjoyed it, please consider telling your friends or posting a short review. Word of mouth is an author's best friend and much appreciated. Jenny and Gabe's story is continued in* Just Destiny.

Turn the page for a sneak preview.

Just Destiny Preview

Prologue

Steve Grant's heart pounded as if it might hammer its way right out of his chest. He took a measured breath, stretched an arm across the back of Annie's chair and settled into his stadium seat. *What's the problem, man? You've faced down Billy Ray Butler and Crush Davis, stared them down across home plate, in front of a sold-out crowd without breaking a sweat; you can do this. It's the right thing to do.*

The band's drums, trumpets and trombones belted out the Michigan fight song. "Let's! Go! Blue!" The Ann Arbor crowd cheered as one.

"Why'd you give up your fifty-yard-line seats for these nosebleeds?" Annie raised her eyebrows.

"Lemme go," the three-year-old behind her shrieked as he strained and bucked in his mother's arms.

Annie winced, covered her ear and gave Steve a knowing look. When they went out without her children, he knew she wanted a break from *all* kids. These seats cost a small fortune; who in the hell brings their kid along? Steve scanned the packed seats around them—not a damn kid in sight. What were the chances they'd be sitting right in front of the only holy terror?

"One of our paralegals, Pete McGaffy, has his dad in town this weekend to celebrate his first year cancer free. Pete helped me a couple of times so when I found out his dad's a huge Michigan fan, I gave them my tickets and got these instead." He glared at the kid beating an annoying tattoo on the back of Annie's chair, tempted to grab the little ankle to still him. "We have a great view of the whole field from here. Besides, I thought you'd enjoy sitting with Notre Dame fans instead of the enemy for a change."

Annie had gone to Notre Dame and was a die-hard Irish fan, where as a Michigan alum, Steve's season tickets bordered the Michigan sideline. She held out her hand for the binoculars and jerked forward as the kid pounded her chair with both of his feet. Stiff backed, Annie scooted forward in her chair.

"Switch seats with me." Steve stood and pulled Annie out of her seat. She should be safe in front of the dad.

Annie stood and threw the little brat that warning look mothers seem to perfect, before slowly lowering herself into the other seat. Not exactly the mood he wanted to set. He hoped it wasn't an omen. *Chill, man. She's gonna love it.*

He looked at the giant scoreboard—five minutes to halftime. Steve settled back in the seat, rubbed tight neck muscles, and rolled his shoulders.

He'd chosen these seats carefully. The first row in club level seating had lots of leg room, a bird's eye view of the whole field, and the cameramen should have no trouble zooming in on them. It was perfe—the boy put a sticky hand on Steve's head and lunged over his shoulder, nearly falling into his lap. Steve caught him and shoved him back at his parents.

"Henry. I'm sooo sorry. Really. Sorry. I..." His mortified mother tried to lift him onto her lap, but the little boy arched his back and bellowed.

"That's enough!" the father said. He handed his wife his beer and reached for the boy at the same time the kid jumped up, knocking her arm.

The halftime buzzer sounded loudly as Steve lunged forward, but he couldn't right the cup before a wave of beer cascaded over the lip, splashing all over Annie's shoulder, arm, and chest.

Annie gasped, jumped up and whirled on the threesome. Fury burned in her eyes as she shook her arm, spraying beer. "Are you freaking kidding me? What's *wrong* with you people? Haven't you ever heard of a babysitter?"

Steve stepped back and stared in horror. The pink of Annie's shirt grew increasingly dark as it soaked up the beer.

"I'm *so* sorry." The woman rummaged in her bag, yanked out some baby wipes and held them out to Annie. "I... please. We'll pay for dry-cleaning."

Annie snatched the wipes, made a few futile dabs at her arm before throwing them on her seat and pushing past Steve.

"Laaadies and geeen-tlemen," The announcer drew out.

Steve grabbed her arm. "Where're you going?"

"Preee-sent-ing the two-hundred thirty-five member Michigan marching Band. Baaa-nd... take the field."

Annie frowned as if he was crazy. "To the bathroom."

"Now? You can't go now."

Eyes widening, she plucked the wet shirt from her chest. "I'm *covered* in beer."

Shit. Shit. Shit. "Uh... there'll be a long line. Just wait a little bit." He turned her toward the field. "Watch the show." He glanced at the forty-seven by eighty-five-foot screen to see the camera zooming in on them. He pointed toward the field. "Look, they're spelling out something."

"I don't care." She tried to pull free.

Steve tightened his grip on her shoulders. "Listen. It's that Bruno Mars song you love."

"What is wrong with you?" She glared. "I'm soaked and smell like a frat party."

Steve pivoted her toward the field and locked his arms around her. "*Look.*"

The band had spelled out "M-A-R-R-Y M-E" and dissolved to reform one last word. "A-N-N-I-E."

The announcer boomed, "Weeeell, Annie?"

Annie looked toward the huge board where the camera had zoomed in on them and they stood larger than life. Her glare melted as awareness set in. She brushed her hair back and a tentative smile flickered across her face.

Steve released her. He wiped damp palms on his thighs, then dropped to one knee and took her hand. "Will you marry me, Annie?"

Hand covering her mouth, Annie dragged her gaze from the huge screen long enough to nod at him. Her glance darted back and forth from the screen to him. She thrust out her left hand. He took the ring box from his pocket, then slid the ring onto her finger.

Annie yanked her hand back and after a quick inspection of the 3-carat marquise, held it up for everybody to see as if she were a winner lofting her trophy. Steve pulled her into his arms for a hug while the crowd cheered and clapped.

Smile, Steve. Even if he couldn't give her his heart, he'd embarrassed himself in front of millions of people and given her her dream proposal. The love would come.

Chapter 1

Even the best-made plans were subject to the whims of fate, and Jenny Harrison believed in embracing Lady Destiny's cues. She grabbed her list and the gallon-size baggie of cookies, whistled for Ritz and rushed through the hedge separating the driveway from their neighbor's. With the golden retriever prancing at her heels, she breezed through Steve's back door, calling out, "Hey, Grant?"

"Kitchen." Steve, with his maroon silk tie tucked into his white dress shirt, leaned over his sink and bit a pickle. He saluted her with the dill. "Lunch?"

"No, thanks, we'll catch something on the road. Save room; I made your favorite, pecan chocolate chip." She held up the cookies.

Steve took the bag. "Mmmm. They're still warm. You didn't have to do that."

"Yes, I did. We really appreciate your taking care of Ritz and the house. With the trial ramping up, I know you're crazy busy."

"No problem." He polished off the pickle and pulled the cookie bag open.

The sweet scent of fresh-baked cookie and warm chocolate commingled with the acetous pickle smell. Jenny winced. Gross. Shaking her head, she laid down the list. "Here's the number of the Saugatuck Inn—in case of an emergency—though we'll both have our cells." She frowned and craned her neck to read the upside down list. "And... you have a key to the house. We won't set the alarm. There should be plenty of dog food in the garage, and I stopped the newspapers." She looked up. "Questions?"

"Jen, you'll only be gone three and a half days." Then at her steady look, he sighed. "Got it."

Jenny reached for her back pocket and fingered the bulky line there, thinking. She couldn't wait to share her good news. Ordinarily she'd want it to be Gabe, but under the circumstances, maybe a test run on Steve might be good.

"What?" He raised his eyebrows and polished off the cookie. "Out with it. You look like the cat who swallowed the canary and got her cream too."

Jenny smiled, whipped the plastic stick from her back pocket and waved it around. "I'm pregnant."

"You're...?" His eyes widened and his jaw dropped. "That's great. Right? Is it great?"

She nodded and smiled. "It's amazing."

"Pregnant? Wow. What'd Gabe say?"

"He doesn't know. I just found out myself. I'm going to tell him this weekend." She grinned a wide silly, grin, then bit her lower lip. "I'm going to have a baby."

"Congratulations, kid. You're gonna be a great mom."

"Thanks." Jenny smiled, still a little shocked. She fingered the stick, staring at the blue line, then slipped it back in her pocket. That wasn't so bad. In just a few minutes Steve had lost that stunned look. It'd be fine. Everything would be fine.

The Lives Between Us
Coming 2015

Grieving the loss of her beloved niece, reporter Skylar Kendall plots revenge on the US Senator who opposed life-saving stem cell research and therapy. She becomes romantically involved with his best friend, putting her in the perfect position to tear the senator's world apart when tragedy strikes. Only, she hadn't counted on falling in love.

Sen. Hastings' tragedy would absolutely *make* Skylar's career and satisfy her thirst for revenge, but can she betray her new love and friends?

Just Beginning Fact or Fiction

I research my books thoroughly and try not to take much "creative license" to fudge facts to suit my story. Below, I've listed real organizations and places in the Grosse Pointe/Detroit area that pop up in *Just Beginning*, and a few other interesting tidbits. Take a look…

The Grosse Pointe Hunt Club is nestled in the middle of a residential area. We used to play tennis there, and one summer I took horseback riding lessons. My children loved going through the barns and seeing all the horses and watching riding events. grossepointehuntclub.com

The Hill is a restaurant in Grosse Pointe Farms and one of my very favorite restaurants for a special lunch or dinner. They take reservations and don't actually hand out pagers when there's a wait. That, I made up. www.thehillgrossepointe.com

Nino Salvaggio is a wonderful market in St. Claire Shores that my family's been going to for decades for fresh fruit, produce, and lunch meats. My children have special memories of shopping at Nino Salvaggio's with Grandma. www.ninosalvaggio.com

Sanders, is a Detroit area institution, and if you've never tried their chocolate or ice-cream toppings, you're missing out! Fred Sanders first opened the store in 1875. In 2002, Morely Candy Makers purchased the Sanders name and original recipes to add to its own. No trip back home is ever complete without a visit to Sanders. My personal favorite is the Dark Chocolate Honeycomb chips— oh—and the assorted creams and Easter bunnies… It also has a special place in my heart because my mom used to work the soda fountain when she was in high school. And occasionally, after a dentist visit with a good no-cavities report, Mom would take us to Sanders for a treat! www.sanderscandy.com

French's Flowers & Gifts is a family operated florist in Livonia that our family has happily used for years. www.frenchsflowers.com

University Liggett School is an amazing private school in Grosse Pointe that both my husband and I attended and is, in fact, where we met. I am dyslexic and wasn't diagnosed until third grade, and if not for the incredible help I received at Liggett from a whole host of excellent, patient teachers, I'm not even sure college would have been a realistic option for me.

Also, in reading the history of ULS, I love that in 1878 the Liggett family established the school as an "accessible school for girls devoted to high standards, proper behavior and preparation for college, as well as life". They were feminists before their time! It wasn't until 1954 that Liggett became co-ed. www.uls.org/page

Dawood Boutique of Grosse Pointe is an elegant boutique that's family owned and operated since 1960. I've always admired and occasionally frequented it when my mom was looking for a special dress for a wedding or dinner dance. www.dawoodgp.com

Christ Child House has been caring for abused and neglected children in the Detroit area since 1948, providing residential services for up to 31 boys, ages 5 through 17. When I started researching foster care and this organization, I quickly understood why this outstanding place had always been one of my mother's favorite causes. I made up John Spears and his multi-million dollar donation for the extension of Christ Child's services to include the Supervised Independent Living house, but I think it'd be a wonderful if a wealthy benefactor would do something like this. I have immense respect for good foster parents. christchildhouse.org

I chose Woodward House because several of my Detroit area friends suggested it and I found Augustus Woodward to be a really interesting visionary. Also, I thought it would be oddly endearing to name the new home after a man who'd never had a family or children. Augustus Woodward was the first Chief Justice of the Michigan Territory; he's credited with playing a prominent role in the planning and reconstruction of Detroit after a devastating fire in 1805 and for spearheading the establishment of the University of Michigan. He was a supporter of freedmen. For more specific information on Augustus Woodward check out his Wikipedia page. en.wikipedia.org/wiki/Augustus_B._Woodward

Chez Lou Lou Salon & Spa is a real salon in The Village in Grosse Pointe Farms that a friend recommended. salonloulou.com

"Learn To Fly" by Larry James is a beautiful poem I found while researching butterfly releases, and it spoke to my heart, so I had to include it in Jenny and Gabe's wedding. Copyright © 2014 – Larry James. Reprinted with permission. Larry's poem is adapted from Larry's Wedding Website and Wedding Blog. Larry James is a non-denominational minister. You'll find more than 475 pages of Wedding ideas, tips, ceremonies, and more at: www.celebrateintimateweddings.com.

SitterCity.com is a real nationwide babysitting site a couple of my daughters used to find good families in need of experienced babysitters when they needed to make a little extra money in college and afterward. www.sittercity.com

The Meadow Brook Theatre is a playhouse in Rochester, Michigan, that I've been to a couple of times on school fieldtrips. www.mbtheatre.org

Canton Express is a restaurant in St. Clair Shores. www.yelp.com/biz/canton-express-saint-clair-shores

Grosse Pointe Academy - Gabe and Jenny were going to be married in the Academy's chapel before they settled on a destination wedding. It's a wonderful independent day school where "students receive the advantage of outstanding academics, an emphasis on moral and spiritual development through a Christian way of life, a wide range of extracurricular activities that challenge the mind and the body." I grew up not far from the academy and spent hours playing on the playground and letting my dad beat me in tennis on their tennis courts. Okay, so maybe I didn't really let him beat me. www.gpacademy.org

Leader Dogs for the Blind in Rochester, Michigan, is a real organization, founded in 1939, that trains dogs for the blind. They provide dogs to ideal candidates at no cost to the blind person. Their funding comes from gifts, endowments and service organizations like the Lions Clubs. When a dog is not able to serve as a Leader Dog, they call it "career changed" and adopt the dog out as a regular pet. When I was in high school, my family got a wonderful German shepherd named Misty this way. www.leaderdog.org/about-us/adopt-a-career-changed-dog

Trevor Allen Photography—Trevor is a Halifax Wedding and Portrait photographer more talented than I can describe. His photos are amazing—so full of emotion. Trevor took the beautiful photo of Mandi and Mark Fanning's wedding rings, and they all kindly allowed me to use them as Jenny and Gabe's for Just Beginning's cover. trevorallen.ca/, facebook.com/trevorallenphotography